THE SALMON
COOKBOOK

THE SALMON
COOKBOOK

DELICIOUS WAYS WITH SALMON AND TROUT, WITH
OVER 150 STEP-BY-STEP RECIPES

JANE BAMFORTH

LORENZ BOOKS

This edition is published by Lorenz Books

Lorenz Books is an imprint of Anness Publishing Ltd
Hermes House, 88–89 Blackfriars Road, London SE1 8HA
tel. 020 7401 2077; fax 020 7633 9499
www.lorenzbooks.com; info@anness.com

© Anness Publishing Ltd 2003, 2004

UK agent: The Manning Partnership Ltd, 6 The Old Dairy, Melcombe Road, Bath BA2 3LR;
tel. 01225 478444; fax 01225 478440; sales@manning-partnership.co.uk

UK distributor: Grantham Book Services Ltd, Isaac Newton Way, Alma Park Industrial Estate, Grantham, Lincs NG31 9SD;
tel. 01476 541080; fax 01476 541061; orders@gbs.tbs-ltd.co.uk

North American agent/distributor: National Book Network, 4501 Forbes Boulevard, Suite 200, Lanham, MD 20706;
tel. 301 459 3366; fax 301 429 5746; www.nbnbooks.com

Australian agent/distributor: Pan Macmillan Australia, Level 18, St Martins Tower, 31 Market St, Sydney, NSW 2000;
tel. 1300 135 113; fax 1300 135 103; customer.service@macmillan.com.au

New Zealand agent/distributor: David Bateman Ltd, 30 Tarndale Grove, Off Bush Road, Albany, Auckland;
tel. (09) 415 7664; fax (09) 415 8892

A CIP catalogue record for this book is available from the British Library.

PUBLISHER: Joanna Lorenz
MANAGING EDITOR: Judith Simons
PROJECT EDITOR: Sarah Ainley
COPY EDITOR: Jenni Fleetwood
DESIGNER: Adelle Morris
INDEXER: Helen Snaith
PRODUCTION CONTROLLER: Stephen Lang
REFERENCE SECTION: Jenni Fleetwood and Kate Whiteman
RECIPES: Catherine Atkinson, Alex Barker, Jane Bamforth, Carla Capalbo, Jacqueline Clarke,
Roz Denny, Matthew Drennan, Joanne Farrow, Christine France, Brian Glover, Becky Johnson,
Christine Ingram, Liz Trigg, Linda Tubby, Kate Whiteman and Elizabeth Wolf-Cohen
PHOTOGRAPHY: Tim Auty, Martin Brigdale, Nicki Dowey, James Duncan, Michelle Garrett,
Dave Jordan, David King, Thomas Odulate, William Lingwood and Sam Stowell
ADDITIONAL PHOTOGRAPHY (pp8, 9, 10, 11): The Anthony Blake Photo Library

Previously published as *Salmon*

1 3 5 7 9 10 8 6 4 2

NOTES
Bracketed terms are intended for American readers.
For all recipes, quantities are given in both metric and imperial measures and, where appropriate,
measures are also given in standard cups and spoons. Follow one set, but not a mixture, because they
are not interchangeable. Standard spoon and cup measures are level. 1 tsp = 5ml, 1 tbsp = 15ml,
1 cup = 250ml/8fl oz. Australian standard tablespoons are 20ml. Australian readers should use 3 tsp in place of 1 tbsp for measuring
small quantities. Medium (US large) eggs are used unless otherwise stated.

CONTENTS

INTRODUCTION

THE KING OF FISH

No fish captures the imagination quite like salmon. Whether it is the romantic vision of a lone fisherman casting his line in a Scottish river on a misty morning, the creature's legendary leap, or its almost mystical migratory habits, salmon inspires a sense of wonder.

The flavour of wild salmon is superb, and although farmed salmon seldom comes close in terms of texture or taste, the cheaper alternative does provide good quality protein to many people who might otherwise be denied the opportunity of trying this delicious fish. Choosing responsibly farmed salmon may also be more environmentally sound in an era when wild Atlantic salmon stocks are falling fast.

HISTORY

There is ample evidence that salmon has been a valuable food source for thousands of years. The Tlingits, who inhabited present-day Alaska some eight thousand years ago, were typical of hunter-gatherer groups living along the east and west coasts of America. For much of the year they caught cod, halibut and herring, along with larger marine mammals, but as the weather

Above: Freshly caught salmon on the shores of Loch Lomond, Scotland.

warmed they moved to their summer camps for one of the most important events of their year: the salmon run. As the fish returned to their native rivers, the hunters trapped them or caught them using primitive hooks and lines. The fish were highly valued as a winter food supply, to supplement the game hunted towards the turn of the year.

Across the Atlantic, salmon was equally highly sought after. Mesolithic fishermen in Ireland are known to have feasted on salmon during the summer months, and to have preserved stocks for winter. In fact, salmon was so highly regarded in Ireland that the fish passed into mythology in tales like the legend of the Salmon of Knowledge.

In Scotland, a country whose name is synonymous with salmon, the importance of the fish was quickly recognized, and William the Lion, who ruled Scotland from 1165 to 1214, introduced legislation to protect salmon.

Two centuries later, in one of the first instances of environmental legislation, the Corporation of Dublin introduced a law forbidding Irish tanners polluting the river Liffey and threatening fish stocks. Salmon are fastidious creatures and will only thrive in pure water.

Throughout the Middle Ages, salmon was a popular food, either braised with spices, potted, salted or made into pies or pastes. In later centuries it became a luxury item, often teamed with other extravagant ingredients, such as lobster. Only recently has salmon once again become affordable.

The Salmon of Knowledge

According to Irish legend, the first person to eat the flesh of the Salmon of Knowledge would be endowed with superhuman intelligence. The fish was a wily creature, almost impossible to capture, but the tale tells how it was eventually landed and cooked by a druid called Finegas. A precocious young fair-haired lad called Fionn MacCumhaill happened by just as the fish was cooked to perfection. Before Finegas could take his first mouthful, Fionn reached out a hand to steal a piece and burnt his thumb in the process. He put his thumb in his mouth to cool it down, and at that moment, all knowledge was his. Fionn became a great hero and his exploits are recounted in dozens of Irish folk tales.

RANGE AND HABITAT

Salmon are native to the northern hemisphere. Their range naturally extends from the Arctic Circle to the Tropic of Cancer, although they have been introduced into Australia, New Zealand, South America and southern Africa. Classified as Atlantic or Pacific salmon, there are several different varieties. Most are anadromous, which means that they migrate from the sea to fresh waters to spawn. There are some non-migratory species in land-locked lakes in Europe and North America.

LIFE CYCLE

The curious life cycle of the salmon has intrigued fishermen and naturalists for generations. A female Atlantic salmon produces an average of around 1400 eggs per 1kg/2¼lb of body weight. When spawning occurs, in early winter, she will scoop out a shallow depression, known as a redd, in the gravel on the river bed. She does this by turning on to her side and flexing and relaxing her body, creating a current that is capable of moving quite large pebbles. When the redd is deep enough, she extrudes some eggs, which are then fertilized by a male salmon. She continues in this way, often making several redds, until all the fertilized eggs have been deposited and covered with gravel.

Right: Fresh sockeyes, a type of Pacific salmon, kept on ice at the fishmonger's.

The eggs hatch about four months later. The tiny hatchlings are first called alevins, then parr, and then smolts. They remain in the river of their birth for up to five years, depending on the variety of salmon, food supply and water temperature, until they are sufficiently mature to journey to the deep-sea feeding grounds. Some may return a year later, as grilse, while others travel further and stay away for several years before returning as adult salmon, weighing up to 14kg/31lb.

The homing instinct, which drives salmon to return to the precise spot where they were spawned, is very mysterious. Some scientists believe that a navigational sense similar to that of migratory birds enables salmon to return to the area of their birth, while chemical imprinting acts like a fine-tuning mechanism, making it possible for them to recognize the smell of their home river and even the exact gravel bed where they originally hatched.

Returning home to spawn is considerably more arduous than the outward journey, as the fish must swim upstream. To do so, many perform astonishing leaps, and the sight of salmon negotiating a waterfall in this way is very impressive.

SALMON FARMING

The first salmon hatcheries, where the eggs from female fish were artificially fertilized and incubated, were developed around the middle of the 19th century, but it was not until the 1970s that commercial salmon farms were established, first in Norway and then soon after in Scotland.

Today, commercial salmon farming is big business, but it is not without problems. Although there are plenty of highly responsible fish farmers, raising fish in a manner that mimics as closely as possible conditions in the wild, there are others who employ intensive methods similar to those used in some factory chicken farms. Such agrochemical fish farmers frequently pollute rivers with pesticides, waste fish food and sewage. The salmon are penned in tightly, making them vulnerable to disease and infestation by fish lice. When they escape, as they often do, they infect wild fish. The escapees also breed with wild fish, putting already compromised natural stocks at risk. Consumers can avoid contributing to this problem by making sure that any farmed salmon they buy comes from a farm with a recognized organic certification.

COOKING

Salmon is a very versatile fish. Whether you serve it raw as sushi, brined as gravlax, or cook it in any of the myriad ways described in this book, it is delicious, nourishing, and an excellent source of the omega-3 fatty acids that are so important for a healthy heart.

THE STORY OF TROUT

Catching a glimpse of quicksilver trout in a quiet pool or lake is one of the delights of the countryside. Not only does this mean that the water is pure – trout, like salmon, are known to loathe a polluted environment – but it also suggests that, with a bit of luck, this delicious and highly versatile fish might be on the menu for supper.

HISTORY

Ever since man first learned to catch trout, these fish have been invaluable as a source of food. Native Americans, ancient Britons and early Europeans all treasured these tasty fish, and it is no surprise that the fish hook was one of man's earliest tools.

Fishing rods were in use around four thousand years ago and it is known that the ancient Macedonians were adept at fly fishing for trout. They used the technique known as dapping, which involves dropping the artificial fly lightly on the surface of the water so that the fish thinks it is the real thing.

In a bid to increase the freshwater trout population, the ancient Chinese encouraged the fish to spawn on mats placed in rivers. The mats were then lifted out and the fertilized eggs were used to stock new breeding sites. The first person to artificially fertilize trout eggs is said to have been a French monk. The eggs were tightly packed in wooden boxes and buried in sand underground until they hatched.

Tickling trout

A time-honoured method for catching trout – especially popular with poachers – is tickling. This requires enormous patience as it involves sliding the hands gently under a trout that is resting under a rock, and lifting out the slippery creature before it can get away. Although the trout escapes more often than not, there are plenty of tales of individuals who perfected this practice and were rewarded with a freshly fried trout for their breakfast or dinner.

Above: Freshly caught sea trout hung up ready for cooking over an open fire.

RANGE AND HABITAT

Like salmon, to which they are related, trout are native to the northern hemisphere but they are also highly successful emigrants. Brown trout are native to Europe but they thrive in America. Conversely, the American rainbow trout has been successfully introduced to many other parts of the world. In New Zealand, for instance, the rainbow trout has acclimatized so successfully that many inhabitants of that country believe it to be one of their own native species.

LIFE CYCLE

There are many similarities between trout and salmon and both spawn in gravel pits, or redds, in fresh water. The young trout hatch after about 30 days. Initially they remain hidden in the gravel, feeding off their yolk sacs, but when this supply of food is exhausted they emerge. At this stage they are known as fry. As they grow, they develop markings, like fingerprints, on the sides of their bodies, and are described as parr, the name deriving from an Old English word for finger. Like young salmon, trout remain in their home waters for an initial period before swimming further afield to feed. Unlike salmon, however, most trout are fairly modest in their aspirations, moving to a larger river or lake rather than the ocean, although some species have adapted to living in salt water as well as fresh. Sea trout, cutthroat trout and steelhead rainbow trout are in this category. When they are several years old, the skins of these anadromous (i.e. migratory) fish become silvery and, like salmon, they are then known as smolts. They spend most of their lives at sea, returning to fresh water to spawn.

When and where individual species spawn depends on the variety of trout, the water temperature and other local conditions. Trout eggs hatch earlier than those of salmon, giving the fry time to establish themselves before their larger relatives appear on the scene.

There is considerable size variation between trout of different species and within the species themselves. The average rainbow trout on sale at the fishmonger's weighs around 350g/12oz but fishermen have reported catching fish in excess of 12kg/26lb. Sea trout that evade capture can survive for many years and grow to over 40kg/88lb, although most fish sold commercially weigh about 3kg/6½lb.

TROUT FARMING

Trout have been raised in captivity since the 1850s, initially with the aim of re-stocking freshwater rivers and lakes, but more recently for supply to the consumer. In the early years of the 20th century, a Danish trout farmer developed a system for introducing a flow of fresh water into his fish ponds to imitate river conditions. This helped reduce disease and led to improved yields. The first commercial fish farm in England was opened in 1950 and there are now more than 300 farms in the United Kingdom alone, mainly in Scotland, North Yorkshire and the south of England. As with salmon, it is very important to buy farmed trout from a responsible producer who cares for

Right: Fly fishing on the Scottish border. This method of catching trout has been popular since ancient times.

the environment as well as for his fish. Some agrochemical farmers pollute rivers with pesticides, waste fish food and sewage. The trout are packed into pens, and this makes them vulnerable to disease and infestation by fish lice.

In the wild, trout flesh is often pale pink, due to its natural diet. Some producers of farmed fish add colorants to the feed to mimic this. Organically farmed trout have creamy white flesh.

COOKING

Frying freshly caught trout over an open fire on the river bank may be the ideal, but there are many other ways of cooking this delicious fish, including poaching in court-bouillon, baking, braising, grilling (broiling) and cooking on a barbecue. Whole trout is easy to eat, as the cooked flesh falls away from the bone, but it can also be flaked and added to salads, rice or pasta dishes.

TYPES OF SALMON

There are several species of this superb fish, identified initially by the names of the northern oceans in which they spend most of their adult lives. Atlantic salmon are generally judged to have the finest flavour, but the various species of Pacific salmon have their admirers too.

ATLANTIC SALMON (Salmo salar)

There is only one species of Atlantic salmon. Its Latin name – *salar* – means leaper, and is a tribute to the creature's athleticism as it travels upstream to the spawning grounds. Atlantic salmon are sleek and muscular, with powerful bodies that contrast with their small heads. On their heads and silvery-blue backs are tiny black crosses. Their sides are silver and the bellies are white. It is quite difficult to tell the sex of immature cock and hen salmon, but during the spawning run, cock salmon develop distinctive hooks or kypes on their lower jaws, making it much easier to tell them apart.

The best salmon are those caught at the start of their spawning run, when they are fat and in prime condition. After leaving the sea, they will not feed again until they return from the spawning grounds, so by the time they get back to sea (if they get back; many salmon die after spawning) they are lean and scrawny.

The average Atlantic salmon weighs about 4.5kg/10lb when mature. The flesh of the wild fish is deep pink in colour, and is firm, succulent and full of flavour.

Salmon roe

The roe of salmon is a beautiful orange-pink colour. It does not have the depth of flavour of sturgeon caviar, but is nonetheless delicious with a squeeze of fresh lemon. The eggs are larger than those of sturgeon and have a delicate, mild flavour and excellent texture. Use them to garnish salmon dishes, or try them with blinis and sour cream. The roe is generally sold in jars, sometimes as *keta*, which is the Russian name for chum salmon.

PACIFIC SALMON (Oncorhynchus)

There are six species of Pacific salmon. Five are native to North America and the sixth, masu, is found in Japan.

Sockeye salmon (Oncorhynchus nerka)

Slender and silvery when at sea, with blue-black shading on their backs, sockeye salmon are very colourful at the spawning stage. Their heads become olive green and their bodies turn bright red. This has earned them the alternative name of red salmon, and they are also known colloquially as bluebacks. The flesh is an intense red, which is not diminished by canning. Rich and flavourful, it has a high fat content. In the canning industry, sockeye salmon has the highest grade. Smaller than some of the other types of Pacific salmon, sockeyes can weigh as much as 7kg/15½lb, but the average fish on sale is around half this size.

Chinook salmon (Oncorhynchus tschawytscha)

Also called the king salmon, this is the largest of the Pacific salmon and takes its common name from the native American tribe for whom they were a vital food source. Chunky in appearance, chinook salmon have silvery bodies with dark backs. These sport sizeable black spots, which are also on the tail. When they spawn, cock chinooks become dark red. The colour is particularly noticeable on the tail fin. The tender, soft-textured flesh ranges from off-white to pinkish-red. The average chinook weighs around 7kg/15½lb, but can grow to over 45kg/100lb.

Coho salmon (Oncorhynchus kisutch)

Alternative names for this fish are silver salmon or hooknose, the latter being a reference to the tapered kype or hook that develops on the lower jaw of males during the spawning season. At this stage, too, the silvery sides of cock cohos develop a band of red. Both males and females have small, irregular black spots on the back and tail. The flesh of coho salmon is pinkish orange, with firm texture. It is not as fatty as Chinook or sockeye salmon, and is seldom canned. A popular fish for farming, especially in the north-western United States, cohos are marketed at a weight of around 275g/10oz.

Chum salmon (Oncorhynchus keta)

At sea, these slim, elongated fish have silver skins with blue-green backs, without the black spots typical of other species. As they near the spawning season, males develop an olive green hue, and red bands appear on their sides. The pale flesh is lower in fat and not as flavourful as some other varieties. Mature chum salmon weigh around 4.5kg/10lb. Also known as keta, they are widely found in Asian waters.

Above: Atlantic salmon steaks (left) and middle cut

Above: Atlantic salmon

Pink salmon *(Oncorhynchus gorbuscha)*

The smallest members of the Pacific salmon family, these have pale silver skins, with large black spots on the back and tail, and smaller scales. During the spawning season, cocks and hens become greenish brown in colour. They have pale pink flesh, which is widely used for canning. The average pink salmon weighs around 1.8kg/4lb.

Masu salmon *(Oncorhynchus masou)*

This type of Pacific salmon is mainly found off the coast of northern Japan. It is a popular game fish, but in recent years stocks have dwindled due to environmental degradation of the rivers where the fish spawn. The flesh of masu salmon is of excellent quality and this, together with the rarity value, makes it an expensive buy.

Nutrition

Salmon is a valuable protein food. It is rich in omega-3 fatty acids, which lower blood triglycerides and cholesterol levels, keeping the heart healthy, and is a good source of Vitamin A and the B-group vitamins. Farmed salmon is fatter than wild salmon, and delivers more omega-3. Smoked salmon is less nutritious, as the smoking process introduces salt and reduces nutrient levels.

CANNED SALMON

This tastes nothing like fresh salmon, and has a different texture, but it is a richer source of calcium because the bones soften during the canning process and can be eaten. Several grades are available, from the cheapest pink salmon to the best quality wild red Alaskan fish. The latter has a better flavour and texture, but pink salmon delivers higher omega-3 values. Use for mousses, quiches and fish cakes.

SMOKED SALMON

The best smoked salmon tastes so good that it would be easy to dedicate an entire cookbook to it. Smoked salmon is made by brining the fish, then dry curing it in sugar with flavourings such as whisky or molasses, and smoking it over oak or other wood chips. Cold smoking involves curing the salmon at a temperature of less than 33°C/91°F and does not actually cook the fish. For hot smoking, the temperature is 70–80°C/158–176°F and the fish is smoked and cooked simultaneously.

Depending on the strength of the cure, the type of wood chip used and the smoking time, the colour can be anything from pale pink to deep red. The quality of smoked salmon varies enormously. Avoid very cheap smoked salmon as it is likely to be thickly cut and so heavily smoked that the delicate flavour is all but overwhelmed. Good smoked salmon should always be moist and succulent.

Right: Smoked salmon

TYPES OF TROUT

There are several different types of trout. Like salmon, they all originated in the northern hemisphere, but are now widely distributed wherever appropriate water and feeding conditions exist. Although some people declare that brown trout tastes better than rainbow trout, the reality is that all types are very similar in flavour, and any variations are determined more by diet and location than variety. The texture of good quality trout is fine and firm.

Most wild trout eat a selection of plankton and small crustaceans, which gives their flesh a beautiful rose colour. In Australia, trout that feed on yabbies are particularly highly prized. Some trout farmers use carotene-rich feed so that their fish develop flesh of a similar colour to that of trout in the wild, but others, especially those who farm organically, avoid this and produce fish with creamy-coloured flesh.

Brown trout *(Salmo trutta)*

Also known as river or lake trout, brown trout are native to Europe, but are now widely distributed throughout the world. In appearance, brown trout vary considerably. Even in the same stretch of water, some will be a silver colour, while others will be almost black. The typical colour is brown with a red adipose (rear top) fin, yellow belly, bright red spots and a liberal sprinkling of black speckles. The flesh is very tasty, but sadly, brown trout are more often caught than bought.

Sea trout *(Salmo trutta)*

Sharp-eyed readers will have noticed that this trout has the same Latin name as brown trout. That's because scientists believe them to be the same fish, despite the differences in size and behaviour. At one time it was thought that sea trout were a separate species, because they are anadromous, like salmon, and spend most of their lives

Above: Brown (right) and rainbow trout

at sea, but it is now thought that they are merely a migratory form of brown trout. Sea trout are always wild, but they do not cost as much as wild salmon. They are sold whole and should be bright and silvery in colour with an almost golden sheen. The fish for sale in fishmongers and supermarkets typically weigh between 2kg/4½lb and 3kg/6½lb, with one fish enough to serve 4–6 people. Sea trout have fine, succulent, dark pink flesh and a delicate, rounded flavour.

Rainbow trout *(Oncorhynchus mykiss,* formerly *Salmo gairdneri)*

Native to North America, this highly successful fish is now found in lakes and streams in Australia, New Zealand, Central and South America, and South Africa. It is the most popular breed for fish farming. The base colour of the body is a creamy white colour, with an iridescent sheen. There is a dense black spotting on the back and sides.

Below: Sea trout

Above: Golden trout

Nutrition

Naturally low in sodium and calories, trout is an excellent food, especially if it is steamed, grilled or cooked in the microwave. It is high in omega-3 fatty acids, which lower blood triglycerides and reduce blood pressure, protecting the body against coronary and cardiovascular disease. Trout is also a useful source of vitamins A, B1, B2, C and D. A 100g/3½oz portion of grilled rainbow trout delivers 631kj/151kcals.

Cutthroat trout *(Oncorhynchus clarki)*

Taking its popular name from the yellow, orange or red slash marks on either side of the lower jaw, this fish has a similar distribution to the rainbow trout, but unlike rainbow trout, most cutthroats migrate to sea when they are fully mature. Much prized by anglers, they have tasty, tender flesh, which ranges from a cream colour to deep red, depending on the local diet.

Golden trout *(Oncorhynchus mykiss aguabonita)*

This is the state fish of California. Golden trout, like coral trout, is a farmed hybrid variety, with vibrant skin and delicious red flesh that is firmer than that of its close relation, rainbow trout. The bright colouring makes both types of trout vulnerable to predators, but as farmed fish they are almost always bred and raised in a protected environment.

SMOKED TROUT

Once dismissed as poor man's smoked salmon, smoked trout is now regarded as a delicious treat in its own right. To prepare it, the fish are first brined, then cured in salt and sugar before being cold or hot smoked over oak or birch chippings. The colour ranges from rose pink to reddish brown and the best smoked trout is beautifully moist, with a more delicate flavour than that of smoked herring or mackerel. Smoked trout is usually sold as skinned fillets, but you will occasionally find them whole. Smoked trout has a wonderful flavour and tastes great with bread and butter. Horseradish cream and capers are often served as accompaniments. The fish also makes a very good pâté, or can be added to omelettes, risottos, quiches or pasta dishes. Allow one fillet per person as an appetizer; two as a main course.

Above: Smoked trout

Right: Trout roe

Left: Coral trout

TROUT ROE

Translucent orange beads of trout roe make a glorious garnish for savoury dishes. It can also be eaten in the same way as caviar, with sour cream and blinis for a delicious hors d'oeuvre to accompany a chilled glass of wine. Try the roe spread on fingers of wholemeal (whole-wheat) toast, or spooned over crème fraîche in tiny pastry cases.

BUYING AND STORING SALMON

When buying salmon, whether you are choosing a whole fish for a special celebration or just buying steaks for a family supper, it pays to buy from a reputable supplier who knows his product. It is surprising how many fishmongers say they don't like fish. If that's the case, shop elsewhere, for an enthusiast is far more likely to take care when buying his fish. The ideal supplier receives daily deliveries of fish, which are kept cold on a bed of regularly replenished crushed ice or in a refrigerated cabinet. Supermarkets can be a good source of salmon. Most develop good relationships with their own suppliers, and are well aware of how important it is to have well trained, helpful staff to advise their customers.

BUYING WHOLE SALMON

Look for a fish that has shiny skin and scales that are firmly attached. The skin should feel cold and firm, and should spring back when lightly pressed. If the indentation remains, the fish is not perfectly fresh. The eyes should be clear and slightly bulbous. Cloudy or sunken eyes are a sign that the fish has been badly handled or is old. The gills should always be bright pink, not a dull brown.

Smell can also be a good indication of freshness. There should be barely any odour except perhaps the faintest aroma of riverweed.

Serving a whole salmon is inevitably a treat, so it makes sense to buy the best you can afford. Wild salmon will be considerably more expensive than farmed, but the taste will be its own reward. Order the fish in good time from your supplier, so that he can obtain it on the day required. Given notice, a good fishmonger will gut, clean and scale the fish, and will also fillet it, if that is what you want. Ask him for the trimmings, as these can be used to make fish stock.

BUYING PORTIONS

Salmon steaks, fillets or cutlets are a good buy. Salmon portions take little time to cook and can be prepared in many different ways, whether steamed, grilled (broiled), fried or baked. One of the most delicious ways of cooking salmon steaks is on a ridged grill (broiling) pan or griddle, with a little butter and oil, a dash of Tabasco and a squeeze of fresh lemon juice. As with whole salmon, buy portions on the

Below: Salmon steaks

day you plan to cook them. Although fish can be kept chilled for up to two days before being eaten, valuable nutrients will be lost if it is left to languish in the refrigerator.

SUSHI

If you are buying salmon to use raw in sushi or sashimi, the advice given about freshness is doubly important. It is vital that you can rely on your supplier to obtain the best possible fish, and for that reason it is better to order the fish in advance. Ask for a chunk from a large salmon, rather than ready-cut steaks. In Japan, fresh salmon is not used for sushi because of the risk of parasite infestation. Smoked salmon is sometimes used instead.

QUANTITIES

Allow about 175g/6oz fish fillet, cutlets or steaks for serving as a main course. There is a lot of wastage on a whole fish, so allow at least 300g/11oz per person when buying fish in this way.

STORING

It is a good idea to put salmon straight into a chiller bag when you buy it, and transfer it to the coldest part of your refrigerator as soon as you get home. If you have a meat keeper, use that for storage, but make sure that the salmon is very well wrapped, so it does not taint anything else in the refrigerator.

FREEZING

Salmon tastes best fresh, but it is sometimes not practical to cook it straight away. In that case, it is better to freeze it. Unlike some more delicate fish, salmon freezes quite well, retaining much of the original texture and taste. If you buy salmon ready-frozen, make sure it comes from a reputable supplier with a rapid turnover. Avoid freezing salmon for more than 1 month, and thaw it gradually, overnight in the refrigerator if possible. If defrosting in the microwave, separate pieces as soon as possible without tearing the flesh. Remove from the microwave when still slightly icy; if fish is thawed too much it will start to dry out.

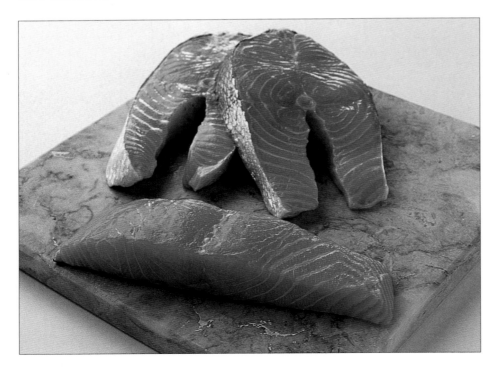

PREPARING SALMON

Many fish suppliers will prepare fresh fish for you on request, but it is not difficult to do at home, given a sharp filleting knife and a little dexterity.

SCALING

If a salmon is going to be cooked whole, and you intend removing the skin before or after cooking it, there is no need to scale it. Scaling is essential if the salmon is to be cut into portions. The supplier will do this for you if you ask him, but if doing the job yourself, remove the fins before you start, as they can be a source of bacteria, and are likely to get in the way when you are descaling the fish. Work in the kitchen sink, to contain the scales, and so that you have access to running water.

1 Wash the whole salmon under cold water. Cut off the three fins on the underbelly, from the head to the tail, then turn the fish over and remove the dorsal fins on the back. Be careful when doing this as fins can be sharp.

2 Using a cloth to hold the fish by the tail, use a fish scaler or the back of a large cook's knife to remove the scales, working from the tail to the head. Rinse the fish and repeat the process as many times as necessary.

GUTTING/CLEANING AND BONING

You may prefer to ask your fish supplier to do this part of the preparation for you because it is a messy job. If you are doing it yourself, work on a stable work surface, and rest the fish on several thicknesses of newspaper topped with a large sheet of greaseproof (waxed) paper. Always make sure you dispose of the fish innards by wrapping them securely and removing them to an outside bin.

If you intend to serve the salmon whole, with the head on, you will need to clean it through the gills. This is slightly trickier than cleaning it by slicing through the belly, but it will preserve the appearance of the fish.

Whichever method of cleaning you choose, it is important to completely remove the gills, which would give an unpleasant, bitter taste if left on. Do this by lifting up the gill flaps, which are located on either side of the head of the fish. Push out the frilly gills and use a sharp knife to cut them off at the back of the head, under the jawbone.

Whether you are planning to cook a whole fish or to divide it into separate pieces, it will then be necessary to remove the backbone and pin bones.

Cleaning through the belly

Make sure you have your work surface well covered before you start. Use a sharp, sturdy knife, such as a filleting knife, which will allow you to make firm, smooth cuts through the fish.

1 Starting at the site of the anal fin at the tail end of the salmon, slit open the belly from tail to head, using a short, sharp filleting knife. Try to work with one clean stroke, rather than several jagged movements.

2 Carefully pull out the salmon innards, severing them at the throat and tail if necessary. Remove the gills and use a knife to scrape out the cavity, removing any blood vessels adjacent to the backbone. If left, these could impart a bitter taste when the salmon is cooked. Wash the cavity carefully with cold running water, then carefully pat the salmon dry with kitchen paper. Double wrap the innards, then put them in a sealed plastic bag in the outside bin.

Essential equipment

If you plan to prepare your own whole fish at home, it is important to make sure you that have all the necessary tools to hand. Cleaning, boning and filleting fish is relatively straightforward once you know the necessary techniques, but trying to do it without the right equipment will make your task more difficult. Fortunately, these are not unusual or expensive items.

Fish scaler The best way to remove scales from salmon skin is with a fish scaler. Brushing the back and sides of the fish with this handy utensil will get rid of scales quickly and easily.

Chef's knife A large heavy knife is invaluable for cutting whole salmon into steaks and cutlets.

Filleting knife For skinning and filleting salmon, use a flexible, long-bladed knife. Sharpen it before you start work on the fish to make sure it cuts cleanly and evenly through fish skin and flesh.

Kitchen scissors Sharp scissors with serrated edges will make short work of removing fish fins and tails.

Cleaning through the gills

This method preserves the appearance of the fish, and this is important if you plan to serve the fish whole. Make sure you have your work surface well covered before you start. Use a sharp, flexible knife, such as a filleting knife, which will allow you to make firm, smooth cuts through the flesh. Remove the gills after cleaning the fish, otherwise they will give the meat a bitter and unpleasant taste.

1 Lay the salmon on its side. Using scissors or a sharp filleting knife, make an incision in the belly, near the tail end of the fish. Locate the end of the innards with your fingertips, and cut through to separate them from the fish.

2 Using a sharp filleting knife, cut through the bone at the head of the fish, under the lower jaw. Open up the gill flaps, then insert your fingers into the cavity and gently pull out the innards. These should come away through the gill flaps, to leave the belly intact. Remove the gills.

3 Wash the cavity in running water and pat dry with kitchen paper. Double wrap the innards and put them in a sealed plastic bag in the outside bin.

Boning via the belly

If you intend stuffing the salmon and serving it whole – which is a particularly delicious way to cook salmon on the barbecue – you will need to remove the backbone. This is less difficult than it sounds. The secret is to neatly cut away the flesh so that the bones can be pulled away easily. You will need a razor-sharp filleting knife and a pair of kitchen tweezers, which are necessary to remove the small pin bones.

1 Having cleaned the salmon through the belly, place it belly up. Holding a filleting knife with the blade pointing up, and starting from the tail end, slice between the rib bones and the flesh on one side so that you free the ribs.

2 Turn the knife over and finish the job on this side by sliding the blade down the ribs to the backbone, gradually working the ribs free of the flesh. Repeat on the other side. Using sharp scissors, cut out the backbone so you can remove it with the ribs.

3 Use tweezers to remove any stray pin bones. The best way to locate these tiny bones is to feel carefully along the length of the belly with your fingertips. The cavity is now ready for stuffing.

Boning a salmon steak

Salmon cutlets or bone-in steaks are often cheaper to buy than fillets but the bone can be removed quite easily. This will give a strip of fish that can be cooked as it is or folded back into the steak shape and tied neatly for frying.

1 Insert a sharp, thin-bladed knife into the salmon cutlet at the top of the bone. Cut around the bone, staying as close to it as possible, until you reach the centre of the V-shape of the cutlet. Try to work in one smooth movement.

2 Repeat on the other side of the cutlet to free the bone completely. Gently pull out the bone. Skin the fish if you want to make it more manageable.

3 To keep the steak shape, fold the flesh and tie it neatly with string (twine).

FILLETING SALMON

If you've never filleted a round fish before, salmon is a good one to start with, as its large robust size makes the job relatively easy.

1 If the salmon has been cleaned through the belly, place it on its side and make a diagonal cut around the head, behind the gill flap. If it was cleaned through the gills, this cut may already have been made.

2 Slice through the skin from the gill down the middle of the back, holding the knife flat. Keep the knife on top of the backbone and slice the flesh away from the ribs in one piece, using long even strokes and leaving as little flesh on the ribs as possible. For a salmon cleaned through the gills, you will first need to make a cut from the gills along the middle of the belly.

Filleting fish

One advantage of filleting salmon yourself is that you are left with the head and bones for making your own fish stock. Wash the head thoroughly and remove the gills before using them for stock.

3 When the first fillet, on one side of the fish, has been removed, turn the salmon over and cut away the second fillet in the same way. Remove any pin bones with tweezers. Use the bones and trimmings for fish stock, if you like, but not the bitter gills.

SKINNING A SALMON FILLET

Round fish fillets such as salmon are skinned in exactly the same way as flat fish such as hake and skate.

1 Lay the fillet skin side down with the tail towards you. Dip your fingers in a little salt to stop them slipping and grip the tail. Angle the knife towards the skin.

2 With a sawing action, cut along the length of the fillet from the tail to the head, folding the flesh forwards as you go and keeping the skin taut.

Cutting salmon escalopes

Escalopes (US scallops) are thin pieces of boneless meat or fish, which are sometimes coated in egg and breadcrumbs before being fried. To cut salmon escalopes, skin a salmon fillet, then, holding the fillet down with your hand, use a large knife to cut the piece diagonally into thin slices. The blade should be almost flat. Hold it at enough of an angle to obtain slices about 1cm/½in thick. These will cook very quickly.

PREPARING FILLETS FOR COOKING

Salmon fillets can be cooked whole and flat, rolled and secured with a cocktail stick or cut into cubes.

1 If you are cooking the fillets whole, trim them with a sharp knife, cutting off very thin flaps of fish along the edges.

2 To cube a skinned salmon fillet, cut along the length of the fillet, making strips of the desired width. Then cut each strip across into cubes.

3 To roll a fillet, roll the head end towards the tail and tuck the tail underneath. Secure with a cocktail stick (toothpick).

BUYING AND PREPARING TROUT

Wild trout is difficult to come by, unless you happen to have a fisherman in the family. Most of the trout on sale in fish shops and supermarkets is farmed, and is likely to be rainbow trout or one of its hybrids. Brown trout is available from some specialist suppliers, and it is always worth trawling the Internet for details of organic fish farmers who will deliver your order. Make sure that the fish will be delivered within 24 hours, in an insulated container, and place a small order in the first instance so that you can satisfy yourself as to the quality of the fish and its condition on receipt.

Frozen trout is also a good buy and the fish is usually in prime condition, having been frozen so quickly that the skins still retain their natural moisture.

Sea trout is not farmed, and you will almost certainly need to order it from your fishmonger or market. This large fish has an excellent flavour and is often substituted for the more expensive salmon. Sea trout are always sold whole.

When buying fresh trout in person, the same rules apply as for any other fresh fish. Look for fish that have shiny, iridescent skins, with a good coating of slime, bright clear eyes and red gills. The skin should feel cold to the touch, and when pressed, should spring back instantly. If any indentation remains, the fish is not as fresh as it might be. Trout are almost always sold whole with the head on. They are very inexpensive.

QUANTITIES

Unless they are particularly large, you should allow one trout per person if you plan to serve it whole. A 2kg/4½lb sea trout will be sufficient to serve 4–6 people. If cooking trout fillets as part of a recipe, follow the quantity given in the instructions.

STORING AND FREEZING

When buying fresh trout, transport it in a chiller bag. Double wrap it when you get home and store it in the coldest part of the refrigerator. Aim to cook it on the same day. If this is not possible, store it for no more than two days, or freeze it. Trout freezes very well. Thaw it slowly, overnight in the refrigerator if possible.

PREPARATION

If you buy trout from a fishmonger or supermarket, it will have been cleaned, but you might be lucky enough to be offered some freshly caught trout on some occasion. In this case it is essential to know how to prepare it.

Trout do not need to be scaled, but it is a good idea to remove the fins as these can harbour bacteria. Cut them off using a strong pair of scissors. Take care with the dorsal fins (those on the back), which can have sharp spines.

CLEANING TROUT

This isn't a pleasant job, but can be performed quickly and easily with a bit of preparation. Start by spreading the work area with newspapers and topping these with greaseproof (waxed) paper.

There are two ways of gutting whole trout: through the belly or through the gills. The former is the more usual method, but gutting through the gills is preferred if splitting the fish open would spoil its appearance. This method might be used for a sea trout that was to be served whole, for instance. In either case, the gills should be removed before the fish is cooked, because they taste bitter. Do this by holding the fish on its back and opening the gill flaps. Push out the frilly gills and cut them off at the back of the head and under the jawbone with a sharp knife.

Cleaning through the belly

This is the usual way of cleaning trout. Assemble your equipment and cover the work surface before you begin.

1 Starting at the site of the anal fin, slit open the belly from tail to head, using a sharp filleting knife.

2 Pull out the innards, severing them at the throat and tail if necessary. If you are planning to stuff the trout, the roes will make a delicious addition.

3 Use a tablespoon to make sure the cavity is empty, removing any blood vessels adjacent to the backbone. Double wrap the innards and throw them away in an outside bin. Wash the cavity, then pat dry with kitchen paper.

Essential equipment
Have the necessary tools to hand before you start to prepare fish at home, as trying to work without the right equipment will make your task more difficult. Fortunately, these are not unusual or expensive items.
Chef's knife A large heavy knife is invaluable for cutting whole trout into steaks and cutlets.
Filleting knife For skinning and filleting trout, use a flexible filleting knife with a long blade. Sharpen it before you start work on the fish to make sure it cuts cleanly and evenly through fish skin and flesh.
Kitchen scissors Sharp scissors with serrated edges will make short work of removing fish fins and tails.

Cleaning through the gills

If you are planning to serve the trout whole, it is better to clean through the gills to preserve its appearance.

1 Lay the fish on its side. Make an incision in the belly, near the tail. Find the ends of the innards and snip through.

2 Cut through the bone under the lower jaw. Open the gill flaps and pull out the innards; they will come away through the flaps. Wash and dry the fish.

Filleting trout

This is a useful technique to learn if you want to cut fillets from whole trout.

1 Lay the trout on a board with its tail towards you. Lift the pectoral fin and make a diagonal cut behind the fin to the top of the head.

2 Insert the knife halfway down the body, as close to the backbone as possible. Cut towards the tail, keeping the knife flat to the bone. Lift up the released fillet, turn the knife towards the head and slide it along the bone to free the fillet completely.

3 Turn the trout over and repeat on the other side. Remove any small pin bones from the fillets with tweezers. Skin the fillets if you like.

Skinning trout fillets

1 Lay the fillet skin side down with the tail towards you. Grip the tail and angle the knife towards the skin.

2 With a slight sawing action, cut along the length of the fillet from tail to head. Keep the skin taut.

Removing pin bones from fillets

There are always some small bones left in a fillet. Run your finger down the fillet to locate these and lift them out with tweezers.

Round fish also have tiny pin bones behind the gill fins. To remove these, make a diagonal cut on either side of the line of bones with a sharp knife. Remove the V-shaped piece of flesh together with the bones.

Boning a trout steak

Trout cutlets or bone-in steaks can be boned to give a strip of fish. This can be cooked as it is or folded back into a steak shape and tied neatly with string ready for pan-frying.

1 Insert a sharp, thin-bladed knife into the trout cutlet at the top of the bone. Cut around the bone until you reach the centre of the V-shape of the cutlet.

2 Repeat on the other side of the steak, to free the bone completely. Gently pull out the bone. Skin the fish if you want to make it more manageable.

3 Fold the skinned flesh into the middle and tie with a length of string to hold the shape.

COOKING SALMON

Despite being quite a substantial, meaty fish, salmon cooks quickly. It can be prepared in a wide number of ways, from poaching to pan-frying, grilling (broiling) to baking and braising. It will emerge from a microwave beautifully moist and full of flavour and can be steamed or smoked with equal success.

Court-bouillon

This stock, which is flavoured with white wine and aromatics, is perfect for poaching salmon. Salt should be added only after cooking the salmon, as it can cause the flesh to stiffen. The recipe makes about 1 litre/ 1³/₄ pints/4 cups.

1 Slice 1 small onion, 2 carrots and the white part of 1 large leek. Put the vegetables in a pan.

2 Add 2 fresh parsley stalks, 2 bay leaves, 2 lemon slices, 300ml/ ¹/₂ pint/1¹/₄ cups dry white wine and 90ml/6 tbsp white wine vinegar. Sprinkle in a few white peppercorns. Add 1 litre/1³/₄ pints/4 cups water. Bring to the boil, lower the heat and simmer for 20 minutes. Strain and leave to cool before using.

Whichever method you choose, it is vital to avoid overcooking salmon. In some circles it is served when the flesh still has a ruby tint, but most people prefer salmon that has just turned opaque. Ideally, the fish should finish cooking on the way to the table, so that when it is touched with the fork, the flesh separates easily into meltingly tender flakes.

It is not possible to give precise timings for cooking salmon, since factors such as the thickness of the fish, the cooking method used and the temperature will all come into play. To ensure that the salmon cooks evenly, remove it from the refrigerator at least 30 minutes before cooking.

Salmon is cooked when its internal temperature is around 63ºC/145ºF, but rather than employ a meat thermometer, which is quite a specialist piece of kitchen equipment, it is best to use a visual check. Gently insert a small sharp knife into the centre of the fish and part the flesh. It should be no longer translucent and should have begun to ease away from the bone. For large pieces of salmon, it may be simpler to press a fork into the thickest part. If the prongs sink into the flesh, meeting only slight resistance near the bone, the salmon is cooked.

POACHING

This is the classic way of cooking salmon. The fish is cooked gently in either water, fish stock or an aromatic court-bouillon, and this ensures that the maximum flavour is retained.

Whole salmon

Use a fish kettle to poach whole salmon. If you do not have a fish kettle you could try to hire one from a local kitchen store, if they offer this service. It is a good idea to measure the length of your fish kettle before you shop for your fish. There's nothing more irritating than bringing home a salmon only to find it will not fit your kettle. If you are not able to obtain a fish kettle, a whole salmon can be wrapped in foil and cooked in the oven. Use the extra-large foil, sometimes known as turkey foil.

Using a fish kettle

1 Remove the metal insert from the fish kettle and place the salmon on this. Lower the salmon into the kettle. Pour over cold court-bouillon, fish stock or water to cover the fish.

2 Add a few fresh herbs, such as parsley, dill or tarragon. Slices of lemon can be laid on top of the salmon.

3 Cover the fish with buttered baking parchment, place the pan over a medium heat and heat slowly until the water just begins to tremble. Simmer until the flesh is just opaque. If you plan to serve the salmon cold, simmer it for only 5 minutes, then remove the kettle from the heat and set it aside without lifting the lid. By the time the poaching liquid has cooled, the salmon will be perfectly cooked.

Butter sauce for poached fish

Poached fish needs very little enhancement other than a simple sauce that has been made from the poaching liquid itself.

1 Remove the cooked fish from the poaching liquid and keep it hot while you make the sauce.

2 Strain the poaching liquid into a pan and place it over a medium heat. Simmer gently until the liquid has reduced by half.

3 Whisk in some cold diced butter or a little double (heavy) cream to make a smooth, velvety sauce. Season with salt and black papper. Pour the sauce over the fish and serve.

Cooking whole salmon in foil

If you do not have a fish kettle, a whole salmon can be baked in the oven. Have ready a large piece of strong foil. Brush on 15ml/1 tbsp oil. Place the salmon on the foil and tuck some lemon slices inside the cavity. Place more lemon slices on top. Wrap the salmon loosely but securely in the foil and support in a roasting pan. Bake in a preheated oven at 150°C/300°F/Gas 2 for 10–15 minutes per 450g/1lb if under 2.3kg/5lb or 8 minutes per 450g/1lb if over that weight. Check frequently towards the end of cooking as timings will vary, depending on your oven and the thickness of the fish. If the salmon is very large, it may be simpler to cook it in sections, then reassemble it for serving. Clever garnishing can cover any joins.

Salmon portions

A large piece of salmon can be cooked in a pan, following the method for poaching in a fish kettle. Small portions are best poached in a dish that is large enough to hold them in a single layer.

1 Place the salmon portions in a shallow flameproof dish. Pour over court-bouillon, light fish stock or water.

2 Cover the fish with buttered baking parchment. Bring the liquid slowly to simmering point. By this time, thin portions may be cooked. Lower the heat, cover and poach thicker portions for 5–10 minutes more, until opaque.

Using the dishwasher

Many cooks claim that the best way to poach salmon is in the dishwasher. The suggested technique involves wrapping the fish in several layers of foil, placing it on the top shelf of the thoroughly clean machine, and then running the dishwasher through the hottest cycle – without detergent, of course. While this might work if the salmon is relatively small and the dishwasher offers an extra-long hot cycle, a test in a standard dishwasher was unsuccessful. The salmon was beautifully moist, but only the thinnest parts were cooked.

Fish stock

It is easy and economical to make fish stock. For 1 litre/1¾ pints/ 4 cups stock you will need about 1kg/2¼lb white fish bones and trimmings from the fishmonger. Do not leave the stock simmering on the stove – after 20 minutes the flavour will deteriorate.

1 Wash any fish heads thoroughly and remove the gills, which would make the stock bitter. Chop the heads and bones if necessary. Put them in a large pan.

2 Slice the white part of 1 leek or ½ fennel bulb. Chop 1 onion and 1 celery stick. Add to the fish heads and bones in the pan.

3 Pour in 150ml/¼ pint/⅔ cup dry white wine and 1 litre/1¾ pints/ 4 cups water. Add 6 white peppercorns and a bouquet garni. Bring to the boil.

4 Lower the heat and simmer for 20 minutes. Remove from the heat, strain through a sieve lined with muslin (cheesecloth) and cool.

BAKING AND BRAISING

If you want to cook salmon slowly along with other vegetables and flavourings, baking and braising are ideal. To ensure the fish cooks evenly, take it out of the refrigerator 30 minutes before cooking. Aim to undercook the fish as the texture will be dry and it will lose its flavour if it is allowed to cook for too long. You can give it a little extra cooking if necessary.

Baking fillets

Salmon steaks, fillets and cutlets can all be baked in the oven. Check the fish frequently because cooking times will vary, depending on the cut and size of the fish, the method of baking and the effectiveness of your oven.

Chunky salmon steaks and cutlets are perfect for baking in a roasting pan in the oven. The temperature should be no higher than 200°C/400°F/Gas 6. Keep the fish moist by coating it in a sauce or olive oil or by wrapping it in foil.

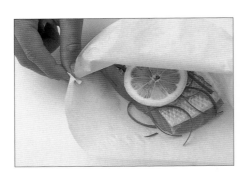

Another way of retaining maximum moisture is to cook the salmon *en papillote*, which means in a foil or paper parcel. Add a couple of slices of lemon and some fresh dill or other herbs. No additional fat is needed, so this is a very healthy option.

Braising fillets

This is an excellent cooking method for larger salmon fillets. Adding the stock helps to keep the fish beautifully moist.

1 Butter a flameproof dish and arrange a thick bed of thinly sliced or shredded vegetables on the base. A mixture of leeks, fennel and carrots works well.

2 Place the fish on top of the vegetables and pour on enough dry white wine, court-bouillon or light fish stock to come nearly halfway up the fish.

3 Sprinkle over 15ml/1 tbsp chopped fresh herbs, then cover with buttered baking parchment and set over a high heat. Bring the liquid to the boil. Braise over a low heat on top of the stove or in an oven preheated to 180°C/350°F/Gas 4 for 10–15 minutes.

FRYING

Pan-frying is particularly well-suited to salmon because the flesh is robust and the flavours will not be diminished. Stir-frying in a wok is just as tasty, but it uses less oil and makes a healthier alternative to pan-frying.

Pan-frying

Salmon tastes absolutely delicious when lightly pan-fried in butter, fruity olive oil or a mixture of the two.

Heat the fat in the pan. When it is very hot, add the fish and seal briefly on both sides. Lower the heat and cook the fish gently until done. If the pieces of fish are large or the recipe is more complex it may be necessary to finish cooking the fish in an oven preheated to 180°C/350°F/Gas 4.

Searing

This method gives the best results with thick fillets of salmon, with the skin on.

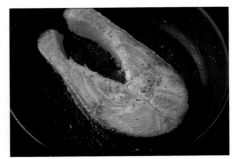

Smear the base of a frying pan or griddle with a little oil and heat until smoking. Brush both sides of the salmon with oil and put into the hot pan, skin down. Sear for 2 minutes, until the skin is golden brown, then turn the fish over and cook the other side.

Stir-frying

This quick Asian cooking style is perfect for many types of fish. Strips of salmon taste delicious stir-fried with thinly sliced spring onions (scallions) and slices of baby fennel. Stir-fry the vegetables briefly in hot oil, then add the salmon strips, lightly moistened with soy sauce, and stir-fry for 1–2 minutes until cooked but still in one piece.

1 Cut the salmon fillets into bitesize strips. Toss in a little cornflour (cornstarch) to prevent them falling apart as they cook in the oil.

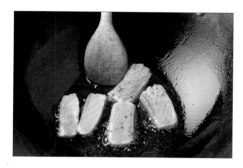

2 Heat vegetable oil in a wok or frying pan over a very high heat. Add the pieces of salmon to the wok and stir-fry for a few moments. You may need to cook the pieces in batches, depending on the amount of fish you wish to cook and the size of your wok.

3 As each batch of salmon pieces is cooked, remove them from the wok and keep warm as you cook further batches.

Deep-frying salmon

Salmon pieces are seldom deep-fried in the way that cod or haddock are. The reason for this is not so much because salmon is not suitable for deep-frying – quite the opposite in fact, because its firm, meaty flesh is perfectly capable of holding its shape – but because frying impairs the special flavour and texture. The exception is when thin strips of salmon fillet are transformed into goujons by coating them in milk and flour and deep-frying them in oil.

Goujons of salmon

Crisp on the outside and succulent and tender within, salmon goujons taste wonderful served with a creamy dipping sauce.

SERVES 4

INGREDIENTS

    1 salmon fillet, about 350g/12oz
    120ml/4fl oz/$\frac{1}{2}$ cup milk
    50g/2oz/$\frac{1}{2}$ cup plain
      (all-purpose) flour
    salt and ground black pepper
    oil, for deep-frying

1 Skin the salmon fillet and cut it into 7.5 x 2.5cm/3 x 1in strips. Pour the milk into a shallow bowl. Season the flour and spread it out in a separate shallow bowl.

2 Dip the salmon strips into the milk, then into the seasoned flour. Shake off the excess flour.

3 Heat the oil for deep-frying to about 185°C/360°F or until a small cube of bread dropped into the oil turns brown in 30 seconds.

4 Lower the salmon strips into the oil, adding four or five at a time. Fry for 3 minutes, turning them occasionally with a slotted spoon, until they have risen to the surface and are golden brown in colour.

5 Lift out each goujon in turn with a slotted spoon and drain on kitchen paper. Keep hot in the oven while you cook successive batches.

ON THE BARBECUE

This is a very good way of cooking salmon. Either marinate steaks or thick fillets (with the skin on) for at least an hour before cooking, or brush them with vegetable or olive oil just before cooking over medium coals. If you are entertaining in large numbers, you could cook a whole salmon on the barbecue. If you have a hinged grill, put the prepared salmon directly on the grill. Otherwise, wrap the salmon in a large sheet of foil. A 2.25kg/5lb salmon will take from 45 minutes to 1 hour to cook, depending on the heat of the coals and whether or not the fish is wrapped in foil.

Marinate the salmon pieces in a mixture of olive oil and lemon juice, making deep slashes in the side of the fish so that the marinade penetrates right the way through and the heat is conducted evenly through the flesh. Leave the fish in the refrigerator to marinate for a minimum of 1 hour.

A ridged griddle set on the barbecue is good for cooking salmon. Grease it lightly with oil to prevent the skin of the salmon from sticking – an oil spray will give the best coverage with the least amount of oil.

GRILLING

When grilling (broiling) salmon steaks or fillets, high heat should be used initially, to seal in the fish juices. Regardless of the recipe, the fish will always benefit from being marinated in a mixture of oil and lemon juice before being grilled. Brush the grill (broiling) rack with oil, and if the fish has not been marinated, brush it with oil too. Turn thick salmon steaks or fillets over once the surface is sealed, and grill the other side until cooked through. Thin fillets will not need to be turned. Cubes of salmon make excellent kebabs.

MICROWAVING

Salmon cooks well in the microwave. Always cover the fish with microwave clear film (plastic wrap). Cook on full power (100 per cent) for the time recommended in your handbook, then give it a resting period so that it finishes cooking by residual heat. As a general guide, thick fillets, steaks and cutlets will take 4–5 minutes and should be left to stand for a further 5 minutes.

Cook salmon fillets in a single layer in a microwave dish. Put thinner parts towards the centre, or tuck a thin end underneath a thicker portion.

ROASTING

Thick pieces of salmon can be roasted successfully. As with grilling it is a good idea to marinate the fish in oil and lemon juice beforehand. Preheat the oven to 230°C/450°F/Gas 8, with the roasting pan inside. Add the pieces of fish, skin side down, to the hot pan. This will sear the skin and help to retain the juices. Fillets will take about 10–12 minutes; steaks 15–20 minutes.

STEAMING

This is the healthiest way of cooking salmon, since no extra fat is required and nutrients are retained, and the steaming process enhances the natural flavour. Salmon cooks quickly this way, but even if you overcook it the fish will retain its shape and remain moist.

1 Half-fill the base pan of a metal steamer with water and bring to the boil. Lower the steamer insert into the base, making sure that it stands well clear of the boiling water.

2 Place the fish in a single layer in the steamer basket, leaving room for the steam to circulate freely. Add fresh herbs with the salmon if you like.

3 Lay a sheet of greaseproof (waxed) paper loosely over the surface of the fish, then cover the pan tightly with a lid or foil. Steam until the fish is just cooked through.

4 Salmon cooks very quickly in a steamer, but take care that the level of the water does not fall too low, or the base of the pan will burn. Check once or twice during cooking and keep a kettle of boiling water on hand to top it up if necessary.

Alternative steaming methods

There are plenty of purpose-made steamers on the market, ranging from the hugely expensive stainless steel models to modest Chinese bamboo baskets. However, you can easily improvise with a large pan, any perforated container, such as a colander or sieve, and some foil. It is important to make sure that the pan is large enough to hold several inches of water.

Whatever the type of steamer you use, remember that the golden rule of steaming is not to allow the boiling liquid to touch the steamer basket or the salmon inside it. This would mean that the fish was boiling in water, and all of its nutritional value would be lost.

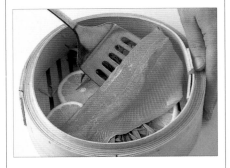

A Chinese bamboo steamer is ideal for steaming salmon. Arrange the fish, skin side up, on a bed of aromatic flavourings, such as lemon slices and fresh herbs, or on finely shredded vegetables. Place the steamer in a wok or on top of a large pan of boiling water and steam until the fish is cooked.

SMOKING

Salmon can be smoked at home, either in a small domestic smoker or a kettle barbecue. Follow the instructions in your handbook. In the kitchen, the Chinese method of tea smoking works well, but it helps if you have an extractor fan to remove excess smoke.

1 Line a wok with foil and sprinkle in 30ml/2 tbsp each of raw long grain rice, sugar and aromatic tea leaves.

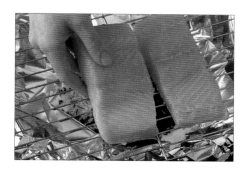

2 Place a wire rack on the wok and add the salmon fillets in a single layer.

3 Cover the wok with a lid or more foil and cook over a very high heat until smoke appears. Lower the heat slightly (some smoke should still escape from the wok) and cook for 10–15 minutes more until the fish is done.

RAW SALMON

Very fresh salmon that has been bought from a reliable fishmonger or supplier can also be served raw, as smoked salmon, sushi or sashimi, or brined to make the delectable Scandinavian speciality known as gravlax.

Home-cured gravlax

Although almost every supermarket sells ready-cured gravlax, it is very easy to prepare at home. For eight people you will need 1–1.2kg/2¼–2½lb of absolutely fresh middle-cut salmon that has already been boned and cut lengthways into two fillets.

1 For the curing mix, mix 30ml/2 tbsp coarse sea salt, 30ml/2 tbsp caster (superfine) sugar, 15–30ml/1–2 tbsp crushed black peppercorns and a handful of chopped fresh dill.

2 Lay one salmon fillet skin side down in a non-metallic dish. Cover with a generous layer of the curing mix. Lay the second fillet on top, skin side up, and sprinkle on the remaining mix. Cover with clear film (plastic wrap).

3 Place a wooden board slightly larger than the non-metallic dish on top of the salmon and weigh it down with heavy cans or weights.

4 Leave in the refrigerator for at least 72 hours, turning the salmon every 12 hours and basting it with the juices that have oozed out. To serve, slice on the diagonal, a little thicker than you would for smoked salmon.

Above: Gravlax

Flavourings for salmon

Salmon is a hugely versatile fish and it works well with a range of flavourings. The following can be used to adapt your own recipes or some of those featured in this book.

Companion flavourings Salmon has a natural affinity for fresh-tasting herbs like parsley, chervil and tarragon. Dill, with its aniseed flavour, is a great favourite, and is essential in the Swedish sugar-and-salt-cured dish, gravlax. Citrus flavourings like lemon and lime are obvious choices, but try lemon grass for a more subtle taste, or that little used but delicious herb, sorrel.

Fusion flavours Aromatics like ginger and galangal go well with salmon, as does fresh garlic. Spring onions (scallions), leeks and shallots are also suitable, and are especially good to use in marinades and sauces. Fennel has a similar flavour to dill, the herb that works so well with salmon, so try roasting salmon on a bed of thinly sliced fennel, with the fronds chopped and added to a sauce or used as a garnish.

Nuts It is well known that almonds go well with trout, but you can try them with salmon too. Brown them in butter or use them in a stuffing for whole salmon. Other nuts you could try include hazelnuts, pine nuts, pistachios and macadamias.

A splash of wine Dry white wine is the obvious choice of alcohol for flavouring salmon, and it is often mixed with court-bouillon. The Medierranean aperitif drinks pastis and ouzo are also appropriate, as they have the slightly aniseed flavour that balances the oiliness of the fish. For warmer flavours, try rice wine such as sake or mirin. Ginger wine could also be used, but don't overdo it, as its powerful flavour could be a bit overwhelming. For an alcohol-free cooking medium, use a good homemade court-bouillon or fish stock or coconut milk.

COOKING TROUT

The secret of cooking trout successfully is the same as that for any other type of fish: less time means more taste. Undercooking can easily be remedied, but fish that is overcooked is dry and flavourless. Although the very best way to cook a fresh wild brown trout is to fry it in butter, farmed rainbow trout can be cooked in a variety of ways.

Court-bouillon

This stock, which is flavoured with white wine and aromatics, is perfect for poaching trout. Salt should be added only after cooking, as it can cause the flesh to stiffen. The recipe makes about 1 litre/1¾ pints/4 cups.

1 Slice 1 small onion, 2 carrots and the white part of 1 large leek. Put the vegetables in a pan.

2 Add 2 fresh parsley stalks, 2 bay leaves, 2 lemon slices, 300ml/½ pint/1¼ cups dry white wine and 90ml/6 tbsp white wine vinegar. Sprinkle in a few white peppercorns. Pour in 1 litre/1¾ pints/4 cups water. Bring to the boil, lower the heat and simmer for 20 minutes. Strain and leave to cool before using.

POACHING

For whole trout, you will need a fish kettle, flameproof dish or roasting pan; for smaller cuts, use an ordinary pan.

1 Remove the metal insert from the fish kettle and place the trout on this. Lower into the kettle. Add a few sprigs of fresh herbs and slices of lemon.

2 Pour cold court-bouillon, light fish stock or water over the trout in the fish kettle, adding enough of the liquid to cover the fish completely.

3 Cover the trout with buttered baking parchment. Bring the liquid slowly to simmering point. If poaching fillets, thin portions may be cooked and can be removed. Lower the heat, cover the pan and poach the uncooked thicker fillets for 5 minutes more or until done.

Fish stock

It is both easy and economical to make fish stock. For 1 litre/1¾ pints/4 cups stock you will need about 1kg/2¼lb white fish bones and trimmings from the fishmonger. Do not leave the stock simmering for too long – after 20 minutes the flavour will start to deteriorate.

1 Wash any fish heads thoroughly and remove the gills, which would make the stock bitter. Chop the heads and bones if necessary. Put them in a large pan.

2 Slice the white part of 1 leek or ½ fennel bulb. Roughly chop 1 onion and 1 celery stick. Add to the fish heads and bones in the pan.

3 Pour in 150ml/¼ pint/⅔ cup dry white wine and 1 litre/1¾ pints/4 cups water. Add 6 whole white peppercorns and a bouquet garni. Bring to the boil.

4 Lower the heat and simmer for 20 minutes. Remove from the heat, strain through a sieve lined with muslin (cheesecloth) and cool.

COOKING "AU BLEU"

This time-honoured way of cooking trout is only for the freshest fish – so fresh that it is alive seconds before you begin the process. The term "au bleu" refers to the steely blue colour the fish skin acquires on being poached.

To cook trout "au bleu" the live fish is taken from the water and immediately stunned by a hit on the back of the head with a blunt object, such as the handle of a heavy cook's knife or a steak mallet. The fish is then cleaned through the gills and laid in a flameproof dish or fish kettle. A mixture of water and white wine vinegar is spooned over to cover it completely, and the fish is then gently simmered over a medium heat until it is cooked. A 150g/5oz trout will take 6–8 minutes, during which time the natural slime that coats the very fresh fish will turn a deep blue colour – from which the cooking method takes its name. Trout prepared in this way is traditionally served hot with hollandaise sauce, or cold with Ravigote sauce – made by mixing oil and vinegar with chopped tomatoes, diced hard-boiled eggs, capers, chopped gherkins and fresh herbs.

ROASTING

Delicate fillets of trout should be treated like white fish, such as sole or whiting, and pan-fried or steamed, but thicker trout fillets and steaks, and whole trout, can be roasted successfully. It is a good idea to marinate them in oil and lemon juice beforehand. Preheat the oven to 230°C/450°F/Gas 8 with the roasting pan inside. Add the fish, skin side down, to the pan. Fillets will take 8–10 minutes; steaks 12–15 minutes.

BAKING AND BRAISING

These are two excellent ways of cooking trout slowly, along with extra flavourings, such as fresh herbs, or vegetables.

Baking trout

Whole trout, steaks or fillets can all be baked in the oven. Slash whole fish to allow the heat to penetrate the flesh.

Lay the fish in a greased baking dish, drizzle with olive oil and add a little liquid. Dry (hard) cider goes well with trout, as do court-bouillon and fish stock. Cover with buttered baking parchment or foil and bake at no more than 200°C/400°F/Gas 6. Whole fish will cook in 20–30 minutes, depending on the thickness. Trout fillets will cook more quickly.

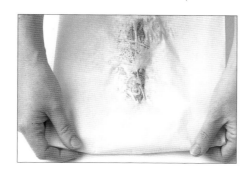

To seal in the flavour and retain moisture, bake the trout *en papillote* in a paper or foil parcel. A stuffing of rice with nuts and sun-dried tomatoes would be an excellent addition. Place the trout on a piece of oiled baking parchment or foil and fill the cavity with the stuffing. Add a drizzle of olive oil. Fold over the paper or foil to enclose the fish completely. Place the parcel on a baking sheet. Bake at 190°C/375°F/Gas 5 for about 20 minutes, until the trout is tender.

Braising trout

This is an ideal way of cooking either whole trout or fillets. Adding the stock helps to keep the fish beautifully moist.

1 Butter a flameproof dish and arrange a thick bed of thinly sliced or shredded vegetables on the base, such as a mixture of leeks, fennel and carrots.

2 Place the fish on top of the vegetables and pour on enough dry white wine, court-bouillon or light fish stock to come nearly halfway up the fish.

3 Scatter over 15ml/1 tbsp chopped fresh herbs, then cover with buttered baking parchment and set over a high heat. Bring the liquid to the boil. Braise over a low heat on top of the stove or in an oven preheated to 180°C/350°F/Gas 4 for 10–15 minutes.

FRYING

Pan-frying is a fabulously tasty way to cook trout, but stir-frying in a wok uses less oil and is a healthier alternative.

Pan-frying

Boned whole trout, steaks and fillets can be pan-fried in butter. Butter burns quite readily; adding a little oil will help prevent this. Coat the fish in seasoned flour before adding it to the melted butter, and fry over a low heat. If using whole trout, cook for 6 minutes on each side, until the skin is crisp and golden brown. After the fish has been removed from the pan, the remaining butter can be used as the basis of a sauce. Add mushrooms, a splash of pastis or ouzo and some double (heavy) cream.

Searing

Smear a frying pan with a little oil and heat until smoking. Brush both sides of the fish with oil and put into the pan skin side down. Sear for 2 minutes until the skin is golden brown, then turn the fish over and cook on the other side.

Stir-frying

Strips of trout fillet can be stir-fried in a hot wok for 1–2 minutes, but take care that they do not disintegrate. Toss the fish strips with a little sweet chilli sauce just before serving.

Deep-frying

Trout pieces are transformed into goujons by coating them in milk and flour and deep-frying in oil.

1 Dip strips of trout fillet into milk, and then into a plate of plain (all-purpose) flour that has been seasoned with salt and ground black pepper. Shake off the excess flour.

2 Heat oil for deep-frying to about 180°C/360°F or until a small cube of bread dropped into the oil turns brown in 30 seconds.

3 Lower the trout strips into the oil and fry for 3 minutes, turning with a slotted spoon, until they rise to the surface. Drain the goujons on kitchen paper and serve with a creamy dipping sauce.

GRILLING

This is one of the best ways of cooking farmed rainbow trout. If grilling (broiling) the trout whole, slash the skin on either side of the fish several times with a sharp knife. This helps to promote fast, even cooking. Marinate whole trout or steaks in a mixture of oil and lemon juice if you like, or simply brush with oil. A light dusting of ground black pepper will give the skin a delicious flavour. Place the trout in a grill (broiler) pan and cook under a medium heat for 5 minutes on each side.

Cooking trout on a barbecue

The oil in trout makes it a good candidate for barbecue cooking. If using thawed frozen trout, pat it dry inside and out with kitchen paper. Brush with oil and sprinkle with salt and ground black pepper. The fish can be cooked directly on a lightly oiled grid, although you may find it easier to turn them over if the fish are placed in a hinged grilling rack. Cook over medium-hot coals for about 10–15 minutes, or until done, and turn once, halfway through cooking. Drizzle with fresh lemon juice just before serving.

Marinate the trout in a mixture of olive oil and lemon juice, making deep slashes in the sides of the fish so that the marinade penetrates right the way through and the heat is conducted evenly. Allow the fish to marinate in the refrigerator for a minimum of 1 hour.

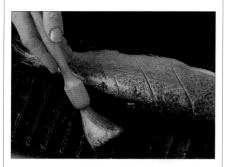

A ridged griddle set on the barbecue is good for cooking trout and will allow you to remove the fish easily. Grease it lightly to prevent the skin of the fish from sticking as it cooks. For the healthiest alternative, an oil spray will give the best coverage with the least amount of oil.

MICROWAVING

Cover the fish with microwave clear film (plastic wrap) and cook on full power (100 per cent) for the time recommended in your handbook, then give it a resting period so that it finishes cooking by residual heat. As a general guide, a whole fish will take 4–7 minutes, depending on whether or not it has been stuffed. Leave to stand for a further 5 minutes before serving.

Slash whole fish several times on either side for even cooking.

Cook fillets of trout in a single layer in a microwave dish. Put thinner parts towards the centre, or tuck a thin end underneath a thicker portion.

STEAMING

As no extra fat is required and all of the nutrients are retained, this is the healthiest way to cook trout.

1 Half-fill the base pan of a steamer with water and bring to the boil. Place the trout fillets in a single layer in the steamer basket, leaving room for the steam to circulate freely.

2 Place a sheet of baking parchment over the fish, then cover the pan and steam until the fish is cooked through. Check the level of water in the steamer occasionally and top up as needed.

SMOKING

Trout can be smoked at home, either in a small domestic smoker or a kettle barbecue. Follow the instructions in your handbook. In the kitchen, the Chinese method of tea smoking works very well, but it helps if you have an extractor fan to remove the excess smoke from the kitchen.

1 Line a wok with foil and sprinkle in 30ml/2 tbsp each of raw long grain rice, sugar and aromatic tea leaves.

2 Place a wire rack on the wok and add the trout fillets in a single layer. Cover with a lid or more foil and cook over a high heat until smoke appears. Lower the heat slightly (some smoke should still escape from the wok) and cook for 6–8 minutes until the trout is done.

No steamer, no problem
If you do not possess a steamer, all is not lost. A good way to cook trout fillets over water is to place them in a single layer on a lightly buttered heatproof plate. Cover this with an inverted heatproof plate of the same size, then lift both plates together and place them over a pan of boiling water. The trout fillets will cook very quickly this way, so check them after about 3–4 minutes.

Smoked Trout Pâté
This tastes great served with crackers or spread on fingers of hot toast.

SERVES 4–6

INGREDIENTS
  450g/1lb smoked trout
    fillets, skinned
  1 small onion, finely chopped
  1 celery stick, thinly sliced
  finely grated rind and juice of
    1 lemon
  200g/7oz cream cheese
  salt and ground black pepper
  fresh dill sprigs, to garnish

1 Tear the trout fillets into chunks and place in the bowl of a blender or food processor. Add the onion, celery and lemon rind. Scrape in the cream cheese and process until the mixture is thick and smooth.

2 Add salt and pepper to taste, then pour in just enough of the lemon juice to balance the flavours. Process briefly to mix. Serve in a small bowl, garnished with the dill.

COOK'S TIPS
• Trout is traditionally served with browned almonds, but this treatment was so widespread in the 1960s and 70s that it became somewhat passé. The flavours do complement each other, however, and recent years have seen a revival of the partnership. Also try hazelnuts, pistachios or pine nuts.
• The flavour of trout is quite robust, and responds well to warm spices like paprika, cayenne and coriander. For blackened trout, the fish are coated in melted butter, then in a mixture of garlic, onion and spices. When cooked, the spice mixture forms a dark crust – a perfect foil for the tender trout inside.
• Frozen trout must be allowed to thaw completely, and fresh trout that has been kept in the refrigerator should be brought to room temperature before cooking.
• To test whether a trout is cooked, insert a knife into the thickest part of the fish and part the flesh. It should look opaque rather than translucent and should readily separate into flakes.

EQUIPMENT

Although it is perfectly possible to prepare and cook fish without special kitchen equipment, there are a few items which make the process much easier. Some, such as the fish kettle, take up quite a lot of storage space; other gadgets, such as the fish scaler, are relatively small, but all will prove invaluable for cooking fish.

KNIVES, SCISSORS AND SCALERS

Chef's knife
A large heavy knife with a 20–25cm/8–10in blade is essential for cutting fish steaks.

Filleting knife
For filleting and skinning fish, you will need a sharp knife with a flexible blade, which is at least 15cm/6in long. This type of knife can also be used for opening shellfish. It is essential to keep a filleting knife razor sharp.

Kitchen scissors
A sturdy, sharp pair of scissors that have a serrated edge are needed for cutting off fins and trimming tails.

Fish scaler
Resembling a rough grater, a fish scaler makes short work of a task that few relish.

PANS

Fish kettle
Long and deep, with rounded edges, this has handles at either end, and a tightly-fitting lid. Inside is a perforated rack or grid on which to lay the fish. This, too, has handles, and enables the cook to lift out the fish flat. Most modern fish kettles are made of stainless steel, but they also come in aluminium,

enamelled steel and copper with a tin-plated interior. Fish kettles are used on the hob (stove top) and are invaluable for cooking whole large fish, such as salmon. Fish kettles can also be used for steaming other foods.

Oval frying pan
Such a simple idea, but intensely practical, this large pan enables you to pan-fry whole fish flat instead of bending them to fit a round pan, spoiling their shape.

Griddle pan
A ribbed cast-iron griddle pan is ideal for searing and grilling fish. They can be round, oval or rectangular. Some of the large griddles need to be used over two electric rings or gas burners on top of a stove.

Steamer
If you steam food frequently, a stainless steel steamer is a good investment. They have a lidded, deep outer pan and a perforated inner basket. Choose a model with the widest basket you can find. Chinese bamboo steaming baskets are an economical alternative. They come in a variety of sizes, from very small dim sum baskets to very wide baskets that are about 35cm/14in across. Chinese steaming baskets can be stacked one on top of each other so that several layers of food can be cooked at one time. Cheapest of all is a small, collapsible, perforated steamer, which unfolds like a flower to fit any pan.

Below: Stainless steel steamer

Below: Chef's knife

Below: Filleting knife

Below: Scissors

Left: Chinese bamboo steamer

Above: Fish kettle

Left: Fish scalers

Below: Griddle pan

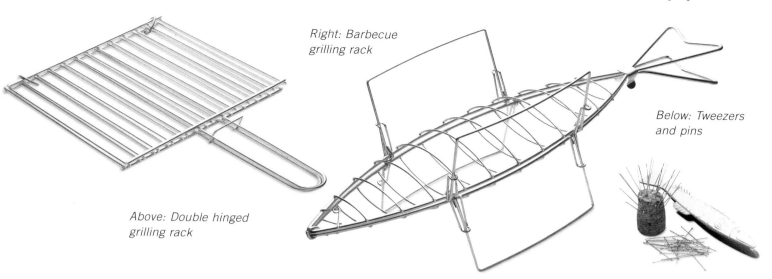

Right: Barbecue grilling rack

Below: Tweezers and pins

Above: Double hinged grilling rack

Wok

A 35cm/14in wok with a lid will be large enough to cope with most types of fish and will prove invaluable in the kitchen. There's no need to reserve this piece of equipment for stir-frying; a wok also makes an effective steamer and can also be used for deep-frying.

SPECIALIST ITEMS

Barbecue grilling racks

A hinged rack in the shape of a fish makes cooking – and turning – a single large fish relatively easy. Also very useful for general purposes is a double-sided hinged grill rack.

These can be square or rectangular and have long handles so that several salmon steaks can be grilled and turned over simultaneously. However, the flat sides do tend to squash the delicate flesh of some fish. Always oil grilling racks before use to prevent the fish from sticking to them.

Fish smoker

The cheapest home-smoker is a lidded metal box with a rack to hold the fish. Smoke produced by placing dampened aromatic oak or other wood chippings, or a sprinkling of fresh herbs, on the coals gives extra flavour to the fish. More convenient (but more expensive) are electric fish smokers. Stove-top models can be used indoors.

OTHER USEFUL UTENSILS

Fish lifter

Resembling an elongated fish slice, the curved and perforated turner is useful for flipping over whole fish during cooking without breaking them.

Fish slice

A fish slice with a sturdy yet flexible blade will make easy work of turning whole fish, steaks and cutlets.

Pins

Use dressmaker's pins with round heads to extract tiny pin bones from salmon and trout. For safety's sake, stick them in a cork when not using.

Tweezers

Use these to extract small bones and pin bones from fish fillets.

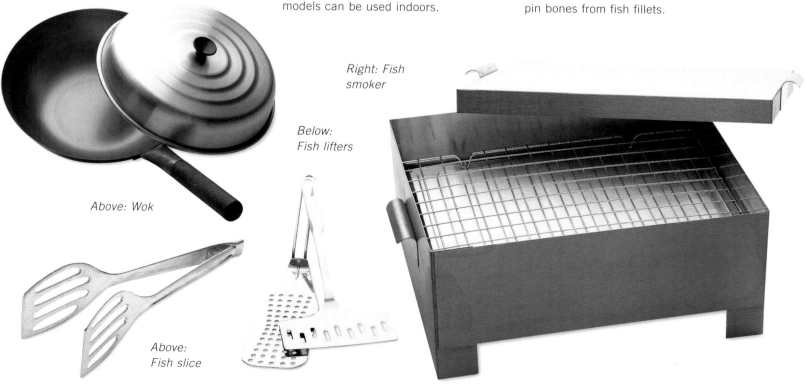

Above: Wok

Below: Fish lifters

Above: Fish slice

Right: Fish smoker

THE RECIPES

SOUPS AND APPETIZERS

One of the many attributes of salmon, aside from its excellent flavour and texture, is the delicate pink colour, and nowhere is this capitalized on more effectively than in the preparation of soups and appetizers. Salmon chowder, for instance, looks so delicious in the bowl that it would seem a shame to disturb it, were it not for the wonderful aroma that rises from the surface. Mousses, terrines and pâtés are just as pretty, especially when smoked salmon is used as a wrapper or garnish. The most dramatic effects, however, come from Japanese kitchens, where very fresh raw salmon is enclosed in jet-black yaki-nori to make superb sushi.

CURRIED SALMON SOUP

A HINT OF MILD CURRY PASTE REALLY ENHANCES THE FLAVOUR OF THIS SOUP, WITHOUT MAKING IT TOO SPICY. GRATED CREAMED COCONUT ADDS A LUXURY TOUCH, WHILE HELPING TO AMALGAMATE THE FLAVOURS. SERVED WITH CHUNKS OF WARM BREAD, THIS MAKES A SUBSTANTIAL APPETIZER.

SERVES 4

INGREDIENTS
   50g/2oz/¼ cup butter
   2 onions, roughly chopped
   10ml/2 tsp mild curry paste
   475ml/16fl oz/2 cups water
   150ml/¼ pint/⅔ cup white wine
   300ml/½ pint/1¼ cups double
     (heavy) cream
   50g/2oz/½ cup creamed coconut,
     grated or 120ml/4fl oz/½ cup
     coconut cream
   2 potatoes, about 350g/12oz, cubed
   450g/1lb salmon fillet, skinned
     and cut into bitesize pieces
   60ml/4 tbsp chopped fresh
     flat-leaf parsley
   salt and ground black pepper

1 Melt the butter in a large pan, add the onions and cook for about 3–4 minutes until beginning to soften. Stir in the curry paste. Cook for 1 minute more.

2 Add the water, wine, cream and creamed coconut or coconut cream, with seasoning. Bring to the boil, stirring until the coconut has dissolved.

3 Add the potatoes to the pan. Simmer, covered, for about 15 minutes or until they are almost tender. Do not allow them to break down into the mixture.

4 Add the fish gently so as not to break it up. Simmer for 2–3 minutes until just cooked. Add the parsley and adjust the seasoning. Serve immediately.

SALMON CHOWDER

DILL IS THE PERFECT PARTNER FOR SALMON IN THIS CREAMY SOUP FROM THE USA. IT TAKES ITS INSPIRATION FROM THE SATISFYING SOUPS THAT ARE TYPICAL OF THE EASTERN SEABOARD OF THE UNITED STATES AND IS BEST SERVED IMMEDIATELY AFTER COOKING, WHEN THE SALMON IS JUST TENDER.

SERVES 4

INGREDIENTS

20g/¾oz/1½ tbsp butter
1 onion, finely chopped
1 leek, finely chopped
1 small fennel bulb, finely chopped
25g/1oz/¼ cup plain
　(all-purpose) flour
1.75 litres/3 pints/7 cups fish stock
2 medium potatoes, cut in
　1cm/½in cubes
450g/1lb salmon fillet, skinned and
　cut into 2cm/¾in cubes
175ml/6fl oz/¾ cup milk
120ml/4fl oz/½ cup whipping cream
30ml/2 tbsp chopped fresh dill
salt and ground black pepper

1 Melt the butter in a large pan. Add the onion, leek and chopped fennel and cook for 6 minutes until softened.

2 Stir in the flour. Reduce the heat to low and cook for 3 minutes, stirring occasionally with a wooden spoon.

3 Add the fish stock and potatoes to the mixture in the pan. Season with a little salt and ground black pepper. Bring to the boil, then reduce the heat, cover and simmer gently for about 20 minutes or until the potatoes are tender when tested with a fork.

4 Add the cubed salmon fillet and simmer gently for 3–5 minutes until it is just cooked.

5 Stir the milk, cream, and chopped dill into the contents of the pan. Cook until just warmed through, stirring occasionally, but do not allow to boil. Adjust the seasoning to taste, then ladle into warmed soup bowls to serve.

SALMON SOUP WITH SALSA AND ROUILLE

THIS SMART FISH SOUP IS THE PERFECT CHOICE FOR SUMMER ENTERTAINING. SORREL IS A GOOD PARTNER FOR SALMON, BUT DILL OR FENNEL ARE EQUALLY DELICIOUS ALTERNATIVES.

SERVES 4

INGREDIENTS
90ml/6 tbsp olive oil
1 onion, chopped
1 leek, chopped
1 celery stick, chopped
1 fennel bulb, roughly chopped
1 red (bell) pepper, seeded
  and sliced
3 garlic cloves, chopped
grated rind and juice of 2 oranges
1 bay leaf
400g/14oz can chopped tomatoes
1.2 litres/2 pints/5 cups fish stock
pinch of cayenne pepper
800g/1¾lb salmon fillet, skinned
300ml/½ pint/1¼ cups double
  (heavy) cream
salt and ground black pepper
4 thin slices baguette, to serve

For the ruby salsa
2 tomatoes, peeled, seeded
  and diced
½ small red onion, very finely
  chopped
15ml/1 tbsp cod's roe
15ml/1 tbsp chopped fresh sorrel

For the rouille
120ml/4fl oz/½ cup mayonnaise
1 garlic clove, crushed
5ml/1 tsp sun-dried tomato paste

COOK'S TIP
For a smart presentation, choose wide, shallow soup plates, so that there is plenty of room for the rouille-topped toast to be accommodated on top of the pieces of flaked salmon. The ruby salsa adds the finishing touch.

1 Heat the oil in a large pan and add the chopped onion, leek, celery, fennel, pepper and garlic. Cover the pan and cook gently for 20 minutes or until all the vegetables have softened. Do not allow the onion and garlic to brown.

2 Add the orange rind and juice, bay leaf and tomatoes. Cover and cook for 4–5 minutes, stirring occasionally. Add the stock and cayenne, cover the pan and simmer for 30 minutes.

3 Add the salmon and cook gently for 8–10 minutes, until just cooked. Using a slotted spoon, remove the salmon and place it on a large plate.

4 Flake the salmon into large pieces, and remove any bones that were missed when the fish was originally filleted. Put the flaked salmon in a dish and set it aside.

5 Meanwhile, make the salsa. Put the diced tomatoes in a bowl and add the finely chopped red onion. Stir in the cod's roe and the chopped fresh sorrel. Transfer the mixture to a serving dish and set it aside.

6 To make the rouille to top the toast, mix the mayonnaise with the crushed garlic and the sun-dried tomato paste in a bowl.

7 Leave the soup to cool slightly, then remove and discard the bay leaf. Purée the soup in a food processor or blender until smooth, then press it through a fine sieve into the rinsed-out pan.

8 Stir in the cream and season well, then add the flaked salmon. Toast the baguette slices under a hot grill (broiler) on both sides and set aside.

9 Reheat the soup gently without letting it boil. Ladle it into bowls and float the toasted baguette slices on top. Add a spoonful of rouille to each slice of baguette and spoon some ruby salsa on top. Serve immediately.

CUCUMBER AND YOGURT SOUP WITH SALSA

CHARRED SALMON BRINGS A HINT OF HEAT TO THE REFRESHING FLAVOURS OF THIS CHILLED SOUP.
GOOD-LOOKING AND BEAUTIFULLY LIGHT, IT MAKES THE PERFECT OPENER FOR AN AL-FRESCO MEAL.

SERVES 4

INGREDIENTS

    3 medium cucumbers
    300ml/½ pint/1¼ cups Greek
      (US strained plain) yogurt
    250ml/8fl oz/1 cup vegetable stock,
      chilled
    120ml/4fl oz/½ cup crème fraîche
    15ml/1 tbsp chopped fresh chervil
    15ml/1 tbsp chopped fresh chives
    15ml/1 tbsp chopped fresh flat-leaf
      parsley
    1 small fresh red chilli, seeded and
      very finely chopped
    a little oil, for brushing
    225g/8oz salmon fillet, skinned and
      cut into eight thin slices
    salt and ground black pepper
    fresh chervil or chives, to garnish

4 Brush a griddle or frying pan with oil and heat until very hot. Add the salmon slices and sear them for 1–2 minutes, then turn over carefully and sear the other side until tender and charred.

5 Ladle the chilled soup into soup bowls. Top each portion with two slices of salmon, then pile a portion of salsa into the centre. Garnish with the chervil or chives and serve.

1 Peel two of the cucumbers and halve them lengthways. Scoop out and discard the seeds, then roughly chop the flesh. Purée the chopped flesh in a food processor or blender.

2 Add the yogurt, stock, crème fraîche, chervil, chives and seasoning, and process until smooth. Pour into a bowl, cover and chill.

3 Peel, halve and seed the remaining cucumber. Cut the flesh into small neat dice. Mix with the chopped parsley and chilli in a bowl. Cover the salsa and chill until required.

NOODLE, PAK CHOI AND SALMON RAMEN

THIS LIGHTLY SPICED JAPANESE NOODLE SOUP IS ENHANCED BY SLICES OF SEARED FRESH SALMON AND CRISP VEGETABLES. THE CONTRASTS IN TEXTURE ARE AS APPEALING AS THE DELICIOUS TASTE.

SERVES 4

INGREDIENTS

   1.5 litres/2½ pints/6 cups good
     vegetable stock
   2.5cm/1in piece fresh root ginger,
     finely sliced
   2 garlic cloves, crushed
   6 spring onions (scallions), sliced
   45ml/3 tbsp soy sauce
   45ml/3 tbsp sake
   450g/1lb salmon fillet, skinned
   5ml/1 tsp groundnut (peanut) oil
   350g/12oz ramen or udon noodles
   4 small heads pak choi (bok choy),
     broken into leaves
   1 fresh red chilli, seeded and sliced
   50g/2oz/1 cup beansprouts
   salt and ground black pepper

1 Pour the stock into a large pan and add the ginger, garlic, and a third of the spring onions.

2 Add the soy sauce and sake. Bring to the boil, then reduce the heat and simmer for 30 minutes.

3 Meanwhile, remove any pin bones from the salmon using tweezers, then cut the salmon on the slant into 12 slices, using a very sharp knife.

4 Brush a ridged griddle or frying pan with the oil and heat until very hot. Sear the salmon slices for 1–2 minutes on each side until tender and marked by the ridges of the pan. Set aside.

COOK'S TIP

To obtain the distinctive stripes on the slices of salmon, it is important that the ridged pan or griddle is very hot before they are added. Avoid moving the slices, or the stripes will become blurred.

5 Cook the ramen or udon noodles in a large pan of boiling water for 4–5 minutes or according to the instructions on the packet. Tip into a colander, drain well and refresh under cold running water. Drain again and set aside.

6 Strain the broth into a clean pan and season, then bring to the boil. Add the pak choi. Using a fork, twist the noodles into four nests and put these into deep bowls. Divide the salmon slices, spring onions, chilli and beansprouts among the bowls. Ladle in the broth.

TROUT BISQUE

*A BISQUE IS A THICK, RICH, SMOOTH SOUP, USUALLY CONTAINING FISH OR SHELLFISH.
THIS WONDERFULLY COLOURED PALE PINK VERSION HAS A DELICIOUSLY CREAMY TEXTURE
WITH A HINT OF SPICINESS. SERVE IT WITH CRUSTY BREAD AND UNSALTED BUTTER.*

SERVES 4

INGREDIENTS

   15ml/1 tbsp olive oil
   1 onion, chopped
   1 red (bell) pepper, finely chopped
   1 garlic clove, crushed
   1 medium potato, diced
   2 tomatoes, skinned and chopped
   300ml/½ pint/1¼ cups fish stock
   225g/8oz trout fillet, skinned
     and diced
   1.5ml/¼ tsp chilli powder
   15ml/1 tbsp chopped fresh
     tarragon
   300ml/½ pint/1¼ cups milk
   30ml/2 tbsp dry sherry
   150ml/¼ pint/⅔ cup double
     (heavy) cream
   salt and ground black pepper
   sprigs of watercress or rocket
     (arugula), to garnish

1 Heat the olive oil in a large pan, add the onion, pepper, garlic and potato. Fry gently for 5 minutes, stirring constantly, until the onion has just softened.

2 Add the tomatoes and stock to the pan, increase the heat and bring to the boil. Then reduce the heat and allow to simmer for 10 minutes or until the vegetables are soft.

3 Add the trout, chilli powder and chopped tarragon. Simmer gently for a further 5 minutes or until the fish is just cooked and is starting to flake when tested with a fork.

4 Remove the pan from the heat, and stir in half the milk. Set aside for 20–30 minutes to allow the contents to cool.

5 Pour the fish and vegetable mixture into a food processor and blend until smooth. Scrape into a clean pan and stir in the sherry and cream, with the remaining milk.

6 Heat the soup gently, stirring, until piping hot. Season to taste, then divide among soup bowls, garnish and serve.

COOK'S TIP
To skin the tomatoes, cut a small cross on the base of each tomato. Pour boiling water over and leave for 1 minute. The skin will then peel off very easily.

CEVICHE

THIS IS A FRUITY FIRST COURSE OF MARINATED FRESH FISH. TAKE CARE IN CHOOSING THE FISH FOR THIS DISH; IT MUST BE AS FRESH AS POSSIBLE AND SERVED ON THE DAY IT IS MADE, SINCE IT IS "COOKED" BY THE ACTION OF THE CITRUS JUICES, RATHER THAN A MORE CONVENTIONAL METHOD.

SERVES 6

INGREDIENTS
  350g/12oz medium cooked
    prawns (shrimp)
  350g/12oz scallops, removed from
    their shells, with corals intact
  175g/6oz tomatoes
  1 mango, about 175g/6oz
  1 red onion, finely chopped
  350g/12oz salmon fillet
  1 fresh red chilli, seeded and chopped
  12 limes
  30ml/2 tbsp caster (superfine) sugar
  2 pink grapefruit
  3 oranges
  salt and ground black pepper

1 Set aside two prawns for the garnish. Peel the remaining prawns and cut the scallops into 1.2cm/½in dice.

2 Dice the tomatoes and place in a bowl. Peel the mango, dice the flesh and add it to the bowl with the red onion. Mix well.

3 Skin the salmon, then remove any pin bones with a pair of tweezers. Cut the fish into small pieces and mix with the tomato, mango and onion. Add the chilli and mix well.

4 Squeeze the juice from eight of the limes and add it to the tomato mixture, with the sugar and a little salt and pepper. Stir, cover and leave to marinate in a cool place for 3 hours.

5 Segment the grapefruit, oranges and remaining limes. Drain off as much excess lime juice as possible and mix the fruit segments into the marinated ingredients. Season to taste and serve, garnished with the reserved prawns.

COOK'S TIP
Skinning the salmon fillet will be much easier if you place the fish in the freezer for about 10 minutes first. Cut down to the skin at the narrow end of the fillet, then, holding that end firmly with your free hand, turn the blade and slice the flesh off the skin.

SALMON <u>WITH</u> CUCUMBER SAUCE

CUCUMBER AND FRESH DILL ARE A PERFECT COMBINATION IN THIS UNUSUAL HOT SAUCE, WHICH REALLY COMPLEMENTS THE BAKED SALMON.

SERVES 6–8

INGREDIENTS
   1.8kg/4lb salmon, cleaned
      and scaled
   melted butter, for brushing
   3 fresh parsley or thyme sprigs
   ½ lemon, halved
   orange slices and salad leaves,
      to serve

For the cucumber sauce
   1 large cucumber, peeled
   25g/1oz/2 tbsp butter
   120ml/4fl oz/½ cup dry white wine
   45ml/3 tbsp finely chopped
      fresh dill
   60ml/4 tbsp sour cream
   salt and ground black pepper

3 Meanwhile, halve the cucumber lengthways, scoop out the seeds, then dice the flesh.

4 Place the cucumber in a colander, toss lightly with salt and leave for about 30 minutes to drain. Rinse well, drain again and pat dry.

5 Heat the butter in a small pan, add the cucumber and cook for 2 minutes until translucent. Add the wine and boil briskly until the cucumber is dry. Stir in the dill and sour cream and season to taste. Fillet the salmon and serve with the cucumber sauce, orange slices and salad leaves.

1 Season the salmon. Brush it inside and out with melted butter. Place the herb sprigs and lemon in the cavity.

2 Wrap the salmon in foil, folding the edges together securely, then bake in a preheated oven at 220°C/425°F/Gas 7 for 15 minutes. Remove the fish from the oven and leave in the foil for 1 hour, then remove the skin from the salmon.

CHILLI AND SALT-CURED SALMON

BUY VERY FRESH FISH FROM A REPUTABLE SOURCE FOR THIS DELICIOUS ALTERNATIVE TO SMOKED SALMON.

SERVES 10

INGREDIENTS

50g/2oz/¼ cup sea salt
45ml/3 tbsp caster (superfine) sugar
5ml/1 tsp chilli powder
5ml/1 tsp ground black pepper
45ml/3 tbsp chopped fresh
  coriander (cilantro)
2 salmon fillets, about 250g/
  9oz each
fresh flat leaf parsley, to garnish
garlic mayonnaise, to serve

1 In a bowl, mix together the salt, sugar, chilli powder, pepper and coriander. Rub the mixture into the salmon flesh.

2 Place one of the fillets, skin side down, in a shallow glass dish. Place the other fillet on top, with the skin side up. Cover with foil, then place a weight on top.

3 Chill for 48 hours, turning the fish every 8 hours or so and basting it with the liquid that forms in the dish.

4 Drain the salmon well and transfer to a board. Using a sharp knife, slice it diagonally into wafer-thin slices. Arrange on plates and garnish with sprigs of parsley. Serve with garlic mayonnaise.

COOK'S TIP

For a garnish for the salt-cured salmon, scrape any remaining fish off the skin. Cut the skin into 1cm/½in wide strips and fry for 1 minute in hot oil until crisp. Drain and cool on kitchen paper.

RICE IN GREEN TEA WITH SALMON

THIS IS A COMMON JAPANESE SNACK TO HAVE AFTER DRINKS AND NIBBLES. IN THE KYOTO REGION, OFFERING THIS DISH TO GUESTS USED TO BE A POLITE WAY OF SAYING THE PARTY WAS OVER. THE GUESTS WERE EXPECTED TO DECLINE THE OFFER AND LEAVE IMMEDIATELY.

SERVES 4

INGREDIENTS

150g/5oz salmon fillet
¼ sheet nori
250g/9oz/1¼ cups Japanese short
  grain rice cooked as advised on
  the packet, using 350ml/12fl oz/
  1½ cups water
15ml/1 tbsp sencha leaves
600ml/1 pint/2½ cups water
5ml/1 tsp wasabi paste or 5ml/1 tsp
  wasabi powder mixed with 1.5ml/
  ¼ tsp water (optional)
20ml/4 tsp shoyu (Japanese soy sauce)
sea salt

1 Place the salmon fillet in a bowl and cover it with salt. If the fillet is thicker than 2.5cm/1in, slice it in half and salt both halves. Leave for 30 minutes

2 Wipe the salt off the salmon with kitchen paper and grill (broil) the fish under a preheated grill (broiler) for about 5 minutes until cooked through.

3 Using scissors, cut the nori into short, narrow strips about 20 x 5mm/ ¾ x ¼in long, or leave as long narrow strips, if you prefer.

4 Remove the skin and any bones from the salmon, then flake the fish.

5 If the cooked rice is warm, put equal amounts into individual rice bowls or soup bowls. If the rice is cold, put it in a sieve and pour hot water from a kettle over it to warm it up. Drain and pour into the bowls. Place the salmon pieces on top of the rice.

6 Put the sencha leaves in a teapot. Bring the water to the boil, remove from the heat and leave to cool slightly. Pour into the teapot and wait for 45 seconds.

7 Strain the tea gently and evenly over the top of the rice and salmon. Add some nori and wasabi, if using, to the top of each portion of rice, then trickle shoyu over and serve.

COOK'S TIP
Sencha are fine green tea leaves available from Japanese food stores and shops or markets selling specialist teas.

SIMPLE ROLLED SUSHI

SALMON MAKES A SUPERB FILLING FOR THESE SIMPLE ROLLS. ALSO KNOWN AS HOSO-MAKI, *THEY MAKE EXCELLENT CANAPÉS. YOU WILL NEED A BAMBOO MAT FOR THE ROLLING PROCESS.*

MAKES 12 ROLLS OR 72 SLICES

INGREDIENTS
400g/14oz/2 cups Japanese short
   grain rice, soaked for 20 minutes
   in water to cover
550ml/18fl oz/2¼ cups cold water
55ml/3½ tbsp rice vinegar
15ml/1 tbsp sugar
10ml/2 tsp salt
6 sheets yaki-nori
200g/7oz very fresh salmon fillet
200g/7oz very fresh tuna, in
   one piece
wasabi paste
½ cucumber, quartered lengthways
   and seeded
salmon roe and pickled ginger,
   to garnish (optional)
shoyu (Japanese soy sauce), to serve

1 Drain the rice, then put it in a pan with the measured water. Bring to the boil, then lower the heat, cover and simmer for 20 minutes, or until all the liquid has been absorbed. Meanwhile, heat the vinegar, sugar and salt in a pan, stir well and cool. Fold into the hot rice, then remove the pan from the heat, cover and leave to stand for 20 minutes.

2 Cut the yaki-nori sheets in half. Cut the salmon and tuna into sticks the length of the long side of the yaki-nori and 1cm/½in square if viewed end-on.

3 Place a sheet of yaki-nori, shiny side down, on a bamboo mat. Divide the rice into 12 portions. Spread one portion over the yaki-nori, leaving a 1cm/½in clear space around the edges.

4 Spread a little wasabi paste in a horizontal line along the middle of the rice and lay one or two sticks of tuna lengthways on this, so that when rolled, the tuna will form a filling.

5 Holding the mat and the edge of the yaki-nori nearest to you, roll up the yaki-nori and rice into a cylinder with the tuna in the middle. Use the mat as a guide – do not roll it into the food. Roll the rice tightly so that it sticks together.

6 Carefully roll the sushi off the mat. Make 11 more rolls in the same way, four for each filling ingredient, but do not use wasabi with the cucumber. Use a wet knife to cut each roll into six slices and stand them on a platter. Garnish the sushi with salmon roe and pickled ginger, if you wish, and serve with shoyu.

SALMON DIP

THIS CREAMY SMOKED SALMON DIP WITH HOT ROSEMARY AND CHILLI POTATO WEDGES AND PEPPER STRIPS CAN BE SERVED AS AN APPETIZER OR AS PART OF A BUFFET LUNCH — A GLASS OF CHILLED SPARKLING WHITE WINE IS THE IDEAL ACCOMPANIMENT. IT ALSO MAKES GOOD PARTY FOOD. HAND IT ROUND WITH TORTILLA CHIPS OR CRUDITÉS WHEN YOUR GUESTS ARRIVE.

SERVES 4

INGREDIENTS
 115g/4oz smoked salmon
 250g/9oz/generous 1 cup
  mascarpone cheese
 60ml/4 tbsp chopped fresh chives
 grated rind and juice of 1 lemon
 1 red (bell) pepper, seeded and cut
  into strips
 1 yellow (bell) pepper, seeded and
  cut into strips
 sea salt and ground black pepper

For the potato wedges
 675g/1½lb large potatoes,
  scrubbed
 60ml/4 tbsp olive oil
 30ml/2 tbsp chopped fresh
  rosemary
 1 fresh red chilli, seeded and
  finely chopped

1 Preheat the oven to 200°C/400°F/ Gas 6. To make the potato wedges, dry the potatoes thoroughly with kitchen paper, then cut them into thick pieces.

VARIATIONS
To give a more intense chilli flavour, roast the potato wedges in a mixture of 30ml/ 2 tbsp chipotle chilli oil and 30ml/2 tbsp olive oil. Leave the seeds in the chilli for extra heat, if you like. If, on the other hand, you don't like hot, spicy flavours, omit the chilli and substitute a finely chopped sweet red (bell) pepper.

2 Pour the oil into a roasting pan and heat it in the oven for 10 minutes. Add the potato wedges to the hot oil, then sprinkle over the chopped fresh rosemary and the finely chopped chilli.

3 Protecting your hand with an oven glove, shake the pan gently to coat the potatoes in the oil, rosemary and chilli. Season well with sea salt and plenty of black pepper. Bake for 50–60 minutes or until tender, turning occasionally to prevent the wedges from sticking to the roasting pan.

4 Cut the smoked salmon into small pieces, using kitchen scissors or a sharp filleting knife.

COOK'S TIP
Slice the potatoes just before cooking, or the cut sides will discolour. It isn't necessary to peel the potatoes if you scrub them thoroughly.

5 Put the mascarpone cheese, chives and lemon rind in a bowl and mix with a fork until thoroughly blended.

6 Add the lemon juice, a little at a time, mixing constantly, so that the mixture is thinned and given a lemony tang, but does not curdle. A reamer is useful for squeezing the lemon, but watch out for the pips (seeds).

7 Add the salmon pieces to the cheese mixture and season with ground black pepper to taste. Transfer into a serving bowl, cover and chill until required.

8 To serve, arrange the pepper strips and potato wedges around the edge of a large serving platter and place the dip to one side or in the centre.

SMOKED SALMON TERRINE WITH LEMONS

THIS MELT-IN-THE-MOUTH SMOKED SALMON TERRINE MAKES A SPECTACULAR FIRST COURSE FOR A SPECIAL DINNER. IF YOU WANT TO SERVE IT WITH WRAPPED INDIVIDUAL LEMON HALVES, AS SUGGESTED IN THE METHOD, YOU WILL NEED SOME MUSLIN AND RAFFIA.

SERVES 6

INGREDIENTS
    4 sheets leaf gelatine
    60ml/4 tbsp water
    400g/14oz smoked salmon, sliced
    300g/11oz/scant 1½ cups
      cream cheese
    120ml/4fl oz/½ cup crème fraîche
    30ml/2 tbsp dill mustard
    juice of 1 lime
    2 lemons, to garnish

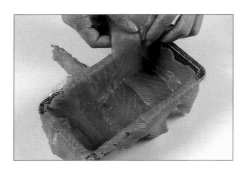

1 Soak the gelatine in the water in a small bowl until softened. Meanwhile, line a 450g/1lb loaf pan with clear film (plastic wrap). Use some of the smoked salmon to line the pan, laying the slices widthways across the base and up the sides and leaving enough hanging over the edge to fold over the top of the filling.

VARIATION
Powdered gelatine can be used instead of the sheets. Substitute 15ml/1 tbsp powdered gelatine. Sprinkle it over the cold water in a heatproof bowl, then set aside until spongy. Place the bowl over simmering water until the gelatine has liquefied completely before adding it to the terrine mixture.

2 Set aside enough of the remaining smoked salmon to make a middle layer the length of the pan. Chop the rest finely by hand or in a food processor. Take care not to over-process the salmon; it must not form a paste.

3 In a bowl, beat the cream cheese, crème fraiche and dill mustard until well combined. Scrape in the chopped salmon and mix with a rubber spatula or a spoon until well combined.

4 Squeeze out the gelatine and put the sheets in a small, heavy pan. Add the lime juice. Place over a low heat until the gelatine has melted, cool slightly, then stir into the salmon mixture.

5 Spoon half the mixture into the lined pan. Lay the reserved smoked salmon slices on the mixture along the length of the pan, then spoon on the rest of the filling and smooth the top.

6 Tap the pan on the surface to expel any trapped air. Fold over the overhanging salmon slices to cover the top. Cover the whole pan with clear film and place in the refrigerator to chill for at least 4 hours, preferably 6–8 hours.

7 If making the lemon garnish, cut one lemon in half widthways. Wrap each half in a small square of muslin (cheesecloth). Gather the muslin at the end of the lemon and tie with raffia.

8 Cut a small "V" from the side of the other lemon. Repeat at 5mm/¼in intervals. Turn out the terrine, then slice. Garnish with the muslin-wrapped lemons and lemon "leaves".

STRIPED FISH TERRINE

ROSE AND CREAM, THE DELICATE COLOURS OF SALMON AND SOLE GIVE THIS TASTY TERRINE A VERY PRETTY APPEARANCE. SERVE IT COLD OR JUST WARM, WITH A HOLLANDAISE SAUCE IF YOU LIKE.

SERVES 8

INGREDIENTS

15ml/1 tbsp sunflower oil
450g/1lb salmon fillet, skinned
450g/1lb sole fillets, skinned
3 egg whites
105ml/7 tbsp double (heavy) cream
15ml/1 tbsp fresh chives,
  finely chopped
juice of 1 lemon
115g/4oz/scant 1 cup fresh or frozen
  peas, cooked
5ml/1 tsp chopped fresh mint leaves
salt, ground white pepper and freshly
  grated nutmeg
thinly sliced cucumber, salad or land
  cress and chives, to garnish

1 Grease a 1 litre/1¾ pint/4 cup loaf pan or terrine with the oil. Slice the salmon thinly; cut it and the sole into long strips, 2.5cm/1in wide. Preheat the oven to 200°C/400°F/Gas 6.

COOK'S TIPS
• Pop the salmon into the freezer about an hour before slicing it. If it is almost frozen, it will be much easier to slice.
• Lining the base of the terrine with a piece of baking parchment before adding the salmon and sole strips will make it easier to turn out.
• If serving the terrine cold, remove it from the refrigerator at least 15 minutes before serving, as the flavour will be diminished if it is too heavily chilled.

2 Line the terrine neatly with alternate slices of salmon and sole, leaving the ends hanging over the edge. You should be left with about a third of the salmon and half the sole.

3 In a grease-free bowl, beat the egg whites with a pinch of salt until they form soft peaks. Purée the remaining sole in a food processor. Spoon into a mixing bowl, season, then fold in two-thirds of the egg whites, followed by two-thirds of the cream. Put half the mixture into a second bowl; stir in the chives. Add nutmeg to the first bowl.

4 Purée the remaining salmon, scrape it into a bowl and add the lemon juice. Fold in the remaining whites and cream.

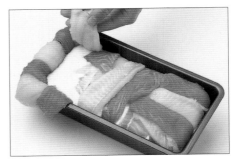

6 Add the salmon mixture, then finish with the sole and nutmeg mixture. Cover with the overhanging fish fillets and make a lid of oiled foil. Stand the terrine in a roasting pan and pour in enough boiling water to come halfway up the sides.

7 Bake for 15–20 minutes, until the top fillets are just cooked and the mousse feels springy. Remove the foil, lay a wire rack over the top of the terrine and invert both rack and terrine on to a lipped baking sheet to catch the cooking juices that drain out. Keep these to make fish stock or soup.

8 Leaving the pan in place, let the terrine stand for about 15 minutes, then turn the terrine by inverting it on to a serving dish and lifting off the pan carefully. Serve warm or lightly chilled, garnished with thinly sliced cucumber, salad or land cress and chives.

THREE FISH MOUSSE

A RICH AND CREAMY MOUSSE WHICH IS FLAVOURED WITH LEMON AND DILL — TWO OF THE CLASSIC
PARTNERS FOR A WIDE RANGE OF FISH AND SHELLFISH. THIS WOULD MAKE A STUNNING FIRST COURSE,
OR IT COULD BE SERVED WITH CRUSTY BREAD FOR A TASTY LUNCH.

SERVES 6–8

INGREDIENTS

15ml/1 tbsp oil
450g/1lb cod fillet, skinned
1 bay leaf
1 slice lemon
6 black peppercorns
275g/10oz thinly sliced
  smoked trout
60ml/4 tbsp cold water
15g/½oz powdered gelatine
175g/6oz cooked peeled prawns
  (shrimp), halved
300ml/½ pint/1¼ cups sour cream
225g/8oz/1 cup cream cheese
30ml/2 tbsp chopped fresh dill
juice of 1 lemon
3 drops Tabasco sauce
salt and ground black pepper
sprigs of fresh herbs, such as
  parsley or dill, and 6–8 lemon
  wedges, to garnish

VARIATION
Any firm-fleshed white fish can be
substituted for the cod, including flat
fish such as brill, halibut and turbot.
Smoked salmon could be used instead
of smoked trout.

COOK'S TIP
If you are unable to use the fish stock
produced when cooking the fish in this
recipe within the next 24 hours, cool
it and then freeze it. Next time you
make a seafood risotto or fish soup, use
it as the basis of the stock.

1 Using a pastry brush, lightly brush a
1.2 litre/2 pint/5 cup ring mould with
the oil. Place the cod, bay leaf, lemon
and peppercorns in a pan. Cover with
cold water and bring to simmering
point. Poach for 10–15 minutes, or until
the fish flakes when tested with a fork.

2 Meanwhile, carefully line the oiled
ring mould with overlapping slices of
smoked trout, leaving plenty hanging
over the edge.

3 Remove the cod from the pan with a
fish slice (metal spatula). Reserve the
stock to use for another recipe. Chop
the cod into bitesize chunks and put it
in a large bowl.

4 Place the measured cold water in a
small heatproof bowl and sprinkle the
gelatine over the surface. Leave for
5 minutes, until spongy, then place
the bowl over a pan of hot water. Stir
until the gelatine has dissolved. Leave
to cool slightly.

5 Add the prawns, sour cream,
cream cheese and dill to the cod in
the bowl. Pour in the lemon juice
and Tabasco sauce. Using a fork,
mash the mixture together until well
combined. Season to taste with salt
and plenty of ground black pepper.

6 Using a large metal spoon, fold the
dissolved gelatine into the fish mixture,
making sure it is evenly incorporated.
Spoon into the lined ring mould and
smooth down the top with the back of
the spoon.

7 Lift the overhanging edges of the
smoked trout and fold them over
the top of the mousse. Cover the
mousse with clear film (plastic wrap)
and chill in the refrigerator for at least
2 hours or until set.

8 To serve, carefully run a round-bladed
knife around the edge of the mousse,
invert a serving plate on top and turn
both over. Shake mould and plate
together, if necessary, until the mousse
drops out on to the plate. Garnish with
the herbs and lemon wedges and serve.

SEA TROUT MOUSSE

THIS DELICIOUSLY CREAMY MOUSSE MAKES A LITTLE SEA TROUT GO A LONG WAY. IF YOU CAN'T LOCATE SEA TROUT, IT IS EQUALLY GOOD MADE WITH SALMON.

SERVES 6

INGREDIENTS
  250g/9oz sea trout fillet
  120ml/4fl oz/½ cup fish stock
  2 sheets leaf gelatine, or
    15ml/1 tbsp powdered gelatine
  juice of ½ lemon
  30ml/2 tbsp dry sherry or dry vermouth
  30ml/2 tbsp freshly grated
    Parmesan cheese
  300ml/½ pint/1¼ cups whipping
    cream
  2 egg whites
  15ml/1 tbsp sunflower oil
  salt and ground white pepper

For the garnish
  5cm/2in piece cucumber, with peel,
    halved and thinly sliced
  fresh dill or chervil

COOK'S TIP
Serve the mousse with Melba toast. Toast thin slices of bread on both sides under the grill (broiler). Cut off the crusts and slice each piece of toast in half horizontally. Return to the grill pan, untoasted sides up, and toast again, taking care not to let it burn.

1 Put the sea trout in a shallow pan. Pour in the fish stock and heat to simmering point. Poach the fish for about 3–4 minutes, until it is lightly cooked. Strain the stock into a jug (pitcher) and leave the fish to cool.

2 Add the gelatine to the hot stock and stir until it has dissolved completely. Set the stock aside until required.

3 When the trout is cool enough to handle, remove the skin and flake the flesh. Pour the stock into a food processor or blender. Process briefly, then gradually add the flaked trout, lemon juice, sherry or vermouth and Parmesan through the feeder tube, continuing to process the mixture until it is smooth. Scrape into a large bowl and leave to cool completely.

4 Lightly whip the cream in a bowl; fold it into the cold trout mixture. Season to taste, then cover with clear film (plastic wrap) and chill until the mousse is just beginning to set. It should have the consistency of mayonnaise.

5 In a grease-free bowl, beat the egg whites with a pinch of salt until they form soft peaks. Using a large metal spoon, stir one-third into the trout mixture to slacken it, then fold in the rest.

6 Lightly grease six ramekins with the sunflower oil. Divide the mousse among the ramekins and level the surface. Chill in the refrigerator for 2–3 hours, until set. Just before serving, arrange a few slices of cucumber and a small herb sprig on each mousse and add a little chopped dill or chervil.

SALMON <u>AND</u> PIKE MOUSSE

WHEN SLICED, THIS LIGHT-TEXTURED RUSSIAN MOUSSE LOAF, PATE IZ SHCHUKI, REVEALS A PRETTY LAYER OF PINK SALMON. FOR A SPECIAL OCCASION, SERVE TOPPED WITH RED SALMON ROE.

SERVES 8

INGREDIENTS
- 10ml/2 tsp oil
- 225g/8oz salmon fillet, skinned
- 600ml/1 pint/2½ cups fish stock
- finely grated rind and juice of
  ½ lemon
- 900g/2lb pike fillets, skinned
- 4 egg whites
- 475ml/16fl oz/2 cups double
  (heavy) cream
- 30ml/2 tbsp chopped fresh dill
- salt and ground black pepper
- red salmon roe or a fresh dill sprig,
  to garnish (optional)

COOK'S TIP
If you have difficulty locating pike, you can substitute turbot, sea bream or sole for the pike in this recipe.

1 Preheat the oven to 180°C/350°F/ Gas 4. Brush a 900g/2lb loaf pan with oil and line with baking parchment.

2 Cut the salmon into 5cm/2in strips. Pour the stock and lemon juice into a pan and bring to the boil, then turn off the heat. Add the salmon strips, cover and leave for 2 minutes. Remove with a slotted spoon.

3 Cut the pike into cubes and process in a food processor or blender until smooth. Lightly whisk the egg whites with a fork. With the motor of the food processor or blender running, slowly pour in the egg whites, then the cream through the feeder tube or lid. Finally, add the lemon rind and dill. Taste the mixture and add a little salt and pepper if you think more seasoning is needed.

4 Spoon half of the pike mixture into the prepared loaf pan. Arrange the poached salmon strips on top, then carefully spoon in the remaining pike mixture.

5 Cover the loaf pan with foil and put in a roasting pan. Add enough boiling water to come halfway up the sides of the loaf pan. Bake for 45–50 minutes, or until firm.

6 Leave on a wire rack to cool, then chill for at least 3 hours. Invert on to a serving plate and remove the lining paper. Serve the mousse in slices. Garnish with red salmon roe or a sprig of fresh dill, if you like. A spoonful of crème fraîche could also be added.

SMOKED SALMON PÂTÉ

THIS LOOKS SOPHISTICATED, BUT IS SURPRISINGLY SIMPLE TO MAKE. THE SMOKED SALMON JACKET ENCLOSES A MOUTHWATERING SALMON PÂTÉ.

SERVES 4

INGREDIENTS

   350g/12oz thinly sliced
     smoked salmon
   150ml/¼ pint/⅔ cup double
     (heavy) cream
   finely grated rind and juice of
     1 lemon
   salt and ground black pepper
   Melba toast, to serve

2 Put the remaining smoked salmon into a food processor and add the cream, lemon rind and three-quarters of the lemon juice. Process until smooth, then taste and add more salt and ground black pepper. If the salmon was quite oily, it may also be necessary to add a little more lemon juice.

3 Pack the lined ramekins with the smoked salmon pâté. Bring over the loose strips of salmon to cover the pâté completely. Cover and chill for at least 30 minutes, then turn out of the moulds, lift off and discard the clear film, and serve with the Melba toast.

COOK'S TIP
Process the salmon in short bursts until it is just smooth. Don't over-process the pâté or it will thicken too much and the texture will be compromised.

VARIATIONS
• Try this with smoked trout, which has a lovely rosy colour and a more delicate flavour than smoked salmon.
• A little horseradish cream makes a good addition to the pate, but don't overdo it, or you won't be able to taste the smoked fish.

1 Line four small ramekins with clear film (plastic wrap). Line the dishes with 115g/4oz of the smoked salmon, cut into strips long enough to flop over the edges.

SMOKED FISH PLATTER WITH HONEY DRESSING

A WIDE VARIETY OF SMOKED FISH IS AVAILABLE TODAY — TROUT, SALMON AND MACKEREL FEATURE IN THIS SIMPLE APPETIZER — BUT ANY SMOKED FISH CAN BE USED. ASK YOUR LOCAL FISHMONGER OR INQUIRE AT THE FISH COUNTER AT THE SUPERMARKET FOR THE BEST BUYS.

SERVES 4

INGREDIENTS
 ½ Charentais melon
 ½ cantaloupe melon
 50g/2oz rocket (arugula)
 75g/3oz hot-smoked trout fillets
 75g/3oz smoked salmon
 75g/3oz smoked mackerel
  with peppercorns

For the dressing
 75ml/5 tbsp extra virgin olive oil
 15ml/1 tbsp white wine vinegar
 5ml/1 tsp wholegrain mustard
 5ml/1 tsp clear honey
 salt and ground black pepper

COOK'S TIP
Among the more unusual types of smoked fish available are smoked halibut and smoked sturgeon. Smoked halibut has translucent white flesh and this, coupled with its delicate flavour, would make it a good addition to the fish platter. Smoked sturgeon would be a real talking point at any dinner table. A luxury fish, comparable with the finest smoked salmon, it is best served solo, so its rich flavour and succulent texture can be fully appreciated.

1 Scoop out and discard all the seeds from the Charentais and cantaloupe melons and cut each melon into four or eight slices, leaving the skin on. Divide the melon slices among four small serving plates, placing the slices neatly to one side.

2 Add a quarter of the rocket leaves to each plate, placing them opposite the melon.

3 Make the honey dressing by combining all the ingredients in a small jug (pitcher). Add plenty of salt and black pepper and whisk with a fork until emulsified.

4 Divide the smoked fish into four portions, breaking or cutting the trout fillets and smoked salmon into bitesize pieces. Peel the skin from the mackerel, then break up the flesh. Arrange the trout fillets, smoked salmon and mackerel over the rocket and melon on each platter. Drizzle the dressing over and serve immediately.

TROUT AND GINGER SALAD

FRESH GRIDDLED TROUT AND SMOKED TROUT ARE DELICIOUS ON THEIR OWN. PUT THEM TOGETHER, ADD A GINGER DRESSING AND YOU HAVE A SENSATIONAL FIRST COURSE THAT IS EASY TO PREPARE.

SERVES 4

INGREDIENTS
15ml/1 tbsp olive oil
115g/4oz trout fillet, skinned
grated rind and juice of ½ lime
1 yellow (bell) pepper, finely
  chopped
1 red (bell) pepper, finely chopped
1 small bunch fresh coriander
  (cilantro), chopped
115g/4oz rocket (arugula)
115g/4oz smoked trout
ground black pepper

For the dressing
15ml/1 tbsp sesame oil
75ml/5 tbsp white wine vinegar
5ml/1 tsp soy sauce
2.5cm/1in piece fresh root ginger,
  peeled and grated

1 Heat a griddle pan, brush it with the oil, then fry the trout fillet for 5–8 minutes, until it is just cooked. Lift the fillet out of the pan and place it in a shallow bowl. Flake the trout into bitesize pieces, sprinkle the lime rind and juice over and set aside.

COOK'S TIP
Peppery flavours go well with trout, so the rocket is an excellent choice. Buy wild rocket if possible as it has a more interesting taste. Alternatively, use watercress or even a red-leaved lettuce.
   This dish can easily be prepared in advance, but don't pour the dressing over the salad until the last minute.

2 Make the dressing by mixing the sesame oil, vinegar, soy sauce and grated root ginger in a small jug (pitcher). Whisk thoroughly until the dressing is well combined.

3 Place the chopped yellow and red peppers, coriander and rocket in a large bowl and toss to combine. Transfer the salad to a serving dish.

4 Using kitchen scissors, cut the smoked trout into bitesize pieces. Arrange the smoked trout and griddled trout fillet on the salad. Sprinkle with black pepper. Whisk the ginger dressing again and drizzle it over the salad before serving.

SMOKED TROUT TARTLETS

CRISP, GOLDEN FILO PASTRY CONTRASTS WITH A CREAMY TROUT AND THREE-CHEESE FILLING IN THESE PRETTY LITTLE TARTLETS.

SERVES 4

INGREDIENTS
   8 x 15cm/6in squares filo pastry
   50g/2oz/¼ cup butter, melted
   50g/2oz Gruyère cheese, grated
   115g/4oz/½ cup mascarpone cheese
   50g/2oz Parmesan cheese, grated
   45ml/3 tbsp milk
   75g/3oz smoked trout
   8 cherry tomatoes, halved
   salt and ground black pepper
   fresh flat leaf parsley and salad
      leaves, to garnish

3 In a large bowl, combine the three cheeses and milk. Season generously with salt and pepper and mix well.

1 Preheat the oven to 180ºC/350ºF/ Gas 4. For each tartlet, place two squares of filo pastry on top of each other at angles to form a star shape. Brush with melted butter and place, buttered side down, in an individual Yorkshire pudding pan or 10cm/4in tartlet pan. Repeat with the remaining filo.

4 Cut the smoked trout into bitesize pieces using kitchen scissors or a knife. Arrange the halved tomatoes and trout in the pastry cases.

5 Spoon the cheese mixture into the cooked pastry cases, gently pressing it down with the back of a spoon. Return the tartlets to the oven and bake for 10–15 minutes more, until the cheese is bubbling and golden brown. Serve immediately on individual plates, garnished with the parsley and a few salad leaves.

2 Support the pans on a baking sheet and brush the pastry with a little more butter. Bake for 5 minutes or until the tartlets are crisp and light golden brown in colour. Remove the tartlets from the oven but leave the oven on.

COOK'S TIPS
• Cover the filo pastry sheets with a damp, clean dishtowel or clear film (plastic wrap) until you are ready to use them, so that they do not dry out.
• Although Gruyère is the preferred cheese for these tartlets, Emmenthal or Jarlsberg could be used instead. Grate the cheese finely with a microplane grater.

SALMON PUFFS

CANNED SALMON IS CONVENIENT AND EASY TO USE. THE FLAVOUR AND TEXTURE ARE PERFECTLY ACCEPTABLE IN DISHES SUCH AS THIS ONE, WHERE THE FISH IS FLAKED AND MIXED WITH OTHER INGREDIENTS, INCLUDING SUN-DRIED TOMATOES, MAYONNAISE, LEMON AND CHOPPED PARSLEY.

SERVES 6–8

INGREDIENTS

    65g/2½oz/9 tbsp plain
     (all-purpose) flour
    50g/2oz/¼ cup butter
    150ml/¼ pint/⅔ cup water
    2 eggs, beaten
For the filling
    200g/7oz can red salmon, drained,
     or 175g/6oz poached salmon
    60ml/4 tbsp mayonnaise
    50g/2oz/⅓ cup sun-dried tomatoes
     in oil, drained and finely chopped
    grated rind and juice of ½ lemon
    30ml/2 tbsp freshly chopped parsley
    salt and ground black pepper
    salad leaves and halved cherry
     tomatoes, to serve

1 Sift the flour on to a sheet of baking parchment. Put the butter and water in a medium pan and heat gently until the butter melts. Bring to the boil and remove from the heat.

2 Immediately tip in all the flour and beat with a wooden spoon until the mixture forms a smooth, glossy paste. Leave the paste in a warm room to cool slightly for 5 minutes.

3 Meanwhile, make the filling. Flake the salmon finely and put it in a bowl. Add the mayonnaise, sun-dried tomatoes, lemon rind and juice. Stir in the parsley, with salt and pepper to taste. Cover and chill until ready to serve.

4 Add the beaten egg gradually to the cooled paste, stirring well after each addition to prevent the mixture from curdling. It may not be necessary to add all the egg; stir in just enough to produce a smooth, shiny mixture that is thick enough to hold its shape. Set the choux pastry aside.

5 Preheat the oven to 190°C/375°F/ Gas 5. Grease a large baking sheet. Carefully spoon the choux pastry into a piping (pastry) bag fitted with a 1cm/½in plain round nozzle.

6 Pipe the pastry on to the baking sheet to make about 24 small rounds, spaced well apart. Bake for 20–25 minutes until the puffs are browned.

7 Remove the puffs from the oven and split them horizontally in half to release the steam. Leave the puffs to cool completely on a wire rack.

8 Just before serving, use a teaspoon to fill each puff with a little of the salmon mixture. Divide the salad leaves and halved tomatoes among individual serving plates and place three or four puffs on each.

COOK'S TIPS
• It is essential that the oven has reached the required temperature before the puffs are baked, as they rely on that first burst of heat for the maximum rise.
• When making choux puffs, whether for a savoury or a sweet dish, always slit them to release the steam. If any uncooked paste remains in the centre, simply remove it and return the puffs to the oven for 2–3 minutes to dry out.

TROUT AND PRAWN POTS

BACON IS OFTEN WRAPPED AROUND WHOLE TROUT TO KEEP THE FLESH MOIST WHEN GRILLING, BUT HERE IT HAS ANOTHER FUNCTION, TO MARRY THE FLAVOURS OF TROUT AND PRAWN.

SERVES 6

INGREDIENTS
  15g/½oz/1 tbsp butter
  15ml/1 tbsp olive oil
  1 small leek, finely chopped
  2 rashers (strips) rindless back
    (lean) bacon, chopped
  115g/4oz cooked peeled prawns
    (shrimp)
  115g/4oz trout fillet, skinned
  150ml/¼ pint/⅔ cup sour cream
  1 egg, beaten
  50g/2oz Cheddar cheese, grated
  salt and ground black pepper
  warm country bread, to serve

1 Heat the butter and oil in a heavy frying pan and fry the leek gently for 5 minutes or until softened, stirring from time to time.

2 Add the bacon to the pan and fry until it is just beginning to turn colour, stirring all the time. Add the prawns, increase the heat and stir-fry the mixture for 5 minutes. Remove from the heat.

3 Cut the trout fillet into bitesize pieces and stir into the bacon and prawn mixture. Season with a little salt, if required, and plenty of pepper. Divide the mixture among six ramekins.

4 Preheat the oven to 190°C/375°F/Gas 5. In a jug (pitcher) beat the sour cream and egg with a fork. Season lightly. Pour one-sixth of the mixture into each ramekin and sprinkle the grated cheese over the top.

5 Bake the pots in the preheated oven for 15 minutes or until the top is golden brown and bubbling. Serve straight from the oven with chunks of warm, crusty bread, if you like.

COOK'S TIPS
Trout and prawn pots can be made several hours in advance and baked just before being served for an easy, fuss-free appetizer. Store the prepared pots in the refrigerator until you are ready to cook them. If the bacon is salty, it may not be necessary to add salt to the trout mixture.

SALMON GOUJONS <u>WITH</u> LIME <u>AND</u> CAPER DIP

THESE SCRUMPTIOUS SALMON STRIPS ARE COATED IN A MIXTURE OF POLENTA AND PAPRIKA BEFORE BEING FRIED. THIS GIVES THEM A REALLY CRISP FINISH WITH A SUBTLE SPICY FLAVOUR.

SERVES 4

INGREDIENTS
    350g/12oz salmon fillet, skinned
    50g/2oz/½ cup plain
      (all-purpose) flour
    2 eggs, beaten
    50g/2oz/⅓ cup polenta
    5ml/1 tsp paprika
    vegetable oil, for deep-frying
    salt and ground black pepper
    lime wedges, to garnish

For the dip
    200ml/7fl oz/scant 1 cup Greek
      (US strained plain) yogurt
    finely grated rind and juice of 1 lime
    30ml/2 tbsp drained capers,
      finely chopped

1 To make the dip, combine all the ingredients in a bowl and mix. Season and spoon into a serving dish. Cover and chill in the refrigerator.

2 Cut the salmon fillets into strips of 7.5 x 2.5cm/3 x 1in. Season the flour and place in a shallow dish. Pour the beaten egg into a separate shallow dish. Combine the polenta and paprika in a third shallow dish.

3 Dip the salmon strips, one at a time, in the seasoned flour, then in the beaten egg and finally in the polenta, making sure they are evenly coated.

4 Heat the oil for deep-frying until it is very hot. Fry the goujons in batches, about four or five at a time, for 3–5 minutes, turning them occasionally with a slotted spoon.

5 Remove the cooked goujons with a slotted spoon and drain well on a double thickness of kitchen paper. Keep the cooked goujons hot in the oven while you cook the remainder.

6 When all the goujons have been cooked, arrange them on a platter. Garnish them with the lime wedges and serve them with the lime and caper dip.

SMOKED TROUT COCOTTES

HOT SMOKED TROUT FILLETS TASTE QUITE DIFFERENT FROM COLD SMOKED TROUT; THEY HAVE A SURPRISINGLY CREAMY TEXTURE AND A WONDERFUL PALE PINK COLOUR. THIS DELICIOUS DISH MAKES A PERFECT LIGHT LUNCH FOR TWO PEOPLE, OR A FIRST COURSE FOR FOUR.

SERVES 2–4

INGREDIENTS
    4 red (bell) peppers
    60ml/4 tbsp olive oil
    150g/5oz hot smoked trout fillets
    30ml/2 tbsp chopped fresh parsley
    175g/6oz/¾ cup crème fraîche
    50g/2oz Parmesan cheese, grated
    salt and ground black pepper
    sun-dried tomato bread, to serve

1 Preheat the oven to 180°C/350°F/ Gas 4. Place the peppers in a roasting pan. Drizzle with olive oil and season well with salt and pepper. Bake for 25–30 minutes or until the pepper skins are blackened. Set aside to cool.

2 Peel the skin off the cooked peppers and discard the core and seeds. Cut the pepper flesh into bitesize pieces.

3 Preheat the oven to 200°C/400°F/ Gas 6. Flake the trout and divide between individual baking dishes. Arrange the pepper pieces in a layer over the fish in each dish.

4 Sprinkle the parsley over the fish and peppers. Spoon the crème fraîche into the dishes and season well. Top with the grated Parmesan cheese.

5 Bake in the preheated oven for about 15 minutes, or until the Parmesan cheese is golden brown and bubbling. Serve with chunks of sun-dried tomato bread, if you like.

COOK'S TIP
If making this dish for a dinner party first course, you can prepare it in advance, if you like. Keep it in the refrigerator and bake just before serving.

BAKED TROUT WITH A GREMOLATA CRUST

A GREMOLATA CRUST IS A COMBINATION OF BREADCRUMBS WITH FINELY CHOPPED PARSLEY, LEMON RIND AND GARLIC. IT IS TRADITIONALLY SPRINKLED OVER THE CLASSIC VEAL DISH, OSSO BUCCO.

SERVES 4

INGREDIENTS
    1 small aubergine (eggplant),
      cubed
    1 red (bell) pepper, finely
      diced
    1 yellow (bell) pepper, finely
      diced
    1 small red onion, finely chopped
    30ml/2 tbsp olive oil
    350g/12oz trout fillets
    juice of 1 lime
    salt and ground black pepper
    chunks of bread, to serve

For the gremolata crust
    grated rind of 1 lemon
    grated rind of 1 lime
    25g/1oz/½ cup fresh breadcrumbs
    30ml/2 tbsp chopped fresh flat
      leaf parsley
    1 garlic clove, finely chopped

1 Preheat the oven to 200°C/400°F/ Gas 6. Place the aubergine, peppers and onion in a roasting pan. Add the oil and stir to coat all the vegetables. Sprinkle with plenty of salt and pepper. Cook for 40 minutes or until the edges of the vegetables have begun to char.

2 Make the gremolata by mixing the lemon and lime rind with the breadcrumbs, chopped parsley and garlic. Add plenty of salt and pepper.

3 Place the trout fillets on top of the vegetables in the roasting pan and cover the surface of the fish with the breadcrumb mixture. Return to the oven for a further 15 minutes or until the fish is fully cooked and the gremolata topping is crunchy.

4 Divide the fish and vegetables among four serving plates and sprinkle the lime juice over to taste. Serve with bread to soak up all the juices.

SALMON AU GRATIN

THIS IS A VERY RICH APPETIZER, PERFECT FOR SERVING BEFORE A RELATIVELY PLAIN MAIN COURSE, SUCH AS A SALAD. THE SALMON IS BAKED IN A LUXURIOUS CREAM AND GRUYÈRE SAUCE.

SERVES 6

INGREDIENTS

350g/12oz salmon fillet, skinned
  and cubed
grated rind and juice of 2 limes
60ml/4 tbsp olive oil
2 small red onions, sliced
2 garlic cloves, finely chopped
bunch of fresh tarragon, chopped
450ml/¾ pint/scant 2 cups double
  (heavy) cream
115g/4oz Gruyère cheese, grated
salt and ground black pepper
country bread, to serve

3 Using a slotted spoon, remove the salmon cubes from the marinade and place them in a clean bowl. Add the chopped tarragon and cream. Season with salt and pepper and mix gently.

1 Place the salmon cubes in a bowl and sprinkle the lime rind and juice over. Toss well and leave to stand for 10 minutes. Meanwhile, use 15ml/1 tbsp of the oil to lightly grease six ramekins.

4 Divide among the ramekins and top with the grated cheese. Support the ramekins on a baking sheet and grill (broil) for 5–6 minutes or until the salmon is cooked and the cheese is golden brown and bubbling. Serve immediately with bread.

2 Preheat the grill (broiler) to high. Heat the remaining oil in a frying pan over a medium heat, add the onion slices and fry for 3 minutes. Add the garlic to the pan and cook for a further 3 minutes, taking care not to let it burn. Divide the onion mixture among the ramekins.

VARIATIONS
• Look out for salmon lardons in specialist delicatessens. These, like bacon lardons, are quite chunky, and work well for a recipe like this. They are popular in France, partly because they are full of flavour and partly for convenience, since they are ready cut.
• Although Gruyère is the preferred cheese for these ramekins, Emmenthal or Jarlsberg could be used instead. Grate the cheese finely – a microplane grater is useful for this.

QUICK FOODS
AND SNACKS

Both salmon and trout cook extremely quickly, so are ideal for those occasions when you want good food fast. In fact, you do not necessarily have to cook the fish — a good meal could be merely a matter of opening a packet. Whether you fancy a sophisticated breakfast of Lox with Bagels and Cream Cheese or a picnic lunch of Cheese Scones with Trout Butter, keeping your favourite smoked fish in the refrigerator makes perfect sense. Almost as quick, and just as tasty, are the meals you can make with fresh fish. Try Egg and Salmon Puff Parcels or Seared Trout Bruschetta for tempting treats.

EGG <u>AND</u> SALMON PUFF PARCELS

THESE ELEGANT PARCELS HIDE A MOUTHWATERING MIXTURE OF FLAVOURS, AND MAKE A DELICIOUS APPETIZER OR LUNCH DISH. SERVE WITH CURRY-FLAVOURED MAYONNAISE OR HOLLANDAISE SAUCE.

SERVES 6

INGREDIENTS
  75g/3oz/scant ½ cup long grain rice
  300ml/½ pint/1¼ cups good-quality
    fish stock
  350g/12oz tail pieces of salmon
  juice of ½ lemon
  15ml/1 tbsp chopped fresh dill
  15ml/1 tbsp chopped fresh parsley
  10ml/2 tsp mild curry powder
  6 small (US medium) eggs,
    soft-boiled and cooled
  425g/15oz flaky or puff pastry,
    thawed if frozen
  1 egg, beaten
  salt and ground black pepper

VARIATION
You could replace the hen's eggs with quail's eggs for a luxury touch.

1 Place the rice in a large pan and cook according to the instructions on the packet, using fish stock instead of water, then drain and cool. Preheat the oven to 220°C/425°F/Gas 7.

2 Place the salmon in a large pan and cover with cold water. Gently heat until the water is not quite simmering and cook the fish for 8–10 minutes until it flakes easily when tested.

3 Lift the salmon out of the pan and remove the bones and skin. Flake the fish into the rice, add the lemon juice, herbs, curry powder and seasoning, and mix well. Peel the eggs.

4 Roll out the pastry and cut into six 15cm/6in squares. Brush the edges with the beaten egg. Place a spoonful of the rice mixture in the middle of each square, push an egg into the centre and top with a little more of the rice mixture. Pull over the pastry corners to the middle to form a neat, square parcel, pressing the joins together with your fingers firmly to seal.

5 Brush the parcels with more beaten egg, place on a baking sheet and bake for 20 minutes, then reduce the oven temperature to 190°C/375°F/Gas 5. Cook for 10 minutes more, until golden and crisp. Cool slightly before serving.

LOX <u>WITH</u> BAGELS <u>AND</u> CREAM CHEESE

THIS GLORIOUSLY COMFORTING, SELF-INDULGENT DISH IS PERFECT FOR A WEEKEND BREAKFAST OR A LIGHT LUNCH WITH FRIENDS. LOX IS THE JEWISH WORD FOR SMOKED SALMON, AND THIS RECIPE IS A REAL JEWISH DELI CLASSIC WHICH YOU CAN EASILY RECREATE AT HOME.

SERVES 2

INGREDIENTS
  2 bagels
  115–175g/4–6oz/½–¾ cup full-fat
  cream cheese
  150g/5oz sliced best smoked salmon
  ground black pepper
  lemon wedges, to serve

1 Preheat the oven to 200°C/400°F/ Gas 6. Put the bagels on a large baking sheet and warm them in the oven for 4–5 minutes.

2 Remove the bagels from the oven, split them in two and spread generously with cream cheese. Pile the salmon on top of the bagels and grind over plenty of black pepper.

3 Squeeze over some lemon juice, then top with the other bagel half and eat while still warm.

4 For an easy and elegant touch, place a wedge of lemon in the centre of a small square of muslin (cheesecloth), bring up the edges to enclose it, tie with fine string and put it on the plate.

COOK'S TIP
It is essential to be generous with the smoked salmon and to use the best cream cheese you can find – absolutely not a low-fat version.

SCRAMBLED EGGS <u>WITH</u> SMOKED SALMON

FOR A LUXURY BREAKFAST, OR A LATE-NIGHT SUPPER, YOU CAN'T BEAT THIS SPECIAL COMBINATION. SERVE IT WITH BUCK'S FIZZ: CHAMPAGNE MIXED WITH FRESHLY SQUEEZED ORANGE JUICE.

SERVES 4

INGREDIENTS
    4 slices of pumpernickel or
       wholemeal (whole-wheat) bread,
       crusts trimmed
    50g/2oz/¼ cup butter
    115g/4oz thinly sliced smoked salmon
    6 eggs
    105ml/7 tbsp crème fraîche or sour
       cream
    salt and ground black pepper
    generous 60ml/4 tbsp salmon roe
       or lumpfish roe and sprigs of dill,
       to garnish

VARIATION
If you are lucky enough to have a truffle,
another treat is to grate a little into the
scrambled eggs. Serve them on toast,
topped with a little chopped fresh chervil.

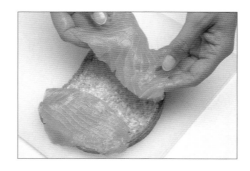

1 Spread the slices of pumpernickel or
wholemeal bread with half of the butter
and arrange the smoked salmon on top.
Cut each slice in half, place two halves
on each serving plate and set aside
while you make the scrambled eggs.

2 Lightly beat the eggs in a bowl and
season with salt and freshly ground
pepper. Melt the remaining butter in
a pan until sizzling, then quickly stir
in the beaten eggs.

3 Stir constantly until the eggs begin to
thicken. Just before they have finished
cooking, remove the saucepan from the
heat and stir in the crème fraîche or
sour cream. Set the eggs aside and
keep warm.

4 Spoon the scrambled eggs on to
the smoked salmon. Top each serving
with a spoonful of salmon roe or
lumpfish roe and serve, garnished
with sprigs of dill.

TROUT BURGERS

THESE HOME-MADE FISH BURGERS REALLY ARE A TREAT. THEY PROVIDE THE IDEAL WAY OF PERSUADING CHILDREN WHO CLAIM THEY DON'T LIKE FISH TO TRY IT. COOK CHILLED BURGERS ON THE BARBECUE, IF YOU PREFER, ON A LIGHTLY OILED GRILL RACK.

MAKES 8

INGREDIENTS
   350g/12oz trout fillet, skinned
   150ml/¼ pint/⅔ cup milk
   150ml/¼ pint/⅔ cup hot fish stock
   4 spring onions (scallions),
      thinly sliced
   350g/12oz cooked potatoes, peeled
   5ml/1 tsp tartare sauce
   1 egg, beaten
   50g/2oz/1 cup fresh white
      breadcrumbs
   60ml/4 tbsp semolina
   salt and ground white pepper
   vegetable oil, for shallow frying

To serve
   120ml/4fl oz/½ cup mayonnaise
   45ml/3 tbsp drained canned
      whole kernel corn
   1 red (bell) pepper, seeded
      and finely diced
   8 burger buns
   4 ripe tomatoes, sliced
   salad leaves

1 Place the trout in a frying pan with the milk, stock and spring onions. Simmer for 5 minutes or until the fish is cooked. Lift it out of the pan and set it aside. Strain the stock through a sieve into a bowl, reserving the spring onions.

COOK'S TIP
Not all children like tartare sauce. If you have any doubts about adding it to the burger mixture, you could substitute tomato ketchup instead.

2 Mash the potatoes roughly and stir in the tartare sauce, egg and breadcrumbs. Flake the trout and add the reserved spring onions. Fold into the potato mixture and season with salt and pepper.

3 Divide the potato mixture into eight and shape into burgers, using your hands. Coat thoroughly in the semolina and pat them into shape. Arrange on a plate and place in the refrigerator for 1 hour, so that they firm up.

4 In a bowl, mix the mayonnaise for serving with the corn kernels and diced red pepper.

5 Heat the oil in a frying pan and fry the burgers for 10 minutes, turning once.

6 To serve, split open the buns and spread a little of the mayonnaise over each half. Fill with a few salad leaves, a couple of tomato slices and a fish burger. Serve immediately.

SALMON AND AVOCADO PIZZA

A MIXTURE OF SMOKED AND FRESH SALMON MAKES A DELICIOUS PIZZA TOPPING WHEN MIXED WITH AVOCADO. CAPERS ADD A TOUCH OF PIQUANCY TO CUT THE RICHNESS OF THE MAJOR INGREDIENTS.

SERVES 3–4

INGREDIENTS
150g/5oz salmon fillet
120ml/4fl oz/½ cup dry white wine
15ml/1 tbsp olive oil
400g/14oz can chopped
   tomatoes, drained
115g/4oz mozzarella cheese, grated
1 small avocado, halved, stoned
   (pitted), peeled and cubed
10ml/2 tsp lemon juice
30ml/2 tbsp crème fraîche or
   sour cream
75g/3oz smoked salmon, cut
   into strips
15ml/1 tbsp drained bottled capers
30ml/2 tbsp chopped fresh chives,
   to garnish
ground black pepper

For the pizza base
175g/6oz/1½ cups strong white
   (bread) flour
1.5ml/¼ tsp salt
5ml/1 tsp easy-blend (rapid-rise)
   dried yeast
120–150ml/4–5fl oz/½–⅔ cup
   lukewarm water
15ml/1 tbsp olive oil

1 Make the pizza base. Sift the flour and salt into a mixing bowl, stir in the yeast, then make a well in the centre.

2 Add the lukewarm water to the well, then add the oil. Mix with a spoon gradually incorporating the flour to make a soft dough.

3 Knead the dough until smooth and elastic, then place in a bowl, cover with clear film (plastic wrap) and leave in a warm place for about 1 hour or until the dough has doubled in bulk.

4 Knock back (punch down) the dough, knead it briefly, then roll it out to a 25–30cm/10–12in round and support on a baking sheet. Push up the edges to make a rim.

5 Preheat the oven to 220°C/425°F/ Gas 7. Place the salmon in a frying pan, pour over the wine and season. Bring slowly to the boil, remove from the heat, cover and cool. (The fish will cook in the cooling liquid.) Skin and flake the salmon, removing any bones.

6 Brush the pizza base with the oil and spread over the drained tomatoes. Sprinkle over 50g/2oz of the mozzarella. Bake for 10 minutes. Meanwhile, toss the avocado in the lemon juice.

7 Dot teaspoonfuls of the crème fraîche or sour cream over the pizza base. Arrange the fresh and smoked salmon, avocado, capers and remaining mozzarella on top. Season with black pepper. Bake for a further 10 minutes until crisp and golden. Sprinkle over the chives and serve immediately.

COOK'S TIPS
• Smoked salmon trimmings are cheaper than smoked salmon slices and could be used for the topping.
• For an unusual addition to this pizza, try Peppadews. These sweet cherry chillies come from South Africa. There are mild and hot varieties, and both are delicious with salmon. Drain them thoroughly before cutting them into strips and adding them to the topping with the avocado and capers.
• When adding the topping, leave the rim of the pizza clear.

CHEESE SCONES WITH TROUT BUTTER

THESE DELICIOUS SCONES ARE TOPPED WITH A RICHLY FLAVOURED SMOKED TROUT AND HORSERADISH BUTTER, WHICH CAN BE PREPARED A DAY AHEAD. THE CHEESE SCONES ARE BEST BAKED ON THE DAY YOU ARE PLANNING TO EAT THEM AS THEY STALE QUITE QUICKLY.

MAKES 6

INGREDIENTS
75g/3oz/¾ cup self-raising (self-rising) flour
75g/3oz/¾ cup plain (all-purpose) flour
5ml/1 tsp baking powder
25g/1oz/2 tbsp butter
75g/3oz Cheddar cheese or Monterey Jack, grated
1 egg, beaten
45ml/3 tbsp milk
salt and ground black pepper
fresh parsley sprigs, to garnish

For the butter
50g/2oz/¼ cup butter, softened
50g/2oz smoked trout
5ml/1 tsp creamed horseradish

COOK'S TIP
For the lightest scones, handle the dough as little as possible, mixing the ingredients together quickly and kneading the dough as briefly as possible. Sifting the flours into the mixing bowl from a height will help to incorporate additional air into the scone mixture.

VARIATIONS
Other hard cheeses, such as Red Leicester or Lancashire, could be used instead of the Cheddar or Monterey Jack for the cheese scones.

1 Make the smoked trout butter. Place the softened butter, smoked trout and creamed horseradish in a food processor. Season to taste with salt and ground black pepper. Process the ingredients until well blended. Transfer to a bowl, cover and chill until needed.

2 Preheat the oven to 220°C/425°F/ Gas 7. To make the scones, sift the flours and baking powder into a mixing bowl. Season the flour with salt and ground black pepper.

3 Rub the butter into the flour with your fingertips until the mixture resembles fine breadcrumbs. Stir in most of the cheese, reserving just enough to sprinkle on top of the scones.

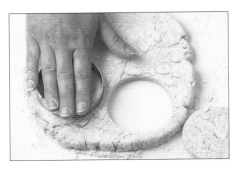

4 Stir in the beaten egg and enough milk to make a smooth, soft dough. Knead the dough gently and turn it out on a floured surface. Roll or pat the dough out to a thickness of 2cm/¾in. Using a plain 7.5cm/3in cutter, stamp out six scones.

5 Place the scones on a well-greased baking sheet, brush with a little milk to glaze and sprinkle the reserved cheese over. Bake for 15–20 minutes or until just turning golden. Cool slightly on a wire rack.

6 Remove the smoked trout butter from the refrigerator 30 minutes before serving. Split the warm scones in half, top with the butter and garnish with the parsley to serve.

GOAT'S CHEESE AND TROUT TOASTIES

THESE LITTLE ROUNDS ARE PACKED FULL OF FLAVOUR — THE GOAT'S CHEESE AND TROUT COMBINE BEAUTIFULLY TO MAKE A DELICIOUS SNACK SUITABLE FOR ANY TIME OF THE DAY.

SERVES 4

INGREDIENTS
    8 thick slices of white bread
    30ml/2 tbsp olive oil
    5ml/1 tsp fresh thyme leaves
    20ml/4 tsp pesto
    50g/2oz smoked trout slices
    4 round goat's cheese slices,
      each about 50g/2oz
    salt and ground black pepper
    cherry tomatoes and fresh basil,
      to serve

COOK'S TIP
The easiest way to crumb a small quantity of bread is with a hand-held grater. Rub the bread down the coarsest side, in the same way as grating cheese. Fresh breadcrumbs can be stored in the freezer until you need them.

1 Preheat the oven to 200°C/400°F/ Gas 6. Using a pastry cutter that is slightly larger than the goat's cheese rounds, cut a circle from each slice of bread.

2 Brush the bread rounds with a little olive oil, scatter with a few thyme leaves and season well. Place the bread rounds on a baking sheet and bake for 5 minutes or until crisp and a light golden colour.

3 Remove the bread from the oven and spread 5ml/1 tsp pesto over half the rounds. Divide the smoked trout among the pesto-topped bread, top with the cheese rounds and season well with black pepper. Top the cheese with the remaining bread circles.

4 Bake the toasties in the oven for 5 minutes more, until the cheese has just started to soften slightly. Remove from the oven and serve immediately with the cherry tomatoes and basil leaves.

VARIATIONS
• Thyme goes particularly well with goat's cheese but other strong herbs can be substituted. Try oregano, marjoram or sage for a completely different taste.
• For a milder flavour, use rounds of under-ripe Brie or Camembert cheese in place of the goat's cheese.

SMOKED SALMON AND SPINACH WRAPS

THE CREAMY TEXTURES OF AVOCADO AND HUMMUS AND THE VIBRANT COLOURS OF RED PEPPER AND BABY SPINACH MAKE THESE DELICIOUS WRAPS A FEAST FOR THE EYES AS WELL AS THE TASTE BUDS!

MAKES 6

INGREDIENTS
    2 red (bell) peppers
    30ml/2 tbsp olive oil
    6 large wheat flour tortillas
    1 avocado
    30ml/2 tbsp lemon juice
    115g/4oz/½ cup hummus
    25g/1oz/3 tbsp pine nuts
    50g/2oz baby spinach leaves
    115g/4oz smoked salmon
    salt and ground black pepper

COOK'S TIP
The peppers can also be charred under the grill (broiler) and the tortillas heated in the microwave.

1 Preheat the oven to 180°C/350°F/ Gas 4. Place the peppers in a roasting pan. Drizzle the olive oil over and season with plenty of salt and black pepper. Bake for 25–30 minutes.

2 Peel the skin off the cooked peppers and discard the core and seeds. Cut the pepper flesh into strips.

3 Place the tortillas on a sheet of foil and seal tightly. Warm in the oven for 10 minutes.

4 Meanwhile, cut the avocado in half, remove the stone (pit) and peel, then slice lengthways. Sprinkle with the lemon juice to prevent the avocado flesh from turning brown.

5 Remove the tortillas from the oven. Spread a quarter of the hummus over each wrap, using a round-bladed knife or slim spatula, then sprinkle the pine nuts evenly over the hummus, but leaving the borders free of nuts.

6 Divide the spinach, salmon and peppers among the topped tortillas, placing them in a line down the centre. Roll up each wrap and serve immediately, while still warm. Offer lemon wedges for squeezing, if you like.

SALMON TORTILLA CONES

WHETHER YOU'RE SNUGGLING UP ON THE SOFA TO WATCH A LATE NIGHT MOVIE OR CATERING FOR A CROWD, THESE SIMPLE YET SOPHISTICATED WRAPS ARE IRRESISTIBLE.

SERVES 4

INGREDIENTS
    115g/4oz/½ cup soft white
      (farmer's) cheese
    30ml/2 tbsp roughly chopped
      fresh dill
    juice of 1 lemon
    1 small red onion
    15ml/1 tbsp drained bottled capers
    30ml/2 tbsp extra virgin olive oil
    30ml/2 tbsp roughly chopped fresh
      flat leaf parsley
    115g/4oz smoked salmon
    8 small or 4 large wheat
      flour tortillas
    salt and ground black pepper
    lemon wedges, for squeezing

3 Cut the smoked salmon into short, thin strips, and add to the red onion mixture. Toss to mix. Season to taste with plenty of pepper.

4 If using small tortillas, leave them whole, but large ones need to be cut in half. Spread a little of the soft cheese mixture on each piece of tortilla and top with the smoked salmon mixture.

1 Place the soft cheese in a small bowl and mix in half the chopped dill. Add a little salt and pepper and just a dash of the lemon juice to taste. Reserve the remaining lemon juice in a dish.

5 Roll up the tortillas into cones and secure with wooden cocktail sticks (toothpicks). Arrange on a serving plate and add some lemon wedges, for squeezing. Serve immediately.

VARIATIONS
Try soft cheese with red pesto, chopped sun-dried tomatoes and smoked salmon, or smoked trout pâté with slices of cucumber.

COOK'S TIP
Look out for tortilla wraps in the supermarket. Thinner than traditional Mexican wheat tortillas, these come in several flavours. The spicy tomato ones would be good for this recipe.

2 Finely chop the red onion. Add the onion, capers and olive oil to the lemon juice. Add the chopped flat leaf parsley and the remaining dill and stir gently.

SMOKED TROUT SOUFFLÉ OMELETTE

HALF OMELETTE, HALF SOUFFLÉ, THIS DELICIOUSLY LIGHT SUPPER DISH IS THE IDEAL CHOICE FOR WHEN YOU'RE JUST COOKING FOR YOURSELF. PACKED WITH FRESH HERBS AND SMOKED TROUT, IT IS FULL OF FLAVOUR. SERVE IT SIMPLY WITH A GLASS OF DRY WHITE WINE, SOME WARM COUNTRY BREAD AND A FRESH SALAD SUCH AS BASIL AND TOMATO.

SERVES 1

INGREDIENTS

  2 eggs, separated
  30ml/2 tbsp water
  25g/1oz/2 tbsp butter
  15ml/1 tbsp chopped fresh parsley
  15ml/1 tbsp chopped fresh chives
  50g/2oz smoked trout, roughly
    chopped
  40g/1½oz Gruyère cheese,
    finely grated
  salt and ground black pepper
  warm bread, to serve

For the tomato and basil salad
  3 plum tomatoes, sliced
  30ml/2 tbsp fresh basil leaves
  5ml/1 tsp balsamic vinegar
  15ml/1 tbsp extra virgin olive oil

COOK'S TIP
For the best results when whisking, the egg whites should be at room temperature. If you store eggs in the refrigerator, remember to take them out 30 minutes or so before you want to use them.

VARIATIONS
• Any fresh herbs, such as chervil, oregano or thyme – or a mixture of all of them – can be substituted for the chives and parsley in this recipe.
• Instead of Gruyère cheese, try another full-flavoured hard cheese, such as Cheddar or Monterey Jack.

1 Make the salad. Arrange the tomato slices on a serving plate and top with the fresh basil leaves. Drizzle the vinegar and oil over and season well. Set aside but do not chill, as the sweet flavour of the tomatoes will be more pronounced at room temperature.

2 Put the egg whites in a mixing bowl and add salt and pepper. Using a hand-held electric mixer or rotary whisk, whisk until they are stiff but not dry. In a separate mixing bowl, whisk the egg yolks with the water until creamy.

3 Using a large metal spoon, add a little of the egg white mixture to the yolks. Fold in carefully to incorporate as much air as possible. Add the remaining white and fold in gently.

4 Preheat the grill (broiler) to high. Melt the butter in an 18cm/7in omelette or frying pan which can safely be used under the grill. Swirl the pan around to grease the sides thoroughly.

5 Pour the egg mixture into the pan and cook over a medium heat, gently shivering the pan from time to time, until the omelette is golden brown on the base and just firm to the touch in the centre.

6 Sprinkle over the chopped herbs, smoked trout and grated cheese.

7 Place the pan under the grill and cook until the egg is just set and the cheese is golden and bubbling. Run a blunt knife around the edge of the pan to release the omelette, then gently score a line right across the centre of the omelette.

8 Fold the omelette in half and slide it carefully on to a hot serving plate. Serve immediately with the tomato and basil salad and warm bread.

TROUT-FILLED PITTAS WITH MUSTARD MAYO

MUSTARD AND TROUT MAY NOT BE AN OBVIOUS COMBINATION OF FLAVOURS, BUT THEY TASTE GREAT WHEN TEAMED TOGETHER IN THESE SIMPLE FILLED PITTA BREADS.

SERVES 4

INGREDIENTS

    175g/6oz hot smoked trout fillets
    6 sun-dried tomatoes in oil, drained
     and finely chopped
    90ml/6 tbsp mayonnaise
    10ml/2 tsp wholegrain mustard
    4 pitta breads
    2 Little Gem (Bibb) lettuces
    1 yellow (bell) pepper, finely diced
    salt and ground black pepper

COOK'S TIP
The pitta breads can be warmed in a toaster if you prefer. Watch them carefully so that they do not burn. They are ready as soon as they start to puff up.

1 Preheat the oven to 180°C/350°F/ Gas 4. To make the filling, flake the trout into small pieces and place in a large mixing bowl.

2 Add the chopped sun-dried tomatoes, mayonnaise and mustard to the trout in the bowl. Season to taste with salt and plenty of ground black pepper. Stir well to combine all the ingredients.

3 Wrap the pitta breads in foil and heat them in the oven for 10 minutes.

4 Chop or shred the lettuces and mix with the yellow pepper in a bowl.

5 Remove the pitta breads from the oven and split each one along one side with a sharp knife. Half fill each pitta with the lettuce and pepper mixture. Add one quarter of the trout mixture and season well before serving.

HOT TROUT WITH RED VEGETABLES

THIS MEDITERRANEAN-STYLE SANDWICH IS SO EASY TO PREPARE AND MAKES A TASTY WEEKEND LUNCH. CHOOSE YOUR FAVOURITE BREAD, BUT MAKE SURE IT IS REALLY FRESH.

3 Peel the skin off the cooked peppers and discard the core and seeds. Cut the pepper flesh into strips. Slice each ciabatta loaf in half vertically, then cut each half in half horizontally.

4 Heat a ridged griddle pan over a medium heat. Lift the trout fillets carefully out of the marinade and fry them for 1–2 minutes, without adding any oil, until just cooked.

5 Mix the pesto and mayonnaise together and spread over the bread. Divide the rocket among four halves of the bread and top with the trout fillet, pepper strips and roasted tomatoes. Place the remaining bread on top and serve.

COOK'S TIPS
• You can use any bread you like but make sure you slice the bread thickly.
• Small loaves of olive-oil bread, such as ciabatta and focaccia, are ideal for these sandwiches. Try the sun-dried tomato and black olive versions, too.
• If you can't find any red pesto, use 30ml/2 tbsp chopped fresh basil mixed with 15ml/1 tbsp sun-dried tomato paste.

SERVES 4

INGREDIENTS
2 red (bell) peppers
8 cherry tomatoes
60ml/4 tbsp extra virgin olive oil
30ml/2 tbsp lemon juice
4 thin trout fillets, each about
  115g/4oz, skinned
2 small ciabatta loaves
15ml/1 tbsp red pesto
30ml/2 tbsp mayonnaise
115g/4oz rocket (arugula)
salt and ground black pepper

1 Preheat the oven to 180°C/350°F/ Gas 4. Place the peppers and tomatoes in a roasting pan and drizzle half the olive oil over. Bake for 25–30 minutes or until the pepper skins are blackened. Set aside to cool.

2 In a small bowl or jug (pitcher), whisk the remaining oil with the lemon juice and a little salt and freshly ground black pepper. Place the trout in a shallow, non-metallic dish and pour over the oil and lemon juice. Turn the fish to make sure they are well coated.

SEARED TROUT BRUSCHETTA

These resemble open sandwiches and are hearty enough to make a satisfying lunchtime snack for four people. If you prefer, cut the loaf into eight and serve as an appetizer.

SERVES 4–8

INGREDIENTS
    1 baguette
    1 garlic clove, halved
    30ml/2 tbsp extra virgin olive oil
    120ml/4fl oz/½ cup crème fraîche or
        sour cream
    15ml/1 tbsp creamed horseradish
    15ml/1 tbsp chopped fresh chives
    4 thin trout fillets, each about
        115g/4oz
    50g/2oz watercress, land cress or
        salad leaves
    salt and ground black pepper
    lemon juice and extra virgin olive oil,
        to serve

3 In a small bowl, mix the crème fraîche or sour cream, horseradish and chives with salt and pepper to taste.

4 Season the trout fillets lightly and brush over a little olive oil. Heat a frying pan until really hot and add the trout, placing the fillets skin side down. Sear for 3 minutes, flip over and cook for 30 seconds more.

5 Place one seared trout fillet on each piece of toasted baguette. Add a generous dollop of the horseradish cream and some watercress, land cress or salad leaves. Serve drizzled with lemon juice and extra olive oil.

1 Preheat the grill (broiler) to high and preheat the oven to 150°C/300°F/Gas 2. Cut the baguette in half horizontally, then cut each half vertically to give four equal-sized pieces altogether.

2 Toast the bread under the grill until lightly browned. Rub the toasted bread all over with the halved garlic clove and drizzle with olive oil. Keep warm in the oven while you prepare the topping.

VARIATIONS
• If you prefer, use 15ml/1 tbsp wholegrain mustard instead of the horseradish in the creamy filling, and substitute chopped fresh flat leaf parsley for the chives.
• Try extra virgin olive oil flavoured with herbs, such as thyme and rosemary, for drizzling over the toasted bread.

MAIN DISHES

We should be eating oily fish like salmon and trout at least two or three times a week, but although many of us intend to do just that, we sometimes get stuck in a recipe rut. There's a limit to how many times a person can serve fisherman's pie or grilled salmon, so this chapter introduces some delicious new recipes to expand your repertoire. Dishes like Herby Salmon Parcels, Pan-fried Citrus Trout with Basil, and Salmon with Stilton are easy to prepare and taste great. Also on the menu are old favourites like Classic Fish Pie and Salmon Fish Cakes — served here with a spicy mayonnaise.

SALMON FISH CAKES

WHOLEGRAIN MUSTARD GIVES THESE EXCELLENT FISH CAKES A SLIGHT TANG, BARELY DETECTABLE BUT QUITE DELICIOUS. THE FLAVOUR IS ECHOED IN THE MAYONNAISE THAT ACCOMPANIES THEM. PEPPERY ROCKET IS THE PERFECT ACCOMPANIMENT.

SERVES 4

INGREDIENTS
450g/1lb cooked salmon fillet
450g/1lb freshly cooked
  potatoes, mashed
25g/1oz/2 tbsp butter, melted
10ml/2 tsp wholegrain mustard
15ml/1 tbsp each chopped fresh dill
  and chopped fresh parsley
grated rind and juice of ½ lemon
15g/½oz/1 tbsp plain
  (all-purpose) flour
1 egg, lightly beaten
150g/5oz/1¼ cups home-made
  dried breadcrumbs
60ml/4 tbsp sunflower oil
salt and ground black pepper
rocket (arugula) leaves and chives,
  to garnish
lemon wedges, to serve

For the spicy mayonnaise
350ml/12fl oz/1½ cups mayonnaise
10ml/2 tsp wholegrain mustard
2.5–5ml/½–1 tsp Worcestershire
  sauce
dash of Tabasco sauce

COOK'S TIP
To make the dried breadcrumbs, crumb day-old white bread in a food processor, or grate it into a bowl. Spread out the crumbs on baking sheets and dry in a very low oven. Process again if you like, to produce fine crumbs.

1 Flake the cooked salmon, discarding any skin and bones. Put it in a bowl with the mashed potato, melted butter and wholegrain mustard, and mix well. Stir in the dill, parsley, lemon rind and juice. Season to taste with salt and pepper.

2 Divide the mixture into eight portions and shape each into a ball, then flatten into a thick disc. Dip the fish cakes first in flour, then in egg and finally in breadcrumbs, making sure that they are evenly coated.

3 Put the salmon fish cakes on a plate and place in the refrigerator to firm up a little. Meanwhile, make the spicy mayonnaise by mixing all the ingredients in a bowl.

4 Heat the oil in a frying pan until it is very hot. Fry the fish cakes in batches until golden brown and crisp all over. As each batch is ready, drain on kitchen paper and keep hot while you fry the rest. Garnish with rocket leaves and chives and serve with the lemon wedges and spicy mayonnaise.

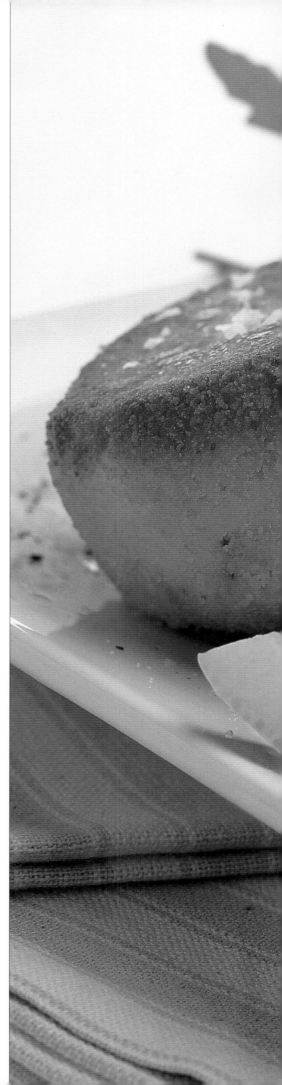

SALMON BAKED <u>WITH</u> POTATOES <u>AND</u> THYME

THIS IS VERY SIMPLE AND ABSOLUTELY DELICIOUS. PEPPER-CRUSTED SALMON FILLETS ARE BAKED ON A BED OF POTATOES AND ONIONS BRAISED IN THYME-FLAVOURED VEGETABLE OR FISH STOCK.

SERVES 4

INGREDIENTS
  675g/1½lb waxy potatoes,
    thinly sliced
  1 onion, thinly sliced
  10ml/2 tsp fresh thyme leaves
  450ml/¾ pint/scant 2 cups vegetable
    or fish stock
  40g/1½oz/3 tbsp butter, finely diced
  4 salmon fillets, each about
    150g/5oz, skinned
  30ml/2 tbsp olive oil
  15ml/1 tbsp black peppercorns,
    roughly crushed
  salt and ground black pepper
  fresh thyme, to garnish
  mangetouts (snow peas) or sugar
    snap peas, to serve

1 Preheat the oven to 190°C/375°F/ Gas 5. Layer the potato and onion slices in a shallow baking dish, such as a lasagne dish, seasoning each layer and sprinkling with thyme. Pour over the stock, dot with butter, cover with foil and place in the oven.

2 Bake the potatoes for 40 minutes then remove the foil and bake for a further 20 minutes, or until they are almost cooked.

3 Meanwhile brush the salmon fillets with olive oil and coat with crushed black peppercorns, pressing them in, if necessary, with the back of a spoon.

4 Place the salmon on top of the potatoes, cover with foil and bake for 15 minutes, or until the salmon is opaque, removing the foil for the last 5 minutes. Garnish with fresh thyme sprigs and serve with mangetouts or sugar snap peas.

SALMON AND BLACK-EYED BEAN STEW

THE ADDITION OF FRESH SALMON TO THIS STEW HELPS TO MAKE IT AN EXTREMELY NOURISHING DISH, AS WELL AS A DELICIOUS WINTER WARMER. THE CANNED BEANS ARE AN ADDED ENERGY BOOST.

SERVES 2

INGREDIENTS

   150g/5oz salmon fillet, skinned and
     any bones removed
   400g/14oz canned black-eyed beans
     (peas) in brine
   50g/2oz fresh shiitake mushrooms,
     stalks removed
   1 small carrot, peeled
   ½ mooli (daikon), peeled
   5g/⅛oz dashi-konbu (dried kelp
     seaweed), about 10cm/4in square
   60ml/4 tbsp water
   15ml/1 tbsp shoyu (Japanese
     soy sauce)
   7.5ml/1½ tsp mirin or dry sherry
   sea salt
   2.5cm/1in fresh root ginger, peeled,
     to garnish

1 Slice the salmon into 1cm/½in-thick strips. Place in a colander, sprinkle with sea salt and leave for 1 hour.

2 Wash away the salt and cut the salmon strips into 1cm/½in cubes. Par-boil in a pan of rapidly boiling water for 30 seconds, then drain. Gently rinse under cold running water to prevent the cubes from cooking further.

3 Slice the ginger for the garnish thinly lengthways, then stack the slices and cut them into thin threads. Soak in cold water for about 30 minutes, then drain well.

4 Drain the can of black-eyed beans into a medium pan. Reserve the beans.

5 Chop all the fresh vegetables into 1cm/½in cubes. Wipe the dashi-konbu with kitchen paper, then snip with scissors. Cut everything as close to the same size as possible.

6 Put the par-boiled salmon, dashi-konbu and vegetables into the pan containing the liquid from the can of beans. Pour the beans on top and add the 60ml/4 tbsp water and 1.5ml/¼ tsp salt. Bring to the boil. Reduce the heat to low and cook for 6 minutes or until the carrot is cooked.

7 Add the shoyu and cook for a further 4 minutes. Add the mirin or sherry and remove the pan from the heat. Mix well. Leave to rest for 1 hour. Serve warm or cold, with the ginger threads.

Salmon <u>with</u> Leeks <u>and</u> Peppers

Cooking salmon in paper parcels is a healthy option. The fish and vegetables cook in their own juices, so both retain all their valuable nutrients.

SERVES 6

INGREDIENTS
25ml/1½ tbsp groundnut (peanut) oil
2 yellow (bell) peppers, seeded and
  thinly sliced
4cm/1½in fresh root ginger, peeled
  and finely shredded
1 large fennel bulb, thinly sliced,
  fronds chopped and reserved
1 fresh green chilli, seeded and
  finely shredded
2 large leeks, cut into 10cm/4in
  lengths and shredded lengthways
30ml/2 tbsp chopped fresh chives
10ml/2 tsp light soy sauce
6 portions salmon fillet, each
  weighing about 150–175g/
  5–6oz, skinned
10ml/2 tsp toasted sesame oil
salt and ground black pepper

1 Heat the oil in a large frying pan. Add the yellow peppers, ginger and fennel bulb and cook, stirring occasionally, for 5–6 minutes, until they are softened, but not browned.

2 Add the chilli and leeks to the pan and cook, stirring occasionally, for about 3 minutes. Stir in half the chopped chives and the soy sauce and season to taste with a little salt and pepper. Set the vegetable mixture aside to cool slightly.

3 Preheat the oven to 190°C/375°F/ Gas 5. Cut six 35cm/14in rounds of baking parchment or foil and set aside.

4 When the vegetable mixture is cool, divide it equally among the paper or foil rounds and top each with a piece of salmon fillet.

5 Drizzle each portion of fish with a little sesame oil and sprinkle with the remaining chives and the chopped fennel fronds. Season with a little more salt and ground black pepper.

6 Fold the baking parchment or foil over to enclose the fish, rolling and twisting the edges together to seal the parcels.

7 Place the parcels on a baking sheet and bake for 15–20 minutes, or until the parcels have puffed up. Carefully transfer the parcels to six warmed plates and serve immediately, to be opened at the table.

CHINESE-STYLE STEAMED TROUT

IF YOU THINK STEAMED TROUT SOUNDS DULL, THINK AGAIN. THIS FISH, MARINATED IN A BLACK BEAN, GINGER AND GARLIC MIXTURE BEFORE BEING MOISTENED WITH RICE WINE AND SOY SAUCE, IS SUPERB.

3 Place a little ginger and garlic inside the cavity of each fish, then lay them on a plate or dish that will fit inside a large steamer. Rub the bean mixture into the fish, working it into the slashes, then sprinkle the remaining ginger and garlic over the top. Cover with clear film (plastic wrap) and place the fish in the refrigerator for at least 30 minutes.

4 Remove the fish from the refrigerator and place the steamer over a pan of boiling water. Sprinkle the rice wine or sherry and half the soy sauce over the fish and place the plate of fish inside the steamer. Steam for 15–20 minutes, or until the fish is cooked and the flesh flakes easily when tested with a fork.

SERVES 6

INGREDIENTS
   2 trout, each about 675–800g/
      1½–1¾lb
   25ml/1½ tbsp salted black beans
   2.5ml/½ tsp granulated sugar
   30ml/2 tbsp finely shredded fresh
      root ginger
   4 garlic cloves, thinly sliced
   30ml/2 tbsp Chinese rice wine or
      dry sherry
   30ml/2 tbsp light soy sauce
   4–6 spring onions (scallions), finely
      shredded or sliced diagonally
   45ml/3 tbsp groundnut (peanut) oil
   10ml/2 tsp sesame oil

1 Wash the fish inside and out under cold running water, then pat dry on kitchen paper. Using a sharp knife, slash 3–4 deep crosses on either side of each fish.

2 Place half the black beans and the sugar in a small bowl and mash together with the back of a fork. When the beans are thoroughly mashed, stir in the remaining whole beans.

5 Using a fish slice (metal spatula), carefully lift the fish on to a warmed serving dish. Sprinkle the fish with the remaining soy sauce, then sprinkle with the shredded or sliced spring onions.

6 In a small pan, heat the groundnut oil until very hot and smoking, then trickle it over the spring onions and fish. Lightly sprinkle the sesame oil over the fish and serve immediately.

PAN-FRIED SALMON WITH MUSHROOM SAUCE

Tarragon has a distinctive aniseed flavour that is great with salmon. Here it is used, not with the fish, but in the exquisite wild and fresh mushroom sauce that accompanies it.

SERVES 4

INGREDIENTS

   50g/2oz/¼ cup butter
   salt and cayenne pepper
   4 salmon steaks, each 175g/6oz
   1 shallot, finely chopped
   175g/6oz/about 2½ cups assorted
     wild and cultivated mushrooms,
     trimmed and sliced
   200ml/7fl oz/scant 1 cup chicken
     or vegetable stock
   10ml/2 tsp cornflour (cornstarch)
   2.5ml/½ tsp mustard powder
   15ml/1 tbsp water
   50ml/3½ tbsp sour cream
   45ml/3 tbsp chopped fresh tarragon
   5ml/1 tsp white wine vinegar

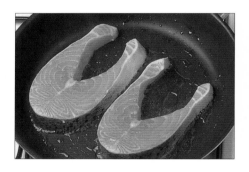

1 Melt half the butter in a large frying pan. Season the salmon, add the steaks to the pan and cook, in batches if necessary, over a medium heat for 8 minutes, turning once. Transfer to a plate, cover and keep warm.

2 Heat the remaining butter in the pan and gently fry the shallot until softened but not coloured. Add the mushrooms and cook until the juices begin to flow.

3 Add the stock and simmer for 2–3 minutes. Put the cornflour and mustard powder in a cup and mix to a paste with the water. Stir into the mushroom mixture and bring to a simmer, stirring until the sauce thickens. Stir in the sour cream, tarragon and vinegar. Season the sauce with salt and cayenne pepper.

4 Spoon the mushroom sauce over each salmon steak and serve with new potatoes and a green salad.

COOK'S TIP
Fresh tarragon will bruise and darken quickly after chopping, so prepare the herb only when you are ready to use it.

TROUT WITH SPINACH AND MUSHROOM SAUCE

SKINNED TROUT FILLETS ARE THE LAZY COOK'S IDEAL INGREDIENT. THEY COOK QUICKLY AND TASTE DELICIOUS, ESPECIALLY WHEN SERVED WITH A RICH SPINACH AND MUSHROOM SAUCE.

SERVES 4

INGREDIENTS

75g/3oz/6 tbsp unsalted
  (sweet) butter
¼ medium onion, chopped
225g/8oz/3 cups field
  (portabello) mushrooms,
  chopped
300ml/½ pint/1¼ cups boiling
  chicken stock
225g/8oz frozen chopped spinach
10ml/2 tsp cornflour (cornstarch)
15ml/1 tbsp water
150ml/¼ pint/⅔ cup crème fraîche
  or sour cream
8 trout fillets, skinned
a pinch of freshly grated nutmeg
salt and ground black pepper
new potatoes, baby carrots and
  baby corn cobs, to serve

3 Mix the cornflour to a paste with the water. Stir into the mushroom mixture. Simmer gently, stirring often, until the sauce thickens.

4 Scrape the sauce into a blender or food processor and process until smooth. Add the crème fraîche or sour cream, nutmeg, salt and pepper. Pour into a serving sauceboat and keep warm.

5 Melt the remaining butter in a large frying pan. Season the trout fillets with salt and ground black pepper and cook for 6 minutes, turning once, until just cooked through. Serve with new potatoes, baby carrots and baby corn cobs. The sauce can be poured over the trout fillets or served separately.

1 To make the sauce, melt 50g/2oz/¼ cup of the butter in a frying pan or wok and fry the onion until soft. Add the mushrooms and cook until the juices begin to run, stirring occasionally with a wooden spoon.

2 Pour the hot stock into the pan, then stir in the frozen spinach and cook, stirring from time to time, until the spinach has thawed completely.

COOK'S TIP
A hand-held electric blender is ideal for processing the spinach and mushroom sauce. If you process the sauce in the pan, you can leave it there to keep warm until you are ready to serve it.

COCONUT SALMON

SALMON IS QUITE A ROBUST FISH, AND RESPONDS WELL TO BEING COOKED WITH STRONG FLAVOURS, AS IN THIS FRAGRANT BLEND OF SPICES, GARLIC AND CHILLI. COCONUT MILK ADDS A MELLOW TOUCH.

SERVES 4

INGREDIENTS

    4 salmon steaks, each about
      175g/6oz
    10ml/2 tsp ground cumin
    10ml/2 tsp chilli powder
    2.5ml/½ tsp ground turmeric
    30ml/2 tbsp white wine vinegar
    1.5ml/¼ tsp salt
    45ml/3 tbsp oil
    1 onion, chopped
    2 fresh green chillies, seeded
      and chopped
    2 garlic cloves, crushed
    2.5cm/1in piece fresh root
      ginger, grated
    5ml/1 tsp ground coriander
    175ml/6fl oz/¾ cup coconut milk
    fresh coriander (cilantro) sprigs,
      to garnish
    rice with spring onions (scallions),
      to serve

1 Arrange the salmon steaks in a single layer in a shallow glass dish. Put 5ml/ 1 tsp of the ground cumin in a bowl and add the chilli powder, turmeric, vinegar and salt. Rub the paste over the salmon steaks and leave to marinate for about 15 minutes.

2 Heat the oil in a large deep frying pan and fry the onion, chillies, garlic and ginger for 5–6 minutes. Put into a food processor or blender and process to a smooth paste.

3 Return the onion paste to the pan. Add the remaining cumin, the coriander and coconut milk. Bring to the boil, reduce the heat and simmer the sauce for 5 minutes, stirring occasionally.

4 Add the salmon steaks. Cover and cook for 15 minutes, until the fish is tender. Transfer to a serving dish and garnish with the fresh coriander. Serve with the rice and spring onions.

TROUT WITH TAMARIND AND CHILLI SAUCE

TROUT IS A VERY ECONOMICAL FISH, BUT CAN TASTE A BIT BLAND. THIS SPICY THAI-INSPIRED SAUCE REALLY GIVES IT A ZING. IF YOU LIKE YOUR FOOD VERY SPICY, ADD AN EXTRA CHILLI.

SERVES 4

INGREDIENTS

4 trout, about 350g/12oz each, cleaned
6 spring onions (scallions), sliced
60ml/4 tbsp soy sauce
15ml/1 tbsp groundnut (peanut) oil
30ml/2 tbsp chopped fresh coriander (cilantro)

For the sauce

50g/2oz tamarind pulp
105ml/7 tbsp boiling water
2 shallots, roughly chopped
1 fresh red chilli, seeded and chopped
1cm/½in piece fresh root ginger, peeled and chopped
5ml/1 tsp soft brown sugar
45ml/3 tbsp Thai fish sauce

1 Slash each trout diagonally four or five times on either side with a sharp knife. Place in one or two shallow dishes.

2 Fill the cavities with spring onions. Douse each fish on both sides with soy sauce, turning the fish over carefully. Sprinkle on any remaining spring onions and set aside until required.

3 Make the sauce. Put the tamarind pulp in a small bowl and pour on the boiling water. Mash with a fork until soft. Tip into a food processor or blender and add the shallots, fresh chilli, ginger, sugar and fish sauce. Whizz to a coarse pulp.

4 Heat the oil in a large frying pan or wok and fry the trout, one at a time if necessary, for about 5 minutes on each side, until the skin is crisp and browned and the flesh cooked. Put on warmed plates and spoon over some sauce. Sprinkle with the coriander and serve.

CLASSIC FISH PIE

ORIGINALLY A FISH PIE WAS BASED ON THE "CATCH OF THE DAY". SALMON WAS SELDOM INCLUDED, AS IT WAS TOO EXPENSIVE. NOW THAT GOOD QUALITY FARMED SALMON IS AVAILABLE — AND AFFORDABLE — IT MAKES AN EXCELLENT ADDITION TO THE OTHER FISH USED.

SERVES 4

INGREDIENTS
    butter, for greasing
    450g/1lb mixed fish, including
      salmon fillets
    finely grated rind of 1 lemon
    450g/1lb floury potatoes, peeled
    25g/1oz/2 tbsp butter
    salt and ground black pepper
    1 egg, beaten

For the sauce
    15g/½oz/1 tbsp butter
    15ml/1 tbsp plain (all-purpose) flour
    150ml/¼ pint/⅔ cup milk
    45ml/3 tbsp chopped fresh parsley

1 Preheat the oven to 220ºC/425ºF/ Gas 7. Grease a baking dish and set aside. Cut the fish into bitesize pieces. Season the fish, sprinkle over the lemon rind and place in the base of the prepared dish.

2 Put the potatoes in a pan. Add cold water to cover and bring to the boil. Cook for 25–30 minutes until tender.

3 Meanwhile, make the sauce. Melt the butter in a pan, add the flour and cook, stirring, for 2–3 minutes. Gradually add the milk, whisking constantly until the mixture boils and thickens to make a smooth white sauce.

4 Stir in the parsley and season to taste. Pour over the fish and mix gently.

5 Drain the potatoes well, return to the pan and mash with the butter.

6 Pipe or spoon the mashed potato on top of the fish mixture. Brush with the beaten egg. Bake for 45 minutes until the potato topping is golden brown. Serve hot.

COOK'S TIP
If using frozen fish thaw it very well and drain it thoroughly, as excess water will ruin the pie.

PAN-FRIED CITRUS TROUT <u>WITH</u> BASIL

THE CLEAN TASTE OF ORANGES AND LEMONS AND THE AROMATIC SCENT OF BASIL COMBINE BEAUTIFULLY IN THIS RECIPE TO CREATE A LIGHT AND TANGY SAUCE FOR TROUT FILLETS.

SERVES 4

INGREDIENTS
4 trout fillets, each about 200g/7oz
2 lemons
3 oranges
105ml/7 tbsp olive oil
45ml/3 tbsp plain (all-purpose) flour
25g/1oz/2 tbsp butter
5ml/1 tsp soft light brown sugar
15g/½ oz/½ cup fresh basil leaves
salt and ground black pepper

1 Arrange the trout fillets in the base of a non-metallic shallow dish. Grate the rind from one lemon and two of the oranges, then squeeze these fruits and pour the combined juices into a jug (pitcher). Slice the remaining fruits and reserve to use as a garnish.

2 Add 75ml/5 tbsp of the oil to the citrus juices. Beat with a fork and pour over the fish. Cover and leave to marinate in the refrigerator for at least 2 hours.

3 Preheat the oven to 150°C/300°F/ Gas 2. Using a fish slice or metal spatula, carefully remove the trout from the marinade. Season the fish and coat each in flour.

4 Heat the remaining oil in a frying pan and add the fish. Fry for 2–3 minutes on each side until cooked, then transfer to a plate and keep hot in the oven.

5 Add the butter and the marinade to the pan and heat gently, stirring until the butter has melted. Season with salt and pepper, then stir in the sugar. Continue cooking gently for 4–5 minutes until the sauce has thickened slightly.

6 Finely shred half the basil leaves and add them to the pan. Pour the sauce over the fish and garnish with the remaining basil and the orange and lemon slices.

COOK'S TIP
Basil leaves bruise easily, so they should always be shredded by hand or used whole rather than cut with a knife.

TROUT WITH CUCUMBER CREAM

*CREAM SAUCES SUIT THE DELICATE FLAVOUR OF TROUT VERY WELL.
THIS ONE INTRODUCES TWO MORE COMPLEMENTARY ELEMENTS,
CUCUMBER AND TARRAGON.*

SERVES 4

INGREDIENTS

    25g/1oz/2 tbsp butter
    8 fresh trout fillets, skinned
    2 large spring onions (scallions),
      white parts only, chopped
    ½ cucumber, peeled, seeded and
      cut into short batons
    5ml/1 tsp cornflour (cornstarch)
    150ml/¼ pint/⅔ cup single
      (light) cream
    50ml/2fl oz/¼ cup dry sherry
    30ml/2 tbsp chopped fresh tarragon
    1 tomato, halved, seeded and
      chopped
    salt and ground black pepper
    new potatoes and green beans,
      to serve

3 Put the cornflour (cornstarch) in a cup and stir in about 30ml/2 tbsp of the cream to make a thin paste.

4 Add the remaining cream to the pan. Stir in the cornflour mixture and the sherry. Heat, stirring constantly, until the mixture thickens.

1 Melt the butter in a large frying pan. Season the trout fillets and cook for 6 minutes, turning once. Transfer to a warm plate, cover and keep hot.

5 Stir in the chopped tarragon. Add the chopped tomato with a little salt and pepper, to taste. Stir until the sauce is thoroughly combined.

2 Add the spring onions and cucumber to the butter remaining in the pan. Cook over a gentle heat, stirring, until soft but not coloured.

6 Place the trout fillets on warmed serving plates. Spoon the sauce over and serve the fish with boiled new potatoes and green beans.

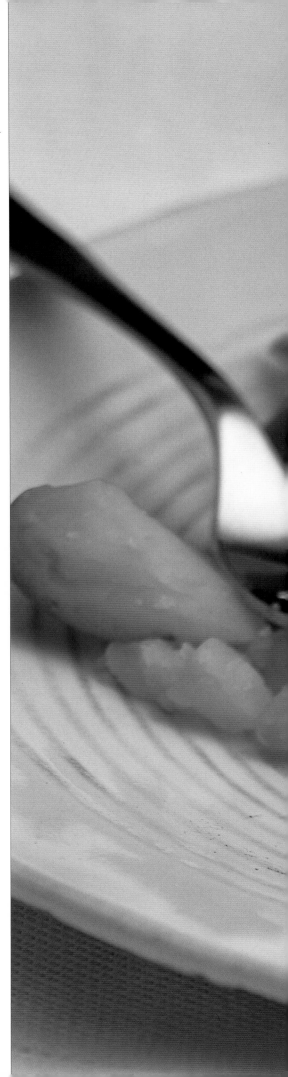

SALMON WITH GREEN PEPPERCORNS

Salmon benefits from being served with a piquant accompaniment. Lemon and lime are the obvious choices, but capers and green peppercorns also serve to counter the rich taste.

SERVES 4

INGREDIENTS

15g/½oz/1 tbsp butter
2–3 shallots, finely chopped
15ml/1 tbsp brandy (optional)
60ml/4 tbsp white wine
90ml/6 tbsp fish or chicken stock
120ml/4fl oz/½ cup whipping cream
30–45ml/2–3 tbsp green peppercorns
  in brine, rinsed
15–30ml/1–2 tbsp vegetable oil
4 pieces salmon fillet, each about
  175g/6oz
salt and ground black pepper
fresh parsley, to garnish

1 Melt the butter in a heavy pan over a medium heat. Add the shallots and cook for 1–2 minutes, until just softened but not coloured.

2 Add the brandy, if using, then pour in the white wine and stock. Bring to the boil. Boil vigorously to reduce by three-quarters, stirring occasionally.

3 Reduce the heat, then add the cream and half the peppercorns, crushing them slightly against the sides of the pan with the back of a spoon. Cook very gently for 4–5 minutes, until the sauce has thickened slightly,

4 Strain the sauce into a clean pan and stir in the remaining peppercorns. Keep the sauce warm over a very low heat, stirring occasionally, while you cook the salmon fillets.

5 Heat the oil in a large, heavy frying pan over a medium-high heat. Lightly season the salmon. When the oil is very hot, add the salmon. Sear the fillets on both sides, then lower the heat and cook for 4–6 minutes, until the flesh is opaque throughout. Arrange the fish on warmed plates and pour over the sauce. Garnish with parsley and serve.

COOK'S TIP
Green peppercorns are available pickled in jars or cans. Keep them on hand for adding to all kinds of sauces and stews. Rinse the peppercorns before use.

TROUT WITH ALMONDS

SOME PEOPLE REGARD THIS DISH AS A CLICHÉ, BUT IF THAT'S TRUE, IT'S A CLICHÉ THAT HAS ENDURED FOR A LONG TIME. THE REASON IS SIMPLE: THIS COMBINATION WORKS EXTREMELY WELL.

SERVES 2

INGREDIENTS
- 2 trout, each about 350g/12oz, cleaned
- 40g/1½oz/⅓ cup plain (all-purpose) flour
- 50g/2oz/¼ cup butter
- 25g/1oz/¼ cup flaked (sliced) almonds
- 30ml/2 tbsp dry white wine
- salt and ground black pepper
- new potatoes and mixed green salad, to serve

3 Add the remaining butter to the pan and cook the almonds, shaking the pan frequently, until just lightly browned.

4 Add the white wine to the pan and boil for 1 minute, stirring constantly, until the sauce is slightly syrupy. Pour or spoon the sauce and almonds over each fish and serve immediately with boiled new potatoes and a green salad.

VARIATION
Other nuts can be used instead of almonds. Hazelnuts are particularly good with trout. The nuts swiftly brown and go crisp, so watch them closely to prevent them burning.

1 Rinse the trout and pat dry. Put the flour in a large plastic bag and season with salt and pepper. Place the trout, one at a time, in the bag and shake to coat with flour. Shake off the excess flour from the fish and discard the remaining flour.

2 Melt half the butter in a large frying pan over a medium heat. When it is foamy, add the trout and cook for 6–7 minutes on each side, until the skin is golden brown and the flesh next to the bone is opaque. Transfer the fish to warmed plates and cover to keep warm.

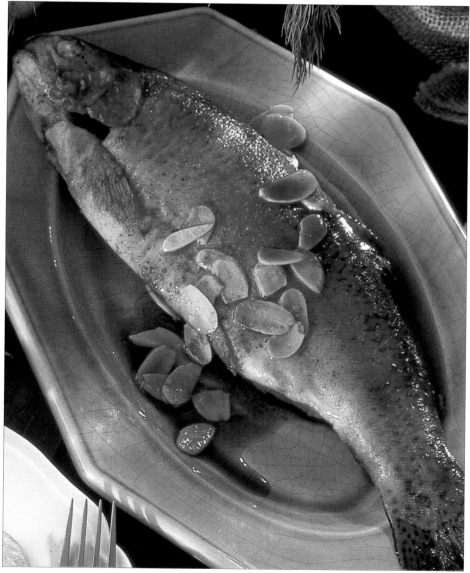

SALMON QUICHE <u>WITH</u> POTATO PASTRY

THERE ARE SO MANY WONDERFUL WAYS OF USING SMOKED SALMON. HERE IT FORMS THE FILLING FOR A LIGHT BUT RICHLY-FLAVOURED QUICHE MADE WITH MELT-IN-THE-MOUTH POTATO PASTRY.

SERVES 6

INGREDIENTS
115g/4oz floury potatoes, diced
225g/8oz/2 cups plain (all-purpose)
    flour, sifted
115g/4oz/½ cup butter, diced
½ egg, beaten
10ml/2 tsp chilled water
salad leaves and chopped fresh dill,
    to serve

For the filling
6 eggs, beaten
150ml/¼ pint/⅔ cup full cream
    (whole) milk
300ml/½ pint/1¼ cups double
    (heavy) cream
30–45ml/2–3 tbsp chopped fresh dill
30ml/2 tbsp drained bottled
    capers, chopped
275g/10oz smoked salmon
salt and ground black pepper

VARIATIONS
These quantities can also be used to make six individual quiches, which are an ideal size to serve as a first course or a light lunch. Prepare them as above, but reduce the cooking time by about 15 minutes. For extra piquancy, sprinkle some finely grated fresh Parmesan cheese over the top of each quiche before baking in the oven.

COOK'S TIP
To ensure the pastry base or the quiche cooks through it is vital to preheat the baking sheet in the oven first.

1 Cook the potatoes in a large pan of lightly salted boiling water for 15 minutes or until tender. Drain well through a colander and return to the pan. Mash the potatoes until smooth and set aside to cool completely.

2 Place the flour in a bowl and rub or cut in the butter to form fine crumbs. Beat in the potatoes and egg. Bring the mixture together, adding chilled water if needed.

3 Roll the pastry out on a floured surface to a 28cm/11in round. Lop the pastry over the rolling pin and ease it into a deep, 23cm/9in round, loose-based, fluted quiche pan. Trim the edges. Chill for 1 hour.

4 Preheat the oven to 200°C/400°F/ Gas 6. Place a baking sheet in the oven to heat it. Using a sharp cook's knife or a pair of kitchen scissors, chop the salmon into bitesize pieces. Place the salmon on a plate and set it aside.

5 Make the filling. In a bowl, beat the eggs with the milk and cream. Stir in the dill and capers and season with pepper. Add in the salmon and stir to combine.

6 Remove the pastry case (pie shell) from the refrigerator, prick the base well and pour the mixture into it. Bake on a baking sheet for 35–45 minutes. Serve warm with mixed salad leaves and some more dill.

SALMON AND PRAWN FLAN

THIS FLAN IS UNUSUAL BECAUSE IT IS MADE WITH RAW SALMON, WHICH MEANS THAT THE FISH STAYS MOIST. COOKING IT THIS WAY GIVES A LOVELY SUCCULENT RESULT. THIS VERSATILE DISH MAY BE SERVED HOT WITH VEGETABLES OR COOLED WITH MIXED SALAD LEAVES AND TOMATO WEDGES.

SERVES 6

INGREDIENTS

    350g/12oz shortcrust pastry,
      thawed if frozen
    225g/8oz salmon fillet, skinned
    225g/8oz cooked peeled prawns
      (shrimp)
    2 eggs, plus 2 egg yolks
    150ml/¼ pint/⅔ cup whipping
      cream
    200ml/7fl oz/scant 1 cup milk
    15ml/1 tbsp chopped fresh dill
    salt, ground black pepper and
      paprika
    lime slices, tomato wedges and
      sprigs of dill, to garnish

VARIATION

For a more economical version of this flan, omit the prawns (shrimp) and use some extra salmon fillet instead, or use a mixture of salmon and trout fillet, or salmon and white fish.

1 Roll out the pastry on a floured work surface and use it to line a 20cm/8in flan dish or tin. Prick the base all over and mark the edges with the tines of the fork. It need not be too neat. Chill in the refrigerator for about 30 minutes.

2 Meanwhile, preheat the oven to 180°C/350°F/Gas 4. Bake the pastry case for about 30 minutes, until golden brown. Reduce the oven temperature to 160°C/325°F/Gas 3.

3 Cut the salmon fillet into 2cm/¾in cubes. Arrange the salmon and prawns evenly in the pastry case. Dust lightly with paprika.

4 In a bowl, beat together the eggs and yolks, cream, milk and dill and season to tasten with salt and ground black pepper. Pour over the salmon and prawns. Bake for about 30 minutes, until the filling is just set. Serve hot or at room temperature, garnished with lime slices, tomato wedges and dill.

BAKED SALMON, CZECH-STYLE

THIS CENTRAL EUROPEAN WAY OF COOKING SALMON IS VERY EASY, AND THE RESULTS ARE EXCELLENT. THE FISH COOKS IN ITS OWN JUICES, WITH CARAWAY SEEDS ADDING THEIR OWN INIMITABLE FLAVOUR.

SERVES 6

INGREDIENTS

1.8kg/4lb whole salmon, cleaned
115g/4oz/½ cup butter, melted
2.5–5ml/½–1 tsp caraway seeds
45ml/3 tbsp lemon juice
salt and ground black pepper
sprigs of flat leaf parsley and lemon
   wedges, to garnish

COOK'S TIP
Take care when slicing off the fins from the salmon as they can be sharp enough to cut fingers.

1 Preheat the oven to 180°C/350°F/ Gas 4. Scale the salmon, remove the head and tail and slice off the fins with a sharp filleting knife, then cut the fish in half lengthways.

2 Place the salmon, skin side down, in a lightly greased roasting pan. Brush with the melted butter. Season generously with salt and ground black pepper, sprinkle over the caraway seeds and drizzle with lemon juice.

3 Cover the salmon loosely with foil and bake for 25 minutes. Remove it from the oven, lift off the foil and test the fish. It is done if it is opaque and flakes easily when tested with the point of a knife. Bake for a little longer if needed.

4 Remove the foil and carefully lift the fish on to a serving plate, using two fish slices or large spatulas. Garnish with flat leaf parsley and lemon wedges. The baked salmon can be served straight away, but also tastes good cold.

GRILLED BUTTERFLIED SALMON

Ask your fishmonger to bone the salmon for butterflying. If you order the fish in advance, and give the supplier plenty of time, most will be happy to oblige.

SERVES 6–8

INGREDIENTS
  25ml/1½ tbsp dried juniper berries
  10ml/2 tsp dried green peppercorns
  5ml/1 tsp caster (superfine) sugar
  45ml/3 tbsp vegetable oil, plus extra
    for greasing
  30ml/2 tbsp lemon juice
  2.25kg/5–5¼lb salmon, scaled,
    cleaned and boned for butterflying
  salt
  lemon wedges and fresh parsley
    sprigs, to garnish

1 Coarsely grind the juniper berries and peppercorns in a spice mill or in a mortar with a pestle. Put the ground spices in a small bowl and stir in the caster sugar, vegetable oil, lemon juice and salt to taste.

COOK'S TIP
It is worth keeping a jar of juniper berries in the spice rack, not merely so you can try this recipe, but also for using with game, or to give chicken or rabbit a gamey flavour. Juniper berries are also delicious with red cabbage.

2 Open the salmon like a book, skin side down. Spread the juniper mixture evenly over the flesh. Fold the salmon closed again and place it on a large plate. Cover and marinate in the refrigerator for at least 1 hour.

3 Preheat the grill (broiler). Open up the salmon again and place it, skin side down, on a large oiled baking sheet. Spoon any juniper mixture left on the plate over the fish.

4 Grill (broil) the salmon, keeping it about 10cm/4in from the heat, for 8–10 minutes or until the salmon is cooked and the flesh is opaque. Serve immediately, garnished with the lemon wedges and parsley.

WHOLE BAKED SALMON

FARMED SALMON HAS MADE THIS FISH MORE AFFORDABLE AND LESS OF A LUXURY BUT A WHOLE SALMON STILL FEATURES AS A CENTREPIECE AT PARTIES. TRADITIONALLY IT IS ACCOMPANIED BY VARIOUS SALADS AND A BOWL OF MAYONNAISE.

SERVES 10 AS PART OF A BUFFET

INGREDIENTS
2.25–2.75kg/5–6lb fresh whole
  salmon, cleaned and scaled
30ml/2 tbsp oil
1 lemon
salt and ground black pepper
lemon wedges, pared cucumber
  ribbons and fresh dill sprigs,
  to garnish

1 Preheat the oven to 150°C/300°F/ Gas 2. Note the weight of the salmon then wash it and dry it well, inside and out. Pour half the oil on to a large piece of strong foil and place the fish in the centre.

2 Put a few slices of lemon inside the salmon and arrange some more on the top. Season well and sprinkle over the remaining oil. Wrap up the foil to make a loose parcel.

COOK'S TIPS
• Use wild salmon if you can afford it, or buy from a farm where the salmon are humanely treated.
• Use extra wide, extra long foil – sometimes described as turkey foil – to wrap the salmon.
• To make the cucumber ribbons, square off but do not peel a cucumber, then draw a potato peeler down its length.

3 Put the parcel on another sheet of foil or a baking sheet and transfer to the oven. Bake for 8 minutes per 450g/1lb. Check the fish towards the end of cooking and remove from the oven when the flesh is opaque right through. Leave to cool in the foil for 15 minutes.

4 Remove the foil, draining any juices into a jug (pitcher). Use in any recipe requiring fish stock. Peel off the salmon skin. When it is cold, slide the salmon on to a large platter and garnish with lemon wedges, cucumber pared into thin ribbons and sprigs of dill.

HERBY SALMON PARCELS

COOKING SALMON, OR ANY FISH, IN A PARCEL HELPS TO KEEP IT MOIST AND SEALS IN ALL THE WONDERFUL FLAVOURS. ADDING LIME AND BASIL TO THE PAPER-WRAPPED SALMON GIVES THE FISH A FRESH, TANGY TASTE.

SERVES 4

INGREDIENTS
    1 lime
    50g/2oz/¼ cup butter, softened
    30ml/2 tbsp finely chopped
        fresh basil
    4 plum tomatoes, sliced
    2 garlic cloves, sliced
    4 salmon fillets, each about
        200g/7oz
    15ml/1 tbsp olive oil

1 Grate the rind from the lime and put it in a small bowl. Cut the lime into eight slices and set aside. Add the butter and basil to the lime rind and mix well. Roll the mixture into a cylinder shape, wrap in greaseproof (waxed) paper or baking parchment and chill in the refrigerator.

2 Preheat the oven to 190°C/375°F/ Gas 5. Cut out sheets of greaseproof paper or baking parchment, each large enough to enclose a salmon fillet easily.

COOK'S TIP
The flavour of the tomatoes is central to the success of this dish. If you can obtain home-grown Italian plum tomatoes, such as San Morzano, so much the better. Alternatively, plump for sweet and juicy cherry tomatoes.

3 Arrange one sliced tomato on each piece of paper or parchment. Sprinkle each with one-quarter of the garlic and season with plenty of salt and pepper.

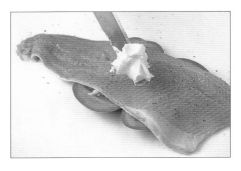

4 Place the salmon fillets on the tomatoes. Cut the chilled, flavoured butter into four equal pieces and place one on each salmon. Top with the reserved lime slices and drizzle the salmon evenly with the olive oil.

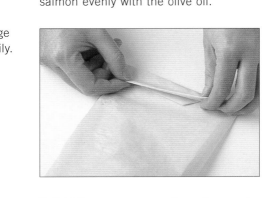

5 Fold the paper or parchment around the topped salmon to make neat parcels. Place on a baking sheet and bake for 20 minutes or until the fish is cooked through.

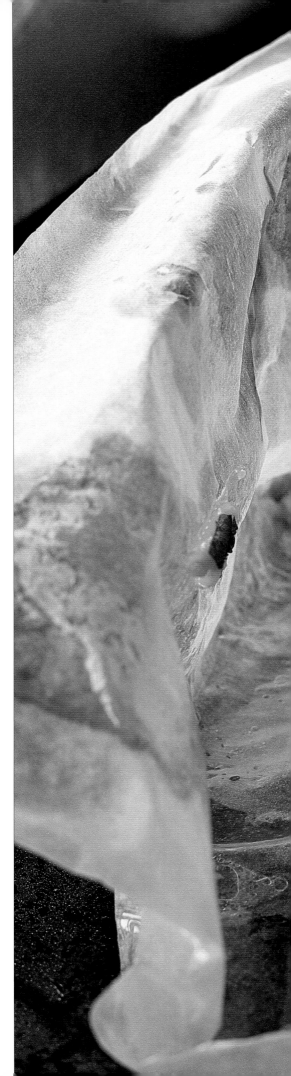

THAI-STYLE TROUT

THE COMBINATION OF CLASSIC THAI AROMATIC INGREDIENTS — GINGER, LEMON GRASS, COCONUT MILK AND LIME — GIVES THIS SIMPLE DISH A FABULOUS FLAVOUR. SERVE WITH PLENTY OF STEAMED THAI FRAGRANT RICE TO SOAK UP THE DELICIOUS SAUCE.

SERVES 4

INGREDIENTS
  200g/7oz spinach leaves
  1 lemon grass stalk, finely chopped
  2.5cm/1in piece fresh root ginger,
    peeled and finely grated
  2 garlic cloves, crushed
  200ml/7fl oz/scant 1 cup coconut milk
  30ml/2 tbsp freshly squeezed
    lime juice
  15ml/1 tbsp soft light brown sugar
  4 trout fillets, each about 200g/7oz
  salt and ground black pepper
  steamed Thai fragrant rice, to serve

COOK'S TIP
To steam Thai fragrant rice, cook it in a pan of salted boiling water for three-quarters of the time noted on the packet. Transfer it to a colander lined with muslin or cheesecloth and steam over simmering water for 5–10 minutes until just tender.

1 Preheat the oven to 200°C/400°F/ Gas 6. Place the spinach in a pan, with just the water that adheres to the leaves after washing. Cover with a lid and cook gently for 3–4 minutes until the leaves have just wilted. Drain the spinach in a colander and press it with the back of a spoon to remove any excess moisture.

2 Transfer the spinach to a mixing bowl and stir in the chopped lemon grass, grated ginger and garlic.

3 Combine the coconut milk, lime juice, sugar and seasoning in a jug (pitcher). Place the trout fillets side by side in a shallow baking dish and pour the coconut milk mixture over.

4 Bake the trout for 20–25 minutes until cooked. Place on individual serving plates, on top of the steamed Thai fragrant rice. Toss the spinach mixture in the juices remaining in the dish, spoon on top of the fish and serve.

TROUT WITH CRUNCHY PEPPERCORNS

BLACK, GREEN AND PINK PEPPERCORNS ADD COLOUR AND TEXTURE TO THIS DISH, AND PROVIDE AN EXPLOSION OF TASTE IN THE MOUTH WHEN CRUNCHED. SERVE THE TROUT FILLETS WITH CREAMY MASHED POTATOES SWIRLED WITH PESTO.

SERVES 4

INGREDIENTS
   60ml/4 tbsp mixed peppercorns
   4 trout fillets, each about 200g/7oz,
   skinned
   60ml/4 tbsp olive oil
   juice of 1 lemon
   fresh basil sprigs, to garnish
   mashed potato with pesto, to serve

COOK'S TIP
Stir a large spoonful of pesto into the mashed potato just before serving, leaving green swirls in the creamy potato.

1 Place the mixed peppercorns in a mortar and crush them lightly with a pestle. Continue until about half the peppercorns are broken.

2 Press one-quarter of the peppercorns on to one side of each trout fillet, using the back of a spoon.

3 Heat the oil in a griddle pan. Place the fish in the pan, coated side up, and fry for 2–3 minutes, using a spatula to press the peppercorns further into the fish as it cooks.

4 Using the spatula, turn the trout fillets over and cook for 2–3 minutes more, until cooked right through. Turn the fillets over again in the pan and sprinkle with the lemon juice.

5 Place each fish on a bed of pesto mash on an individual plate and garnish with the basil sprigs.

STUFFED TROUT WITH TARRAGON SAUCE

TARRAGON AND TROUT MAKE A MARVELLOUS TEAM. HERE WHOLE TROUT ARE FILLED WITH A HERBY STUFFING BEFORE BEING BAKED IN WINE AND SERVED WITH A CREAMY TARRAGON SAUCE. REMOVING THE SKIN BEFORE SERVING REVEALS THE ATTRACTIVE PALE PINK TROUT FLESH.

SERVES 4

INGREDIENTS
90ml/6 tbsp fresh white
  breadcrumbs
30ml/2 tbsp chopped fresh
  tarragon
1 egg, beaten
4 whole trout, each about
  200g/7oz, cleaned and boned
  for stuffing
1 small onion, sliced
150ml/¼ pint/⅔ cup dry
  white wine
8 fresh tarragon sprigs
25g/1oz/2 tbsp butter
15ml/1 tbsp plain (all-purpose) flour
150ml/¼ pint/⅔ cup single
  (light) cream
salt and ground black pepper
new potatoes and a selection of
  steamed green vegetables, to serve

COOK'S TIPS
• For a low-fat version that still tastes delicious, use skimmed milk instead of cream in this recipe and serve with plain boiled potatoes.
• Fresh tarragon leaves can be infused (steeped) in boiling water for about 10 minutes to make a refreshing tisane.

1 Preheat the oven to 190°C/375°F/ Gas 5. Mix the breadcrumbs with half the chopped tarragon in a bowl. Season with salt and pepper, then bind the mixture together with the beaten egg.

2 Spread a layer of tarragon stuffing inside the cavity of each trout, pressing the mixture down firmly to mould it to the shape of the cavity. Season the trout well.

3 Place the trout in a single layer in a shallow baking dish. Add the onion slices and wine to the dish and top each fish with a sprig of tarragon. Cover the dish tightly with foil. Bake for 20–25 minutes or until tender.

4 Carefully remove the cooked trout from the dish, reserving the cooking liquid. Remove the heads, tails and skin, then place the fish in a hot ovenproof dish. Cover with foil and keep warm in the oven.

5 Strain the cooking liquid into a measuring jug (cup) and if necessary make up with water to give 150ml/ ¼ pint/⅔ cup of liquid.

6 Melt the butter in a pan, stir in the flour and cook, stirring constantly, for 1–2 minutes. Gradually add the cooking liquid, stirring constantly. Add the cream in the same way and bring to the boil. Continue to stir as the mixture thickens to a smooth sauce. Season with salt and black pepper and add the remaining chopped tarragon.

7 Blanch the remaining tarragon sprigs by plunging them briefly into a pan of boiling water. Drain well.

8 Place the trout on warmed individual serving plates, pour over the tarragon sauce and garnish with the blanched tarragon sprigs. Serve with buttered new potatoes and a selection of steamed green vegetables.

POACHED TROUT WITH FENNEL

*COOKING TROUT, FENNEL AND POTATOES TOGETHER IN ONE DISH
MAKES FOR AN EASY SUPPER — SIMPLY ADD YOUR FAVOURITE
STEAMED GREEN VEGETABLES TO COMPLETE THE MEAL.*

SERVES 2

INGREDIENTS

1 small fennel bulb, about 175g/6oz,
    with fronds
25g/1oz/2 tbsp butter, plus extra
    for greasing
350g/12oz potatoes, peeled and
    thinly sliced
1 bay leaf
60ml/4 tbsp dry vermouth
60ml/4 tbsp water
2 trout, about 225g/8oz each, cleaned
lemon and lime slices, to garnish
steamed green vegetables, to serve

1 Preheat the oven to 180°C/350°F/
Gas 4. Cut the feathery green fronds
from the fennel, chop very finely and
set aside. Slice the fennel bulb thinly.

2 Grease a shallow baking dish with
butter and spread out the fennel bulb
slices to cover the base of the dish.

3 Spread out the potato slices on top
of the fennel and top with the bay leaf.
Pour the vermouth and water over the
vegetables. Season to taste.

4 Cover the dish tightly with foil and
bake in the oven for 35–40 minutes.

5 Remove the dish from the oven and
lift off the foil. Place the trout on top
of the vegetables and dot with butter.
Replace the foil and bake for 20–25
minutes more, until the trout are cooked
and the vegetables are tender.

6 Remove the foil and sprinkle the
reserved chopped fennel over the fish.
Garnish with the lemon and lime slices.
Serve immediately, with the steamed
green vegetables.

COOK'S TIP
Dry vermouth has a concentrated flavour
that works very well in this recipe, and
the herbs that are an intrinsic part of it
are more than a match for the robust
flavour of the fennel.

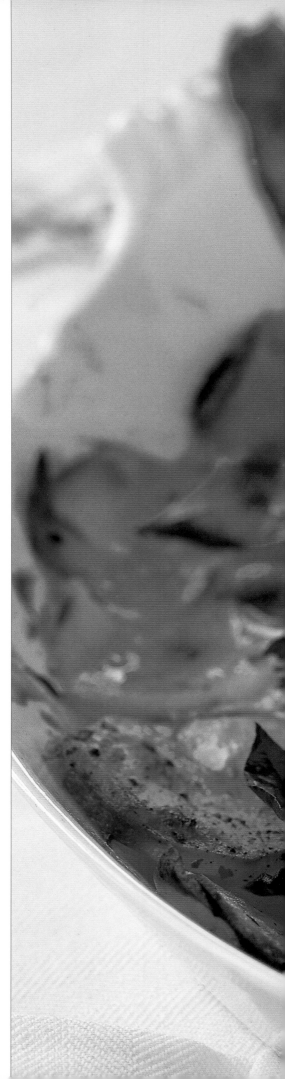

SALMON WITH STILTON

A RICH BLUE STILTON AND HERB BUTTER MAKES A FLAVOURSOME SAUCE FOR SALMON STEAKS BAKED IN WINE. SERVE THIS TOTALLY MOUTHWATERING MELANGE WITH NEW POTATOES, STIR-FRIED RED AND YELLOW PEPPERS AND MANGETOUTS.

SERVES 4

INGREDIENTS
    115g/4oz Stilton cheese
    25g/1oz/2 tbsp butter, softened
    15ml/1 tbsp chopped fresh chives,
      plus extra, to garnish
    15ml/1 tbsp chopped fresh
      thyme leaves
    1 garlic clove, crushed
    30ml/2 tbsp olive oil
    4 salmon steaks
    60ml/4 tbsp dry white wine
    salt and ground black pepper
    new potatoes and stir-fried red and
      yellow (bell) peppers and
      mangetouts (snow peas), to serve

1 Crumble the Stilton and place it in a food processor with the softened butter. Process until smooth. Scrape the Stilton butter into a small bowl.

2 Stir in the 15ml/1 tbsp chives, with the thyme and garlic. Season to taste. Stilton is salty, so you will probably only need to add pepper. Preheat the oven to 180°C/350°F/Gas 4.

3 Place the butter on a piece of foil and shape into an oblong. Wrap this in the foil and seal tightly. Chill the butter by placing it in the refrigerator until it is firm.

4 Brush a sheet of foil, large enough to enclose all the steaks, with olive oil. Support the foil on a baking sheet. Place the steaks on the foil, drizzle the wine over, season and seal the foil tightly. Bake for 20–30 minutes or until cooked through.

5 Unwrap the chilled butter and cut it into four equal portions. Remove the salmon from the oven, carefully open the package and use a fish slice (metal spatula) to transfer each steak to a warmed serving plate.

6 Top each salmon steak with a portion of butter and garnish with the extra chives. Serve immediately with new potatoes and stir-fried red and yellow peppers and mangetouts.

COOK'S TIPS
• If your food processor has a mini bowl for small quantities, use that when making the Stilton butter.
• When wrapping the salmon steaks, turn the foil joins over twice to ensure a tight seal.

SALMON COULIBIAC

THIS IS A COMPLICATED RUSSIAN DISH THAT TAKES A LOT OF PREPARATION, BUT IT IS WELL WORTH IT. TRADITIONALLY, STURGEON IS USED, BUT SALMON MAKES AN EXCELLENT ALTERNATIVE.

SERVES 8

INGREDIENTS
    butter, for greasing
    flour, for dusting
    450g/1lb puff pastry
    1 egg, beaten
    salt and ground black pepper
    lemon wedges and fresh dill sprigs,
      to garnish

For the filling
    50g/2oz/¼ cup butter
    350g/12oz/5 cups chestnut
      mushrooms, sliced
    105ml/7 tbsp white wine
    juice of ½ lemon
    675g/1½lb salmon fillet, skinned
    115g/4oz/scant ½ cup long grain rice
    30ml/2 tbsp chopped fresh dill
    1 large onion, chopped
    4 hard-boiled eggs, shelled
      and sliced

1 First make the filling. Melt most of the butter in a frying pan that is large enough to accommodate the salmon. Add the mushrooms and cook for 3 minutes. Pour in 60ml/4 tbsp of the wine and boil for 2 minutes, then simmer for 5 minutes. Stir in almost all of the remaining wine and the lemon juice.

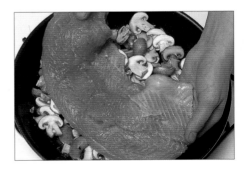

2 Place the salmon on top of the cooked mushrooms, cover with foil and steam gently for 8–10 minutes, until just cooked. Remove the salmon from the pan and set aside.

3 With a slotted spoon, transfer the mushrooms to a bowl. Pour the cooking liquid into a large pan. Add the rice and cook for 10–15 minutes, until tender, adding water or more wine if needed.

4 Remove from the heat and stir in the dill and seasoning. Melt the remaining butter and fry the onion until golden brown. Set aside.

5 Grease a large baking sheet. Using baking parchment, cut out a fish-shaped template that will fit easily on the baking sheet. Roll out just less than half the pastry and use the template to cut a fish shape. Place on the baking sheet.

6 Leaving the edges clear, spread out half the mushrooms on the pastry and top with half the rice, half the onion and half the eggs. Place the salmon on top, cutting it to fit if necessary, then repeat the layers in reverse.

7 Roll out the remaining pastry and cut a slightly larger fish shape than before, so that it will cover the filling. Brush the base pastry rim with beaten egg, fit the pastry top in place and seal the edges. Chill for 1 hour.

8 Preheat the oven to 220ºC/425ºF/Gas 7. Cut four small slits in the top of the pastry, brush with more egg and bake for 10 minutes. Reduce the oven temperature to 190ºC/375ºF/Gas 5 and bake for 30 minutes more, until golden. Garnish with lemon and dill and serve.

PEPPERED SALMON STEAKS

PINK PEPPERCORNS NOT ONLY MATCH THE DELICATE COLOUR OF SALMON, BUT ALSO COMPLEMENT ITS FLAVOUR. THIS IS A LIGHT DISH, WHICH LOOKS VERY PRETTY WITH ITS SMOKED SALMON TOPPING.

2 Sprinkle the dill over the leeks and courgettes and put the salmon steaks in a single layer on top.

3 Place the pink peppercorns in a mortar and crush them lightly with a pestle until about half the corns are broken. Top the salmon with the peppercorns and the bay leaves.

4 Pour the wine over the steaks and dot with the butter. Season well, cover tightly using foil and bake for 20–25 minutes.

SERVES 4

INGREDIENTS

   1 leek, cut into fine strips
   2 courgettes (zucchini), cut into
    fine strips
   15ml/1 tbsp olive oil
   15ml/1 tbsp chopped fresh dill
   4 salmon steaks
   10ml/2 tsp pink peppercorns
   8 small bay leaves
   150ml/¼ pint/⅔ cup dry white wine
   15g/½oz/1 tbsp butter
   50g/2oz smoked salmon
   20ml/4 tsp salmon roe
   salt and ground black pepper

1 Preheat the oven to 190°C/375°F/ Gas 5. Mix the leek and courgette strips with the oil in a bowl. Toss to coat, then spread out on the base of a shallow baking dish.

5 Cut the smoked salmon into strips. Serve each steak on a bed of the braised leek and courgette mixture and top each portion with smoked salmon strips and salmon roe.

TROUT WITH FILO PASTRY AND ALMOND CRUST

BEAUTIFUL PRESENTATION IS A REAL PLUS WHEN IT COMES TO SERVING FISH, AND THIS TROUT IS AS PRETTY AS A PICTURE WITH ITS FILO WRAPPING DUSTED WITH ALMONDS. ALMONDS ARE USED IN THE DELICIOUS STUFFING, TOO, MAKING THIS A TASTY AND FILLING MAIN COURSE.

SERVES 4

INGREDIENTS
  4 whole trout, each about
    175g/6oz, cleaned
  40g/1½oz/3 tbsp butter
  1 small onion, finely chopped
  115g/4oz/1 cup ground almonds
  30ml/2 tbsp chopped fresh
    parsley
  finely grated rind of 1 lemon
  12 sheets filo pastry
  salt and ground black pepper
  lemon slices and parsley sprigs,
    to garnish

VARIATIONS
• It is well known that almonds go particularly well with trout but you could try this recipe with other nuts too. Hazelnuts, pine nuts, pistachios and macadamias would provide an interesting variation.
• Other fresh-tasting herbs such as chervil or tarragon can be used in place of the parsley.

COOK'S TIP
Before working with filo pastry, remove it from the refrigerator and leave, still in its wrapper, for 15 minutes at room temperature. Once the filo pastry sheets have been removed from the packet, they should be covered with a damp, clean dishtowel or clear film (plastic wrap) until needed, so that they do not dry out. If they become too brittle they will not wrap easily around the fish. Any unused filo pastry can be stored in the refrigerator for up to 1 week. It would also freeze well.

1 Preheat the oven to 200°C/400°F/ Gas 6. Season the trout generously with salt and black pepper.

2 Melt 25g/1oz/2 tbsp of the butter in a large pan and cook the onion for 1–2 minutes until soft and translucent. Do not allow the onion to brown.

3 Stir 75g/3oz/¾ cup of the ground almonds into the onions in the pan, then add the chopped parsley and the lemon rind. Stir well to combine.

4 Gently stuff the cavity of each trout with one-quarter of the mixture. Press the mixture down firmly to mould it to the shape of the cavity.

5 Melt the remaining butter. Cut three sheets of filo pastry into long strips and brush with the melted butter.

6 Wrap the strips around one fish, with the buttered side inside. Leave the head and the tail free. Place on a baking sheet. Wrap the remaining trout.

7 Brush the top of the pastry casing with melted butter and sprinkle the remaining ground almonds over the fish. Bake for 20–25 minutes until the pastry is golden brown.

8 Place on warmed individual serving dishes, garnish with the lemon slices and parsley sprigs and serve.

TROUT AND SOLE PARCELS WITH VERMOUTH

TWO TYPES OF FISH, BOTH DELICATE BUT WITH DIFFERENT FLAVOURS, MAKE A WONDERFUL DISH WHEN SANDWICHED WITH A WATERCRESS FILLING AND SERVED WITH A SAUCE SPIKED WITH VERMOUTH.

SERVES 4

INGREDIENTS

1 bunch watercress or rocket (arugula)
1 courgette (zucchini), grated
5ml/1 tsp Tabasco sauce
grated rind and juice of 1 lemon
450g/1lb trout fillets, skinned
450g/1lb sole fillets, skinned
50g/2oz/¼ cup butter
150ml/¼ pint/⅔ cup fish stock
120ml/4fl oz/½ cup dry white
   vermouth
salt and ground black pepper
watercress or rocket (arugula) sprigs,
   to garnish

1 Preheat the oven to 200°C/400°F/ Gas 6. Strip the watercress or rocket leaves from the stalks and chop them finely. Place them in a bowl with the grated courgette, Tabasco sauce, lemon rind and juice. Season with salt and pepper to taste.

2 Season the trout and sole fillets on both sides with salt and pepper. Cover each sole fillet in turn with the watercress or rocket mixture. Top with the trout fillets.

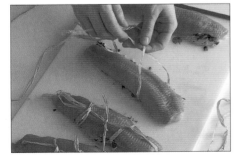

3 Tie the fish "sandwiches" into neat parcels with raffia or string (twine). Arrange the fish parcels side by side in a shallow flameproof dish and dot all over with the butter.

4 Pour the stock and vermouth over, cover and bake for 20 minutes until the fish is tender. Carefully lift the fish parcels on to a serving platter and keep them hot.

5 Transfer the flameproof dish to the top of the stove and cook the stock mixture until it has reduced by half. Pour the sauce over the fish, garnish with watercress or rocket and serve.

COOK'S TIP
If the fish fillets are of uneven sizes, trim the larger piece. Finely chop the trimmings and add to the stuffing.

SALMON WITH WHISKY AND CREAM

THIS DISH COMBINES TWO OF THE FINEST FLAVOURS OF SCOTLAND — SALMON AND WHISKY. IT TAKES VERY LITTLE TIME TO MAKE, SO COOK IT AT THE LAST MOMENT. SERVE QUITE PLAINLY.

SERVES 4

INGREDIENTS

4 thin pieces of salmon fillet, about 175g/6oz each
5ml/1 tsp chopped fresh thyme leaves
50g/2oz/¼ cup butter
75ml/5 tbsp whisky
150ml/¼ pint/⅔ cup double (heavy) cream
juice of ½ lemon (optional)
salt and ground black pepper
fresh dill sprigs, to garnish

1 Season the salmon with salt, pepper and thyme. Melt half the butter in a frying pan large enough to hold two pieces of salmon side by side.

2 When the butter is foaming, fry the first two pieces of salmon for 2–3 minutes on each side, until they are golden on the outside and just cooked through.

3 Pour in 30ml/2 tbsp of the whisky and ignite it. When the flames have died down, carefully transfer the salmon to a plate and keep it hot. Heat the remaining butter and cook the second two pieces of salmon in the same way. Keep them hot.

4 Pour the cream into the pan and bring to the boil, stirring constantly and scraping up the cooking juices from the base of the pan. Allow to bubble until reduced and slightly thickened, then season and add the last of the whisky and a squeeze of lemon if you like.

5 Place the salmon pieces on individual warmed plates, pour the sauce over and garnish with dill. New potatoes and crisp green beans are good with this.

RICE, NOODLES AND PASTA

You don't need a lot of salmon to make an impact in a pasta dish. Penne with Cream and Smoked Salmon, for instance, uses just a few slices of smoked salmon, but when the slices are cut into strips and tossed with cream, pasta, butter and fresh thyme, the results are superb. Salmon is very good with rice, too, whether as a classic risotto, in Creamy Fish Pilau or as the basis of that popular all-in-one dish, Salmon and Rice Gratin.

CREAMY FISH PILAU

THIS SALMON DISH IS FUSION FOOD AT ITS MOST EXCITING — THE METHOD COMES FROM INDIA AND USES THAT COUNTRY'S BASMATI RICE, BUT THE WINE AND CREAM SAUCE IS FRENCH IN FLAVOUR.

SERVES 4–6

INGREDIENTS

 450g/1lb fresh mussels, scrubbed
 350ml/12fl oz/1½ cups white wine
 fresh flat leaf parsley sprig
 about 675g/1½lb salmon
 225g/8oz scallops
 about 15ml/1 tbsp olive oil
 40g/1½oz/3 tbsp butter
 2 shallots, finely chopped
 225g/8oz/3 cups button (white)
  mushrooms
 275g/10oz/1½ cups basmati rice,
  soaked in cold water for 30 minutes
 300ml/½ pint/1¼ cups fish stock
 150ml/¼ pint/⅔ cup double
  (heavy) cream
 15ml/1 tbsp chopped fresh parsley
 225g/8oz large cooked prawns
  (shrimp), peeled and deveined
 salt and ground black pepper
 fresh flat leaf parsley sprigs,
  to garnish

1 Preheat the oven to 160°C/325°F/ Gas 3. Place the mussels in a pan with 90ml/6 tbsp of the wine and the parsley. Cover and cook for 4–5 minutes until the mussels have opened. Drain, reserving the cooking liquid. Remove the mussels from their shells, discarding any that have not opened.

2 Cut the salmon into bitesize pieces. Detach the corals from the scallops and cut the white scallop flesh into thick pieces of equal width.

3 Heat half the oil and all the butter and fry the shallots and mushrooms for 3–4 minutes. Transfer to a bowl. Heat the remaining oil and fry the rice for 2–3 minutes. Spoon into a casserole.

4 Pour the stock, remaining wine and reserved mussel liquid into a frying pan, and bring to the boil. Off the heat, stir in the cream and parsley. Season lightly. Pour over the rice, then add the salmon and the scallop flesh, together with the mushroom mixture. Stir carefully to mix.

5 Cover the casserole tightly. Bake for 30–35 minutes, then add the scallop corals, replace the cover and cook for 4 minutes more. Add the mussels and prawns, cover and cook for 3–4 minutes until the seafood is heated through and the rice is tender. Serve garnished with the parsley sprigs.

SALMON AND RICE GRATIN

THIS ALL-IN-ONE SUPPER DISH IS IDEAL FOR INFORMAL ENTERTAINING AS IT CAN BE MADE AHEAD OF TIME AND REHEATED FOR ABOUT HALF AN HOUR BEFORE BEING SERVED WITH A TOSSED SALAD.

SERVES 6

INGREDIENTS

675g/1½lb fresh salmon fillet, skinned
1 bay leaf
a few parsley stalks
1 litre/1¾ pints/4 cups water
400g/14oz/2 cups basmati rice,
   soaked in cold water for 30 minutes
30–45ml/2–3 tbsp chopped fresh
   parsley, plus extra to garnish
175g/6oz/1½ cups grated
   Cheddar cheese
3 hard-boiled eggs, chopped
salt and ground black pepper

For the sauce
1 litre/1¾ pints/4 cups milk
40g/1½oz/⅓ cup plain
   (all-purpose) flour
40g/1½oz/3 tbsp butter
5ml/1 tsp mild curry paste or
   Dijon mustard

4 Remove the pan from the heat and, without lifting the lid, allow the rice to stand undisturbed for 5 minutes.

5 Meanwhile, make the sauce. Mix the milk, flour and butter in a pan. Bring to the boil over a low heat, whisking constantly until the sauce is smooth and thick. Stir in the curry paste or mustard, with salt and pepper to taste. Reduce the heat and simmer the sauce for 2 minutes, whisking occasionally.

6 Preheat the grill (broiler). Remove the sauce from the heat and stir in the chopped parsley and rice, with half the cheese. Using a large metal spoon, fold in the flaked fish and eggs.

7 Spoon into a shallow gratin dish and sprinkle with the rest of the cheese. Heat under the grill until the topping is golden brown and bubbling. Serve in individual dishes, garnished with chopped parsley.

1 Put the salmon in a wide, shallow pan. Add the bay leaf and parsley stalks, with salt and pepper. Pour in the water and bring to simmering point. Poach the fish for about 12 minutes until just tender.

2 Lift the fish out of the pan using a slotted spoon, then strain the liquid into a clean pan. Leave the fish to cool, then remove any visible bones and flake the flesh gently with a fork.

3 Drain the rice and add it to the pan containing the fish-poaching liquid. Bring to the boil, then reduce the heat, cover and simmer for 10 minutes.

SALMON RISOTTO WITH CUCUMBER

THIS SIMPLE RISOTTO IS COOKED ALL IN ONE GO, AND IS THEREFORE EASIER TO MAKE THAN THE USUAL RISOTTO. NEVERTHELESS, IT IS VERY CREAMY AND THE SALMON GIVES IT SUPERB FLAVOUR.

SERVES 4

INGREDIENTS

25g/1oz/2 tbsp butter
small bunch of spring onions
  (scallions), white parts only, chopped
½ cucumber, peeled, seeded
  and chopped
350g/12oz/1¾ cups risotto rice
1.2 litres/2 pints/5 cups hot fish or
  chicken stock
150ml/¼ pint/⅔ cup dry white wine
450g/1lb salmon fillet, skinned
  and diced
45ml/3 tbsp chopped fresh tarragon
salt and ground black pepper

3 Stir in the diced salmon and then season. Continue cooking for a further 5 minutes, stirring occasionally, then switch off the heat. Cover the pan and leave the risotto to stand for 5 minutes.

4 Remove the lid from the pan, add the chopped tarragon to the rice and mix lightly. Spoon into a warmed bowl and serve. Offer extra chopped tarragon on the side, if you like.

1 Heat the butter and cook the spring onions and cucumber. Cook for 2 minutes without letting the onions brown.

2 Stir in the rice, then pour in the stock and wine. Bring to the boil, then lower the heat and simmer, uncovered, for 10 minutes, stirring occasionally.

VARIATION
Carnaroli rice would be excellent in this risotto, although if it is not available, arborio rice can be used instead.

TROUT WITH RICE, TOMATOES AND NUTS

THIS RECIPE COMES FROM NORTHERN SPAIN, WHERE TROUT IS VERY POPULAR. IF YOU FILLET THE FISH BEFORE YOU BAKE IT, IT COOKS MORE EVENLY AND NO BONES GET IN THE WAY OF THE STUFFING.

SERVES 4

INGREDIENTS

2 fresh trout, each about 500g/1¼lb
75g/3oz/¾ cup mixed unsalted cashew nuts, pine nuts, almonds and hazelnuts
25ml/1½ tbsp olive oil, plus extra for drizzling
1 small onion, finely chopped
10ml/2 tsp grated fresh root ginger
175g/6oz/1½ cups cooked white long grain rice
4 tomatoes, peeled and very finely chopped
4 sun-dried tomatoes in oil, drained and chopped
30ml/2 tbsp chopped fresh tarragon
2 fresh tarragon sprigs
salt and ground black pepper
dressed green leaves, to serve

3 Heat the oil in a small frying pan and fry the onion for 3–4 minutes until soft. Stir in the ginger, cook for 1 minute more, then spoon into a mixing bowl.

4 Add the rice to the mixture in the bowl, then stir in the chopped tomatoes, sun-dried tomatoes, toasted nuts and chopped tarragon. Season the stuffing with plenty of salt and black pepper.

5 Place each of the trout in turn on a large piece of oiled foil and spoon the stuffing into the cavity. Add a sprig of tarragon and a drizzle of olive oil.

6 Fold the foil over to enclose each trout and put the parcels in a large roasting pan. Bake for 20–25 minutes until the fish is tender. Cut the fish into thick slices. Serve with the green salad.

1 Using a sharp knife, fillet the trout. Check the cavity for any remaining tiny bones and remove these with tweezers.

2 Preheat the oven to 190°C/375°F/ Gas 5. Spread out the nuts in a baking tray and bake for 3–4 minutes, shaking the tray occasionally. Chop the nuts.

TROUT AND PROSCIUTTO RISOTTO ROLLS

THIS MAKES A DELICIOUS AND ELEGANT MEAL. THE RISOTTO — MADE WITH PORCINI MUSHROOMS AND PRAWNS — IS A FINE MATCH FOR THE ROBUST FLAVOUR OF THE TROUT ROLLS.

SERVES 4

INGREDIENTS
   4 trout fillets, skinned
   4 slices prosciutto
   capers, to garnish

For the risotto
   30ml/2 tbsp olive oil
   8 large raw prawns (shrimp),
      peeled and deveined
   1 medium onion, chopped
   225g/8oz/generous 1 cup risotto rice
   about 105ml/7 tbsp white wine
   about 750ml/1¼ pints/3 cups
      simmering fish or chicken stock
   15g/½oz/2 tbsp dried porcini or
      chanterelle mushrooms, soaked for
      10 minutes in warm water to cover
   salt and ground black pepper

2 Add the chopped onion to the oil remaining in the pan and fry over a gentle heat for 3–4 minutes until soft. Add the rice and stir for 3–4 minutes until the grains are evenly coated in oil. Add 75ml/5 tbsp of the wine and then the stock, a little at a time, stirring over a gentle heat and allowing the rice to absorb the liquid before adding more.

4 Remove the pan from the heat and stir in the prawns. Preheat the oven to 190°C/375°F/Gas 5.

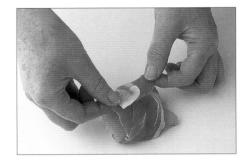

5 Take a trout fillet, place a spoonful of risotto at one end and roll up. Wrap each fillet in a slice of prosciutto and place in a greased baking dish.

1 First make the risotto. Heat the oil in a large, heavy saucepan or deep frying pan and fry the prawns very briefly until flecked with pink. Lift out with a slotted spoon and transfer to a plate.

3 Strain the mushrooms, reserving the liquid, and cut the larger ones in half. Towards the end of cooking, stir the mushrooms into the risotto with 15ml/1 tbsp of the reserved mushroom liquid. The rice should be soft and creamy, with just a little "bite" in the centre of the grain. If necessary, add a little more stock or mushroom liquid and cook for a few minutes more. Season to taste with salt and pepper.

6 Spoon any remaining risotto around the fish fillets and sprinkle over the rest of the wine. Cover loosely with foil and bake for 15–20 minutes until the fish is tender. Spoon the risotto on to a platter, top with the trout rolls and garnish with capers. Serve immediately.

COOK'S TIP
There are no hard and fast rules about which type of risotto to use for this dish. Almost any risotto recipe could be used, although a vegetable or seafood risotto would be particularly suitable.

TROUT WITH BLACK RICE

PINK TROUT FILLETS COOKED WITH GINGER, GARLIC AND CHILLI MAKE A STUNNING CONTRAST TO THE NUTTY BLACK RICE.

SERVES 2

INGREDIENTS

    2.5cm/1in piece fresh root ginger,
      peeled and grated
    1 garlic clove, crushed
    1 fresh red chilli, seeded and
      finely chopped
    30ml/2 tbsp soy sauce
    2 trout fillets, each about 200g/7oz
    oil, for greasing

For the rice
    15ml/1 tbsp sesame oil
    50g/2oz/¾ cup fresh shiitake
      mushrooms, sliced
    8 spring onions (scallions),
      finely chopped
    150g/5oz/¾ cup black rice
    4 slices fresh root ginger
    900ml/1½ pints/3¾ cups
      boiling water

1 Make the rice. Heat the sesame oil in a pan and fry the mushrooms with half the spring onions for 2–3 minutes.

2 Add the rice and sliced ginger to the pan and stir well. Cover with the boiling water and bring to the boil. Reduce the heat, cover and simmer for 25–30 minutes or until the rice is tender. Drain well and cover to keep warm.

COOK'S TIP
Do not have the heat too high when heating the sesame oil, as it smokes readily. If you prefer, you can mix 10ml/2 tsp groundnut (peanut) oil with 5ml/1 tsp sesame oil.

3 While the rice is cooking, preheat the oven to 200°C/400°F/Gas 6. In a small bowl mix together the grated ginger, garlic, chilli and soy sauce.

4 Place the fish, skin side up, in a lightly oiled shallow baking dish. Using a sharp knife, make several slits in the skin of the fish, then spread the ginger paste all over the fillets.

5 Cover the dish tightly with foil and cook in the oven for 20–25 minutes or until the trout fillets are cooked through.

6 Divide the rice between two warmed serving plates. Remove the ginger. Lay the fish on top and sprinkle over the reserved spring onions, to garnish.

SMOKED TROUT RISOTTO

THE MOST IMPORTANT POINT TO REMEMBER WHEN YOU'RE MAKING RISOTTO IS THAT YOU NEED TO BE PATIENT. THE RICE NEEDS CONSTANT STIRRING AND ONCE ALL THE LIQUID HAS BEEN ABSORBED IT IS BEST SERVED STRAIGHT AWAY.

SERVES 4

INGREDIENTS

1.2 litres/2 pints/5 cups hot
   fish stock
30ml/2 tbsp olive oil
1 medium onion, finely chopped
400g/14oz/2 cups risotto rice,
   preferably arborio
150ml/¼ pint/⅔ cup dry
   white wine
45ml/3 tbsp crème fraîche or
   sour cream
45ml/3 tbsp grated Parmesan
   cheese, plus extra, to serve
350g/12oz smoked trout, roughly
   chopped
60ml/4 tbsp chopped fresh chervil
salt and ground black pepper
fresh chervil sprigs, to garnish

COOK'S TIPS
• To make Italian risotto it is essential to use a risotto rice. This special, fat short grain rice is unlike ordinary short grain rice in that it retains its texture while giving dishes a beautiful creaminess. Italian arborio rice, which originates from the Po valley region of northern Italy, is particularly favoured for its nutty flavour. This is the most widely available variety, but you may also find carnaroli and vialone nano in specialist shops, and these would also be suitable.
• For best results, use a well-flavoured fish stock. A home-made stock is best of all but you could use a good fresh stock for convenience if time is short.
• Parmesan cheese is a key ingredient in any Italian risotto. Avoid ready-grated Parmesan and opt for a chunk freshly cut off the block. It is more expensive but it will keep for a long time in the refrigerator and there is no substitute for the flavour.
• During cooking, adjust the heat so that the risotto bubbles merrily. Do not let it boil or the stock will evaporate before it can be absorbed by the rice.

1 For the creamiest risotto the stock needs to be hot when it is added to the rice, so keep it simmering in a pan on top of the stove, next to the risotto pan.

2 Heat the oil in a large pan: a paella pan or a large, heavy pan would be ideal. Add the chopped onion and fry it gently over a low heat for about 5 minutes until softened. Do not allow the onion to brown.

3 Add the rice to the pan and stir well with a wooden spoon to coat each grain thoroughly in oil. Cook over a low heat for 2–3 minutes until the rice grains have turned translucent.

4 Pour the white wine over the rice in the pan, stirring constantly. Continue to stir for 1–2 minutes until all of the wine has been absorbed.

5 Keeping the pan over a medium heat, add the hot stock, a ladleful at a time, stirring all the time.

6 Add another ladleful of stock to the rice only when the previous quantity has been absorbed, and continue in this way until all the stock has been used up. This will take around 20 minutes. As the rice cooks the mixture will thicken – the risotto is cooked when the rice has a velvety texture. When you taste them, the grains of rice should still have a bit of bite in the centre.

7 Remove the pan from the heat and stir in the crème fraîche or sour cream and the grated Parmesan cheese. Add three-quarters of the chopped smoked trout and the chopped chervil. Season with plenty of salt and black pepper and stir well to mix. Cover the pan and leave to stand for about 2 minutes.

8 Divide the risotto among four warmed serving plates, top with the remaining smoked trout and garnish with the fresh chervil sprigs. Extra grated Parmesan cheese can be offered separately.

MALAYSIAN STEAMED TROUT WITH NOODLES

THIS SIMPLE DISH, SERVED ON A BED OF NOODLES, CAN BE PREPARED EXTREMELY QUICKLY. IT IS SUITABLE FOR ANY FISH FILLETS.

2 Mix together the coconut, lime rind and chopped coriander and spread one-quarter of the mixture over each trout fillet. Sandwich another trout fillet on top.

3 Mix the lime juice with the oils, adjusting the quantity of chilli oil to your own taste, and drizzle the mixture over the trout "sandwiches".

4 Prepare a steamer. Fold up the edges of the paper and pleat them over the trout to make parcels, making sure they are well sealed.

5 Place in the steamer insert and steam over the simmering water for about 10–15 minutes, depending on the thickness of the trout fillets.

6 Meanwhile, cook the noodles in a large pan of boiling water for 5–8 minutes, until just tender. Drain, toss with a little chilli oil, if you like, and divide among four warmed plates. Remove each trout "sandwich" from its wrapper and place on top of the noodles. Garnish with the lime slices and coriander.

SERVES 4

INGREDIENTS
    8 pink trout fillets of even thickness,
      about 115g/4oz each, skinned
    45ml/3 tbsp grated creamed coconut
      or desiccated (dry unsweetened
      shredded) coconut
    grated rind and juice of 2 limes
    45ml/3 tbsp chopped fresh coriander
      (cilantro)
    15ml/1 tbsp groundnut (peanut) oil
    2.5–5ml/½–1 tsp chilli oil
    350g/12oz broad egg noodles
    salt and ground black pepper
    lime slices and coriander, to garnish

VARIATION
Use the flesh from a coconut to make a tasty alternative garnish. Having rinsed the flesh with cold water, cut off thin slices using a swivel-bladed vegetable peeler. Toast the slices under a medium grill (broiler) until the coconut has curled and the edges have turned golden. Sprinkle the shavings over the trout fillets before serving.

1 Cut four rectangles of baking parchment, each about twice the size of the trout fillets. Place a fillet on each piece and season lightly.

SMOKED TROUT <u>AND</u> NOODLE SALAD

IT IS IMPORTANT TO USE RIPE JUICY TOMATOES FOR THIS FRESH-TASTING SALAD. FOR A SPECIAL OCCASION YOU COULD REPLACE THE SMOKED TROUT WITH SMOKED SALMON.

SERVES 4

INGREDIENTS
    225g/8oz somen noodles
    2 smoked trout, skinned and
        boned
    2 hard-boiled eggs, chopped
    30ml/2 tbsp snipped chives
    lime halves, to serve (optional)

For the dressing
    6 ripe plum tomatoes
    2 shallots, finely chopped
    30ml/2 tbsp tiny capers, rinsed
    30ml/2 tbsp chopped fresh tarragon
    finely grated rind and juice of
        ½ orange
    60ml/4 tbsp extra virgin olive oil
    salt and ground black pepper

1 To make the dressing, cut the tomatoes in half, remove the cores, and cut the flesh into chunks.

2 Place in a bowl with the shallots, capers, tarragon, orange rind, orange juice and olive oil. Season with salt and ground black pepper, and mix well. Leave the dressing to marinate at room temperature for 1–2 hours.

3 Cook the noodles in a large saucepan of boiling water until just tender. Drain and rinse under cold running water. Drain again well.

4 Toss the noodles with the tomato and onion dressing, then add salt and ground black pepper to taste. Arrange the noodles on a large serving platter or individual plates.

5 Flake the smoked trout over the noodles, then sprinkle the coarsely chopped eggs and snipped chives over the top. Serve the lime halves on the side, if you like.

COOK'S TIP
Choose tomatoes that are firm, bright in colour and have a matt texture, avoiding any with blotched or cracked skins.

STIR-FRIED NOODLES WITH SOY SALMON

TERIYAKI SAUCE FORMS THE MARINADE FOR THE SALMON IN THIS RECIPE. SERVED WITH SOFT-FRIED NOODLES, IT MAKES A STUNNING DISH.

SERVES 4

INGREDIENTS

    350g/12oz salmon fillet,
      skinned
    30ml/2 tbsp shoyu (Japanese
      soy sauce)
    30ml/2 tbsp sake
    60ml/4 tbsp mirin or sweet sherry
    5ml/1 tsp soft light brown sugar
    10ml/2 tsp grated fresh root ginger
    3 garlic cloves, 1 crushed, and 2
      sliced into rounds
    30ml/2 tbsp groundnut
      (peanut) oil
    225g/8oz dried egg noodles, cooked
      and drained
    50g/2oz/1 cup alfalfa sprouts
    30ml/2 tbsp sesame seeds,
      lightly toasted

1 Using a sharp cook's knife, slice the salmon thinly. Spread out the slices in a large, shallow dish, keeping them in a single layer if possible.

2 In a bowl, mix together the soy sauce, sake, mirin or sherry, sugar, ginger and crushed garlic. Pour over the salmon, cover and leave for 30 minutes.

3 Preheat the grill (broiler). Drain the salmon, reserving the marinade. Place the salmon in a layer on a baking sheet. Cook under the grill for 2–3 minutes.

4 Meanwhile, heat a wok until hot, add the oil and swirl it around. Add the garlic rounds and cook until golden brown. Remove the garlic and discard.

5 Add the cooked noodles and reserved marinade to the wok and stir-fry for 3–4 minutes until the marinade has reduced to a syrupy glaze and coats the noodles.

6 Toss in the alfalfa sprouts. Transfer immediately to warmed serving plates and top with the salmon. Sprinkle over the toasted sesame seeds. Serve at once.

BUCKWHEAT NOODLES WITH SMOKED TROUT

THE LIGHT, CRISP TEXTURE OF THE PAK CHOI BALANCES THE STRONG, EARTHY FLAVOURS OF THE MUSHROOMS AND BUCKWHEAT NOODLES AND THE SMOKINESS OF THE TROUT.

SERVES 4

INGREDIENTS

   350g/12oz buckwheat noodles
   30ml/2 tbsp vegetable oil
   115g/4oz/1½ cup fresh shiitake
      mushrooms, stems trimmed,
      quartered
   2 garlic cloves, finely chopped
   15ml/1 tbsp grated fresh root
      ginger
   225g/8oz pak choi (bok choy)
   1 spring onion (scallion), finely
      sliced diagonally
   15ml/1 tbsp dark sesame oil
   30ml/2 tbsp mirin or sweet sherry
   30ml/2 tbsp soy sauce
   2 smoked trout, skinned and boned
   salt and ground black pepper
   30ml/2 tbsp coriander (cilantro)
      leaves and 10ml/2 tsp sesame
      seeds, toasted, to garnish

1 Cook the buckwheat noodles in a pan of boiling water for 7–10 minutes, or until just tender, following the instructions on the packet.

2 Meanwhile, heat the vegetable oil in a large frying pan. Add the shiitake mushrooms and sauté over a medium heat for 3 minutes. Add the garlic, ginger and pak choi, and continue to sauté for 2 minutes.

COOK'S TIP
Mirin is sweet, cooking sake, available from Japanese food stores.

3 Drain the noodles and add them to the vegetables in the frying pan with the spring onion, sesame oil, mirin or sherry and soy sauce. Toss the mixture thoroughly and season with salt and black pepper to taste.

4 Break the trout into bitesize pieces. Arrange the noodle mixture on individual serving plates. Place the smoked trout on top of the noodles. Garnish with coriander leaves and sesame seeds, and serve immediately.

ASIAN SEARED SALMON

SALMON FILLETS ONLY TAKE A FEW MINUTES TO COOK, BUT MAKE SURE YOU ALLOW ENOUGH TIME FOR THE FISH TO SOAK UP ALL THE FLAVOURS OF THE MARINADE BEFORE YOU START COOKING.

SERVES 4

INGREDIENTS
   grated rind and juice of 1 lime
   15ml/1 tbsp soy sauce
   2 spring onions (scallions), sliced
   1 fresh red chilli, seeded and
      finely chopped
   2.5cm/1in piece fresh root ginger,
      peeled and grated
   1 lemon grass stalk, finely chopped
   4 salmon fillets, each about
      175g/6oz
   30ml/2 tbsp olive oil
   salt and ground black pepper
   45ml/3 tbsp fresh coriander
      (cilantro), to garnish

For the noodles
   250g/9oz medium egg noodles
   30ml/2 tbsp olive oil
   1 carrot, cut into fine strips
   1 red (bell) pepper, seeded and cut
      into fine strips
   1 yellow (bell) pepper, seeded and
      cut into fine strips
   115g/4oz mangetouts (snow peas)
   15ml/1 tbsp sesame oil

1 Put the grated lime rind in a jug (pitcher) and pour in the lime juice. Add the soy sauce, spring onions, chilli, ginger and lemon grass. Season with pepper and stir well. Place the salmon in a shallow non-metallic dish and pour the lime mixture over. Cover and marinate in the refrigerator for at least 30 minutes.

2 Bring a large pan of lightly salted water to the boil and cook the noodles according to the instructions on the packet. Drain well and set aside.

COOK'S TIP
Fresh root ginger is a wonderful ingredient. Thin slices can be added to boiling water to make a refreshing tea, and grated ginger makes a great addition to curries and stir-fries. Ginger freezes successfully and can be shaved or grated from frozen.

3 Brush a griddle pan with 15ml/1 tbsp of the olive oil and heat until hot. Remove the fish from the marinade, pat dry and add to the griddle pan. Cook the salmon fillets for 6 minutes, turning once.

4 When the salmon is almost cooked, add to the remaining marinade in a separate pan and heat through.

5 While the fish is cooking, heat the remaining oil in a wok or large frying pan. Add the carrot and stir-fry for 3 minutes. Add the drained noodles, pepper strips and mangetouts and toss over the heat for 2 minutes more. Drizzle the sesame oil over and season well.

6 Serve the salmon on a bed of noodles and vegetables. Garnish with coriander.

PENNE <u>WITH</u> CREAM <u>AND</u> SMOKED SALMON

NO SUPPER DISH COULD BE SIMPLER. FRESHLY COOKED PASTA IS TOSSED WITH CREAM, SMOKED SALMON AND THYME. FROM START TO FINISH IT TAKES UNDER 15 MINUTES TO MAKE.

SERVES 4

INGREDIENTS
   350g/12oz/3 cups dried penne
   115g/4oz thinly sliced
     smoked salmon
   2–3 fresh thyme sprigs
   25g/1oz/2 tbsp butter
   150ml/¼ pint/⅔ cup double
     (heavy) cream
   salt and ground black pepper

VARIATION
Substitute low fat cream cheese for half the cream in the sauce, for a less rich mixture that still tastes very good.

1 Bring a large pan of lightly salted water to the boil. Add the pasta and cook for about 12 minutes, or according to the instructions on the packet, until the penne are tender but still firm to the bite.

2 Meanwhile, using kitchen scissors or a small, sharp knife, cut the smoked salmon into thin strips, each about 5mm/¼in wide, and place on a plate. Strip the leaves from the thyme sprigs.

3 Melt the butter in a large pan. Stir in the cream with a quarter of the salmon and thyme leaves, then season with pepper. Heat gently for 3–4 minutes, stirring constantly. Do not allow the sauce to boil. Taste for seasoning.

4 Drain the pasta, return it to the pan, and toss it in the cream and salmon sauce. Divide among four warmed bowls and top with the remaining salmon and thyme leaves. Serve immediately.

SPAGHETTI WITH SALMON AND PRAWNS

THIS IS A LOVELY, FRESH-TASTING PASTA DISH, PERFECT FOR AN AL-FRESCO MEAL IN SUMMER.
SERVE IT AS A MAIN COURSE LUNCH WITH WARM ITALIAN BREAD AND A DRY WHITE WINE.

SERVES 4

INGREDIENTS
   300g/11oz salmon fillet
   200ml/7fl oz/scant 1 cup dry
    white wine
   a few fresh basil sprigs, plus extra basil
    leaves, to garnish
   6 ripe Italian plum tomatoes,
    peeled and finely chopped
   150ml/¼ pint/⅔ cup double
    (heavy) cream
   350g/12oz/3 cups fresh or
    dried spaghetti
   115g/4oz/⅔ cup peeled cooked prawns
    (shrimp), thawed and thoroughly
    dried if frozen
   salt and ground black pepper

COOK'S TIP
Check the salmon fillet carefully for
small bones when you are flaking the
flesh. Although the salmon is already
filleted, you will always find a few stray
"pin" bones. Pick them out carefully
using tweezers or your fingertips.

1 Put the salmon, skin side up, in a
wide shallow pan. Pour over the wine,
then add the basil. Sprinkle the fish
with salt and pepper. Bring the wine to
the boil, cover the pan and simmer
gently for 5 minutes. Lift the fish out of
the pan and set it aside to cool a little.

2 Add the tomatoes and cream to
the liquid remaining in the pan and
bring to the boil. Stir well, then reduce
the heat and simmer, uncovered, for
10–15 minutes. Meanwhile, cook the
pasta according to the instructions
on the packet.

3 Flake the fish into large chunks,
discarding the skin and any bones.
Add the fish to the sauce with the
prawns, shaking the pan until they
are well coated. Check the seasoning.

4 Drain the pasta and put it in a
warmed bowl. Pour the sauce over
the pasta and toss to combine.
Serve immediately, garnished with
fresh basil leaves.

FUSILLI WITH SMOKED TROUT

IN ITS CREAMY SAUCE, THE SMOKED TROUT BLENDS BEAUTIFULLY WITH THE STILL CRISP-TENDER VEGETABLES IN THIS CLASSIC PASTA DISH.

SERVES 4–6

INGREDIENTS

    2 carrots, cut into matchsticks
    1 leek, cut into matchsticks
    2 celery sticks, cut into matchsticks
    150ml/¼ pint/⅔ cup vegetable stock
    225g/8oz smoked trout fillets,
      skinned and cut into strips
    200g/7oz cream cheese
    150ml/¼ pint/⅔ cup medium sweet
      white wine or fish stock
    15ml/1 tbsp chopped fresh dill
      or fennel
    225g/8oz/2 cups long curly fusilli
      or other dried pasta shapes
    salt and ground black pepper
    fresh dill sprigs, to garnish

3 Cook the fusilli in a pan of salted boiling water according to the instructions on the packet. When the pasta is tender, but still firm to the bite, drain it thoroughly, and return it to the pan.

4 Add the sauce, toss lightly and transfer to a serving bowl. Top with the cooked vegetables and trout. Serve immediately, garnished with the dill sprigs.

1 Put the carrot, leek and celery matchsticks into a pan and add the stock. Bring to the boil and cook quickly for 4–5 minutes, until most of the stock has evaporated. Remove from the heat and add the smoked trout.

2 Put the cream cheese and wine or fish stock into a pan over a medium heat, and whisk until smooth. Add the dill or fennel and salt and pepper.

FARFALLE <u>WITH</u> SMOKED SALMON <u>AND</u> DILL

This quick, luxurious sauce for pasta has become very fashionable in Italy, but wherever you have it, it will taste delicious. Dill is the classic herb for cooking with fish, but if you don't like its aniseed flavour, substitute parsley or a little fresh tarragon.

SERVES 4

INGREDIENTS

6 spring onions (scallions), sliced
50g/2oz/¼ cup butter
90ml/6 tbsp dry white wine
  or vermouth
450ml/¾ pint/scant 2 cups double
  (heavy) cream
freshly grated nutmeg
225g/8oz smoked salmon
30ml/2 tbsp chopped fresh dill
freshly squeezed lemon juice
450g/1lb/4 cups farfalle
salt and ground black pepper
fresh dill sprigs, to garnish

1 Using a sharp cook's knife, slice the spring onions finely. Melt the butter in a large pan and fry the spring onions for about 1 minute, stirring occasionally, until softened.

2 Add the wine or vermouth and boil hard to reduce to about 30ml/2 tbsp. Stir in the cream and add salt, pepper and nutmeg to taste. Bring to the boil, then simmer for 2–3 minutes until slightly thickened.

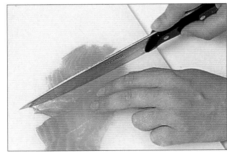

3 Cut the smoked salmon slices into 2.5cm/1in squares and stir into the sauce, together with the dill. Add a little lemon juice to taste. Keep warm.

4 Cook the pasta in a large pan of boiling salted water, following the instructions on the packet. Drain well. Toss with the sauce. Spoon into serving bowls and serve immediately, garnished with sprigs of dill.

SMOKED TROUT PASTA SALAD

CHOOSE HOLLOW PASTA SHAPES, SUCH AS SHELLS OR PENNE, WHICH TRAP THE CREAMY FILLING, CREATING TASTY MOUTHFULS OF TROUT, FENNEL AND SPRING ONION. THE ADDITION OF DILL IS NOT ONLY ATTRACTIVE, BUT ALSO GIVES THIS SALAD A DISTINCTIVE ANISEED FLAVOUR.

SERVES 8

INGREDIENTS

15g/½oz/1 tbsp butter
1 bulb fennel, finely chopped
6 spring onions (scallions), 2 very
 finely chopped and 4 thinly sliced
225g/8oz smoked trout fillets,
 skinned and flaked
45ml/3 tbsp chopped fresh dill
120ml/4fl oz/½ cup mayonnaise
10ml/2 tsp lemon juice
30ml/2 tbsp whipping cream
450g/1lb small pasta shapes,
 such as shells
salt and ground black pepper
fresh dill sprigs, to garnish

1 Melt the butter in a small frying pan. Add the fennel and finely chopped spring onions and fry over a medium heat for 3–5 minutes. Transfer to a large bowl and leave to cool slightly.

2 Add the sliced spring onions, trout, dill, mayonnaise, lemon juice and cream to the bowl with the fennel. Season lightly with salt and pepper and mix gently until well blended.

3 Bring a large pan of lightly salted water to the boil. Add the pasta. Cook according to the instructions on the packet until *al dente*. Drain thoroughly in a colander and leave to cool.

4 Add the pasta to the vegetable and trout mixture and toss to coat evenly. Taste for seasoning. Serve the salad lightly chilled or at room temperature, garnished with the sprigs of dill.

VARIATIONS

This pasta salad works well with any type of fresh, cooked fish fillets, including salmon. Alternatively, you can use a 200g/7oz can of tuna in water in place of the trout.

PASTA WITH SMOKED SALMON

This is a pretty pasta dish that tastes as good as it looks. The light texture of the cucumber perfectly complements the smoked salmon and the pastel colours look very attractive against the creamy swirls of tagliatelle.

SERVES 4

INGREDIENTS

350g/12oz/3 cups dried or
  fresh tagliatelle
½ cucumber
75g/3oz/6 tbsp butter
grated rind of 1 orange
30ml/2 tbsp chopped fresh dill
300ml/½ pint/1¼ cups single
  (light) cream
15ml/1 tbsp orange juice
115g/4oz smoked salmon, skinned
salt and ground black pepper

1 Bring a large pan of lightly salted water to the boil and add the pasta. If using dried pasta, cook for about 12 minutes or for the time recommended on the packet. If using fresh pasta, cook for 2–3 minutes, or until just tender but still firm to the bite.

2 Using a sharp knife, cut the cucumber in half lengthways, then use a small spoon to scoop out and discard the cucumber seeds. Turn the cucumber on to the flat side and slice it thinly in crescent shapes.

COOK'S TIP
If the cost of smoked salmon deters you from using it too often, consider buying salmon pieces or off-cuts. These aren't inferior in any way, but because they are either too small or too awkwardly shaped to look good in a packet, they are much cheaper than the neater slices.

3 Melt the butter in a heavy pan, add the grated orange rind and fresh dill and stir well. Add the cucumber and cook over a low heat for about 2 minutes, stirring from time to time with a wooden spoon.

4 Stir in the cream and orange juice, with salt and pepper to taste. Reduce the heat to the lowest setting and cook gently for 1 minute.

5 Cut the salmon into thin strips. Stir these into the sauce and heat through.

6 Drain the pasta thoroughly and return it to the pan. Add the sauce and toss to combine. Spoon into a dish or into individual shallow pasta plates and serve.

CREAMY LEMON AND SALMON PAPPARDELLE

THIS IS A FANTASTIC ALL-IN-ONE SUPPER DISH THAT TASTES GREAT AND IS MADE IN JUST A FEW MINUTES — IDEAL FOR WHEN YOU'RE REALLY HUNGRY BUT HAVEN'T MUCH TIME. SERVE IT WITH A ROCKET SALAD DRESSED WITH EXTRA VIRGIN OLIVE OIL, BALSAMIC VINEGAR AND BLACK PEPPER.

SERVES 4

INGREDIENTS
    500g/1¼lb fresh pappardelle or
        tagliatelle
    300ml/½ pint/1¼ cups single
        (light) cream
    grated rind and juice of 2 lemons
    225g/8oz smoked salmon pieces
    2.5ml/½ tsp grated nutmeg
    60ml/4 tbsp chopped fresh parsley
    salt and ground black pepper
    fresh Parmesan cheese shavings,
        to garnish
    rocket (arugula) salad, to serve

1 Bring a large pan of lightly salted water to the boil and cook the pappardelle or tagliatelle for 3–5 minutes, or according to the instructions on the packet, until risen to the surface of the boiling water and just tender. Drain well.

2 Add the cream, lemon rind and juice to the pan and heat through gently until piping hot. Return the cooked pappardelle to the pan and stir thoroughly to coat the pasta with the creamy mixture.

3 Add the salmon pieces, grated nutmeg, chopped parsley and plenty of ground black pepper to the sauce in the pan and stir well to combine.

4 Divide the pasta among four warmed serving plates and top with the fresh Parmesan shavings. Serve immediately with the rocket salad.

SMOKED TROUT CANNELLONI

ONE OF THE MOST POPULAR PASTA DISHES, CANNELLONI USUALLY HAS A MEAT AND TOMATO FILLING, OR ONE BASED ON SPINACH AND RICOTTA CHEESE. SMOKED TROUT MAKES A DELICIOUS CHANGE IN THIS LOW-FAT VERSION.

SERVES 4–6

INGREDIENTS

1 large onion, finely chopped
1 garlic clove, crushed
60ml/4 tbsp vegetable stock
2 x 400g/14oz cans chopped
  tomatoes
2.5ml/½ tsp dried mixed herbs
1 smoked trout, about 400g/14oz,
  or 225g/8oz fillets
75g/3oz/½ cup frozen peas, thawed
75g/3oz/1½ cups fresh breadcrumbs
16 no pre-cook cannelloni tubes
salt and ground black pepper

For the sauce
25g/1oz/2 tbsp butter
25g/1oz/¼ cup plain (all-purpose)
  flour
350ml/12fl oz/1½ cups skimmed
  milk
freshly grated nutmeg
25ml/1½ tbsp freshly grated
  Parmesan cheese

1 Put the onion, garlic clove and stock in a large pan. Cover and simmer for 3 minutes. Remove the lid and cook until the stock has reduced entirely.

2 Stir in the tomatoes and dried herbs. Simmer uncovered for 10 minutes, or until the mixture is very thick.

3 Skin the trout with a sharp knife. Flake the flesh, discarding any bones. Put the fish in a bowl and add the tomato mixture, peas and breadcrumbs. Mix well, then season with salt and pepper.

4 Spoon the filling generously into the cannelloni tubes and arrange them in an ovenproof dish. Preheat the oven to 190°C/375°F/Gas 5.

5 Make the sauce. Put the butter, flour and milk into a pan and cook over a medium heat, whisking constantly, until the sauce boils and thickens. Simmer for 2–3 minutes, stirring all the time. Season to taste with salt, freshly ground black pepper and grated nutmeg.

6 Pour the sauce over the stuffed cannelloni and sprinkle with the grated Parmesan cheese. Bake for 30–45 minutes, or until the top is golden and bubbling. Serve immediately.

COOK'S TIP
Smoked trout can be bought as fillets or as whole fish. Look for them in the chiller cabinet of the supermarket.

SEAFOOD LASAGNE

THIS DISH CAN BE AS SIMPLE OR AS ELEGANT AS YOU LIKE. FOR A DINNER PARTY, DRESS IT UP WITH SCALLOPS, MUSSELS OR PRAWNS AND A REALLY GENEROUS PINCH OF SAFFRON IN THE SAUCE; FOR A FAMILY SUPPER, USE SIMPLE FISH SUCH AS COD AND SMOKED HADDOCK.

SERVES 8

INGREDIENTS

350g/12oz monkfish
350g/12oz salmon fillet
350g/12oz undyed smoked haddock
1 litre/1¾ pints/4 cups milk
500ml/17fl oz/2¼ cups fish stock
2 bay leaves or a good pinch of
   saffron threads
1 small onion, halved
75g/3oz/6 tbsp butter, plus extra
   for greasing
45ml/3 tbsp plain (all-purpose) flour
150g/5oz/2 cups mushrooms,
   sliced
225–300g/8–11oz no pre-cook or
   fresh lasagne
60ml/4 tbsp freshly grated
   Parmesan cheese
salt, ground black pepper, grated
   nutmeg and paprika
rocket (arugula) leaves,
   to garnish

For the tomato sauce
30ml/2 tbsp olive oil
1 red onion, finely chopped
1 garlic clove, finely chopped
400g/14oz can chopped tomatoes
15ml/1 tbsp tomato purée (paste)
15ml/1 tbsp torn fresh basil leaves

1 Make the tomato sauce. Heat the oil in a pan and fry the onion and garlic over a low heat for 5 minutes, until softened and golden. Stir in the tomatoes and tomato purée and simmer for 20–30 minutes, stirring occasionally. Season and stir in the basil.

2 Put all the fish in a shallow flameproof dish or pan with the milk, stock, bay leaves or saffron and onion. Bring to the boil over a medium heat; poach for 5 minutes, until almost cooked.

3 When the fish is almost cold, lift it out of the pan and place on a board. Strain the liquid and reserve it. Remove skin and any bones, then flake the fish.

4 Preheat the oven to 180°C/350°F/Gas 4. Melt the butter in a pan and stir in the flour. Cook for 2 minutes, stirring. Gradually add the poaching liquid and bring to the boil, stirring. Stir in the mushrooms. Cook for 2–3 minutes, then season with salt, pepper and nutmeg.

5 Lightly grease a shallow ovenproof dish. Spoon a thin layer of the mushroom sauce over the base of the dish and spread it with a spatula. Stir the fish into the remaining mushroom sauce in the pan.

6 Make a layer of lasagne, then a layer of fish and sauce. Add another layer of lasagne, then spread over all the tomato sauce. Continue to layer the lasagne and fish, finishing with a layer of fish and sauce.

7 Sprinkle over the grated Parmesan cheese. Bake for 30–45 minutes, until bubbling and golden. Remove from the oven and leave to stand for 10 minutes. Sprinkle with paprika. Garnish with rocket leaves and serve.

COOK'S TIP
Use fresh lasagne, if available. Cook the sheets in a large pan of lightly salted boiling water for 3 minutes. Do not overcrowd the pan or the sheets will stick together.

LIGHT AND HEALTHY

Low in calories, but high in the essential fatty acids that are vital for good health, salmon is an important ingredient in a healthy diet. That doesn't mean, however, that all the recipes in this book are tailored to those who are trying to trim their weight. Elsewhere you'll find cream sauces, pastry and flavoured butters, but in this chapter the emphasis is on sensible eating. Dishes include Haddock and Smoked Salmon Terrine, Rice Cakes with Smoked Salmon, and Marinated Salmon with Avocado — delicious but without a hint of self-denial.

GARLIC BAKED TROUT WITH AVOCADO SALAD

PACKED FULL OF FLAVOUR AND WITH PLENTY OF VITAMINS AND MINERALS, THIS BAKED TROUT IS A VERSATILE MAIN DISH. SERVE IT AS SOON AS THE TROUT COMES OUT OF THE OVEN, WITH NEW POTATOES, OR COLD WITH COUNTRY BREAD. IF THE LATTER, DRESS THE SALAD JUST BEFORE SERVING.

SERVES 4

INGREDIENTS
6 plum tomatoes, halved
2 garlic cloves, thinly sliced
15g/½oz/½ cup fresh basil leaves
45ml/3 tbsp olive oil
4 trout fillets, each about
  200g/7oz, skinned
2 avocados
juice of 1 lime
75g/3oz watercress, land cress
  or rocket (arugula)
salt and ground black pepper
lime wedges, to garnish

VARIATION
If you want to add extra piquancy to this dish, serve it with a spoonful of chunky avocado salsa. To make the salsa, halve 1 ripe avocado and remove the stone (pit). Peel and dice the flesh and toss in 5ml/1 tsp lemon juice, in a bowl, to prevent the avocado browning. Dice a 2.5cm/1in piece of cucumber and add to the avocado. Finely chop half a red chilli and stir well so that all the ingredients are combined. Cover with clear film (plastic wrap) until ready to serve.

COOK'S TIP
To remove the stone from an avocado, cut the avocado in half lengthways, then tap the stone with the blade of a sharp knife. When you pull the knife away from the avocado the stone will come away from the flesh.

1 Preheat the oven to 180°C/350°F/ Gas 4. Place the tomatoes on a baking tray lined with baking parchment.

2 Sprinkle the garlic and basil over the tomatoes and season well with black pepper. Drizzle 15ml/1 tbsp of the olive oil over and bake for 25 minutes. Remove from the oven.

3 Using a spatula, move the tomato halves closer together, if necessary, to make room for the trout. Place the fillets on the baking tray. Return the tray to the oven for a further 15 minutes.

4 Test the fish with a fork to check it is cooked through: if the flesh flakes easily it is ready. Remove the baking tray from the oven.

5 Meanwhile, cut the avocados in half, remove the stone (pit) and peel, then slice the flesh lengthways into fine pieces.

6 In a small jug (pitcher), whisk the lime juice with the remaining olive oil. Season the dressing with salt and plenty of ground black pepper.

7 Divide the watercress, land cress or rocket among four individual serving plates. Top with the avocado slices. Drizzle the lime dressing over.

8 Using a fish slice, lift the cooked trout fillets carefully off the baking tray and place them on a board.

9 Arrange the cooked tomatoes over the salad leaves and pour over any cooking juices that have accumulated on the baking parchment.

10 Flake the trout into bitesize pieces and divide among the plates, arranging it attractively amongst the salad leaves. Garnish the plates with the lime wedges and serve.

TROUT WITH ORANGE SAUCE

STUFFING TROUT WITH MUSHROOMS AND PARSLEY NOT ONLY ADDS A NEW FLAVOUR DIMENSION BUT ALSO MAKES THE MEAL MORE SUBSTANTIAL. TANGY ORANGE SAUCE IS A PERFECT ACCOMPANIMENT.

SERVES 4

INGREDIENTS
    4 whole trout, each about
      175g/6oz, cleaned
    25g/1oz/2 tbsp butter
    1 small onion, finely chopped
    50g/2oz/¾ cup button (white)
      mushrooms, chopped
    25g/1oz/½ cup fresh white
      breadcrumbs
    30ml/2 tbsp chopped fresh
      parsley
    1 egg, beaten
    juice of 2 oranges
    salt and ground black pepper
    fresh dill sprigs, to garnish

For the orange sauce
    25g/1oz/2 tbsp butter
    pinch of caster (superfine) sugar
    1 orange, thinly sliced
    juice of 1 orange
    juice of ½ lemon

1 Remove the heads and gills from the trout. Rinse the cavities thoroughly and bone the fish to make them easier to stuff.

2 Preheat the oven to 190ºC/375ºF/ Gas 5. Melt the butter in a small pan, and fry the onion over a medium heat for 4–5 minutes until translucent.

3 Add the mushrooms to the pan and fry for a further minute. Remove from the heat and stir in the breadcrumbs, parsley and egg. Season with plenty of salt and black pepper.

4 Stuff each trout with one-quarter of the mixture, pressing the mixture firmly to distribute evenly and enclose it securely in the fish.

5 Season the trout well and place in a single layer in a shallow baking dish. Pour over the orange juice. Cover the dish with foil. Cook for 20–25 minutes or until the trout are cooked through.

6 Meanwhile, make the sauce. Melt the butter in a frying pan and add the sugar. Add the orange slices to the pan and brown on both sides. Add the orange and lemon juice and stir well. Cook for 2–3 minutes, then remove from the heat.

7 Carefully lift the cooked trout out of the dish, reserving the cooking liquid. Place the fish on a hot serving dish, cover with foil and keep warm in the oven.

8 Add the cooking liquid to the sauce in the frying pan and stir well. Garnish the stuffed trout with the orange slices and dill sprigs, then pour the orange sauce over and serve.

SMOKED TROUT SALAD

HORSERADISH IS AS GOOD A PARTNER TO SMOKED TROUT AS IT IS TO ROAST BEEF. IN THIS RECIPE IT IS MIXED WITH YOGURT, MUSTARD POWDER, OIL AND VINEGAR TO MAKE A DELICIOUSLY PIQUANT LIGHT SALAD DRESSING THAT COMPLEMENTS THE SMOKED TROUT PERFECTLY.

SERVES 4

INGREDIENTS
  1 oakleaf or other red lettuce
  225g/8oz small tomatoes, cut into
    thin wedges
  ½ cucumber, peeled and thinly
    sliced
  4 smoked trout fillets, each about
    200g/7oz, skinned and flaked

For the dressing
  pinch of mustard powder
  15–20ml/3–4 tsp white wine vinegar
  30ml/2 tbsp light olive oil
  100ml/3½fl oz/scant ½ cup natural
    (plain) yogurt
  about 30ml/2 tbsp grated fresh or
    bottled horseradish
  pinch of caster (superfine) sugar

1 Make the dressing. Mix the mustard powder and white wine vinegar in a bowl, then gradually whisk in the olive oil, yogurt, horseradish and sugar. Set aside for 30 minutes to allow all the flavours to develop.

COOK'S TIP
Fresh grated horseradish varies in potency. If it is very strong, whisk only half the suggested amount into the dressing. If the only horseradish you can find is the creamed variety, you can still use it in the recipe, but mix it with the yogurt first.

2 Place the lettuce leaves in a large bowl. Stir the dressing again, then pour half of it over the leaves and toss them lightly using two wooden spoons.

3 Arrange the lettuce on four individual plates with the tomatoes, cucumber and trout. Spoon over the remaining dressing and serve immediately.

RICE CAKES WITH SMOKED SALMON

THESE ELEGANT RICE CAKES ARE MADE USING A RISOTTO BASE. YOU COULD SKIP THIS STAGE AND USE LEFTOVER SEAFOOD OR MUSHROOM RISOTTO INSTEAD. A TOMATO RISOTTO WOULD ALSO WORK WELL.

SERVES 4

INGREDIENTS

  30ml/2 tbsp olive oil
  1 medium onion, chopped
  225g/8oz/generous 1 cup risotto rice
  about 90ml/6 tbsp white wine
  about 750ml/1¼ pints/3 cups fish or
    chicken stock
  15g/½oz/2 tbsp dried porcini
    mushrooms, soaked for 10 minutes
    in warm water to cover
  15ml/1 tbsp chopped fresh parsley
  15ml/1 tbsp chopped fresh chives
  5ml/1 tsp chopped fresh dill
  1 egg, lightly beaten
  about 45ml/3 tbsp ground rice, plus
    extra for dusting
  oil, for frying
  60ml/4 tbsp sour cream
  175g/6oz smoked salmon
  salt and ground black pepper
  radicchio and oakleaf salad, tossed in
    French dressing, to serve

3 Add the beaten egg, then stir in enough ground rice to bind the mixture – it should be soft but manageable. Dust your hands with ground rice and shape the mixture into four patties, each about 13cm/5in in diameter and about 2cm/¾in thick.

4 Heat the oil and fry the rice cakes for 4–5 minutes until browned on both sides. Drain and cool slightly. Place each rice cake on a plate and top with 15ml/1 tbsp sour cream. Twist two or three slices of smoked salmon on top, and serve with a dressed salad garnish.

1 Heat the olive oil in a pan and fry the onion for 3–4 minutes until soft. Add the rice and cook, stirring, until the grains are thoroughly coated in oil. Pour in the wine and stock, a little at a time, stirring constantly over a gentle heat until each quantity of liquid has been absorbed before adding more.

2 Drain the mushrooms and chop them into small pieces. When the rice is tender, and all the liquid has been absorbed, stir in the mushrooms, parsley, chives and dill, with salt and pepper to taste. Remove from the heat and set aside for a few minutes to cool.

SPICED TROUT SALAD

MOST OF THE PREPARATION FOR THIS DELICIOUS SALAD IS DONE IN ADVANCE SO IT IS AN IDEAL DISH TO COME HOME TO AFTER A DAY ON THE BEACH OR AN AFTERNOON WALK. THE TROUT IS MARINATED IN A MIXTURE OF CORIANDER, GINGER AND CHILLI AND SERVED WITH COLD BABY ROAST POTATOES.

SERVES 4

INGREDIENTS
   2.5cm/1in piece fresh root ginger,
     peeled and finely grated
   1 garlic clove, crushed
   5ml/1 tsp hot chilli powder
   15ml/1 tbsp coriander seeds,
     lightly crushed
   grated rind and juice of 2 lemons
   60ml/4 tbsp olive oil
   450g/1lb trout fillet, skinned
   900g/2lb new potatoes
   5–10ml/1–2 tsp sea salt
   ground black pepper
   15ml/1 tbsp whole or chopped fresh
     chives, to garnish

1 Mix the ginger, garlic, chilli powder, coriander seeds and lemon rind in a bowl. Whisk in the lemon juice with 15ml/1 tbsp of the olive oil to make a marinade.

2 Place the trout in a shallow, non-metallic dish and cover with the marinade. Turn the fish to make sure they are well coated, cover with clear film (plastic wrap) and chill for at least 2 hours or overnight.

COOK'S TIP
Look for firm pieces of fresh root ginger, with smooth skin. If bought really fresh, root ginger will keep for up to two weeks in a cool, dry place, away from strong light. Root ginger freezes successfully and can be shaved or grated straight from the freezer.

3 Preheat the oven to 200°C/400°F/Gas 6. Place the potatoes in a roasting pan, toss them in 30ml/2 tbsp olive oil and season with salt and pepper. Roast for 45 minutes or until tender. Remove from the oven and set aside to cool.

4 Reduce the oven temperature to 190°C/375°F/Gas 5. Remove the trout from the marinade and place in a roasting pan. Bake for 20 minutes or until cooked through. Remove from the oven and leave to cool.

5 Cut the potatoes into chunks, flake the trout into bitesize pieces and toss them together in a serving dish with the remaining olive oil. Sprinkle with the chives and serve.

VARIATION
If you don't like spicy hot food, omit the chilli powder in the marinade – the trout tastes equally good without it.

MARINATED SALMON WITH AVOCADO

USE ONLY THE FRESHEST OF SALMON FOR THIS DELICIOUS SALAD. THE MARINADE OF LEMON AND DASHI-KONBU "COOKS" THE SALMON, WHICH IS SERVED WITH AVOCADO, ALMONDS AND SALAD LEAVES.

2 Pour the lemon juice and put two of the dashi-konbu pieces into a wide shallow plastic container. Lay the salmon fillets in the base and sprinkle with the rest of the dashi-konbu. Marinate for 15 minutes, then turn once and leave for 15 minutes more. Drain and pat dry with kitchen paper.

3 Holding a very sharp knife at an angle, cut the salmon into 5mm/¼in thick slices against the grain.

4 Halve the avocado and brush the cut surface with a little of the remaining salmon marinade. Remove the avocado stone (pit) and skin, then carefully slice to the same thickness as the salmon.

SERVES 4

INGREDIENTS
   250g/9oz very fresh salmon tail, skinned and filleted
   juice of 1 lemon
   10cm/4in dashi-konbu (dried kelp seaweed), wiped with a damp cloth and cut into 4 strips
   1 ripe avocado
   4 shiso leaves, stalks removed and cut in half lengthways
   about 115g/4oz mixed leaves such as lamb's lettuce, frisée or rocket (arugula)
   45ml/3 tbsp flaked or sliced almonds, toasted in a dry frying pan

For the miso mayonnaise
   90ml/6 tbsp good-quality mayonnaise
   15ml/1 tbsp shiro miso
   ground black pepper
   15ml/1 tbsp lemon juice

1 Cut the first salmon fillet in half crossways at the tail end where the fillet is not wider than 4cm/1½in. Next, cut the wider part in half lengthways. This means the fillet from one side is cut into three. Cut the other fillet into three pieces in the same way.

COOK'S TIP
Shiro miso, fermented soya bean paste, can be bought at Japanese food stores.

5 Make miso mayonnaise by mixing the mayonnaise, shiro miso and pepper in a small bowl. Spread about 5ml/1 tsp on to the back of each of the shiso leaves, then mix the remainder with the lemon juice to loosen the mayonnaise.

6 Arrange the salad on four plates. Top with the avocado, salmon, shiso leaves and almonds. Drizzle over the remaining miso mayonnaise. Serve immediately.

HADDOCK AND SMOKED SALMON TERRINE

THIS SUBSTANTIAL TERRINE MAKES A SUPERB DISH FOR A SUMMER BUFFET, ACCOMPANIED BY DILL MAYONNAISE OR A FRESH MANGO SALSA.

SERVES 6–8

INGREDIENTS
  15ml/1 tbsp sunflower oil,
    for greasing
  350g/12oz oak-smoked salmon
  900g/2lb haddock fillets, skinned
  2 eggs, lightly beaten
  105ml/7 tbsp low-fat crème fraîche
    or sour cream
  30ml/2 tbsp drained bottled capers
  30ml/2 tbsp drained soft green or
    pink peppercorns
  salt and ground white pepper
  low-fat crème fraîche or sour cream,
    peppercorns and fresh dill and
    rocket (arugula), to garnish

3 Combine the eggs, crème fraîche or sour cream, capers and soft peppercorns in a bowl. Season with salt and white pepper, then stir in the small pieces of haddock. Spoon half the mixture into the mould. Smooth the surface with a spatula.

6 Tap the terrine to settle the contents, then stand it in a roasting pan and pour in boiling water to come halfway up the sides of the terrine. Place in the oven and cook for 45 minutes–1 hour, until the filling is just set.

1 Preheat the oven to 200°C/400°F/Gas 6. Grease a 1 litre/1¾ pint/4 cup loaf pan or terrine. Use some of the salmon to line the pan or terrine; let some of the ends overhang the mould. Reserve the remaining smoked salmon.

4 Wrap the long haddock fillets in the reserved smoked salmon. Don't worry if there isn't enough salmon to cover them completely. Lay the wrapped haddock fillets on top of the fish mixture in the pan or terrine.

7 Take the terrine out of the roasting pan, but do not remove the foil cover. Place two or three large heavy cans on the foil to weight it and leave until cold. Chill in the refrigerator for 24 hours.

8 About 1 hour before serving, remove the terrine from the refrigerator, lift off the weights and remove the foil. Carefully invert the terrine on to a serving plate and lift off the pan or terrine.

9 Cut the terrine into thick slices, using a sharp knife. Serve, garnished with crème fraîche or sour cream, peppercorns and fronds of dill and rocket leaves.

2 Cut two long slices of haddock the length of the pan or terrine and set aside. Cut the rest of the haddock into small pieces. Season all the haddock with salt and pepper.

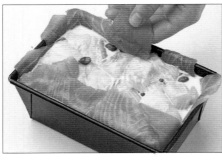

5 Fill the pan or terrine with the rest of the fish mixture, smooth the surface and fold the overhanging pieces of smoked salmon over the top. Cover tightly with a double thickness of foil.

COOK'S TIP
A perfectly clean house brick, wrapped in clear film (plastic wrap) can be used instead of the cans to weight the terrine.

LEMONY SALMON LOAF WITH CUCUMBER

CHOOSE CANNED RED SALMON RATHER THAN THE PINK VARIETY FOR THIS EASY ALL-IN-ONE LOAF AS THE FLAVOUR AND TEXTURE ARE MUCH IMPROVED. THIS LOAF IS IDEAL FOR PICNICS OR IT CAN BE SERVED WITH THE CUCUMBER SAUCE AS A LIGHT SUMMER LUNCH OR SUPPER DISH.

SERVES 4–6

INGREDIENTS
150ml/¼ pint/⅔ cup milk
2 eggs, beaten
115g/4oz/2 cups fresh white
  breadcrumbs
butter, for greasing
75g/3oz celery
400g/14oz can salmon, drained
grated rind and juice of 1 lemon
salt and ground black pepper
lemon slices, to garnish

For the sauce
1 cucumber, peeled, seeded
  and chopped
25g/1oz/2 tbsp butter
15ml/1 tbsp plain (all-purpose)
  flour
rind and juice of ½ lemon
1 egg yolk

1 Mix the milk, eggs and breadcrumbs in a large bowl and leave to stand for 10 minutes.

2 Preheat the oven to 180°C/350°F/ Gas 4. Grease a 450g/1lb loaf tin (pan) with butter. Chop the celery finely and set it aside.

3 Place the drained salmon in a bowl and flake with a fork. Add to the breadcrumb mixture with the chopped celery, grated lemon rind and juice. Season with salt and pepper to taste.

4 Stir the mixture until evenly blended. Pour into the prepared loaf tin and bake for 1 hour or until a skewer inserted into the centre of the loaf comes out clean. Leave the loaf in the tin to cool slightly.

5 Make the sauce. Place the cucumber pieces in a small pan, cover with cold water and simmer until just tender. Using a slotted spoon, remove the cucumber and set it aside. Pour the cooking liquid into a measuring jug (cup). Add enough water to make up the liquid to 300ml/½ pint/1¼ cups.

6 Melt the butter in the clean pan. Stir in the flour using a wooden spoon. Cook, stirring constantly, for 1 minute, then gradually add the reserved liquid, stirring until it boils and thickens.

7 Add the lemon rind and juice to the sauce in the pan, then stir in the cooked cucumber. Beat the egg yolk in a separate container and stir in a little of the hot sauce. Pour into the pan and heat gently, without boiling, until the sauce thickens a little more. Season to taste with salt and ground black pepper.

8 Using a spatula, loosen the salmon loaf from the sides of the tin and invert it on a serving dish. Garnish the loaf with lemon slices. Serve the warm cucumber sauce on the side.

VARIATION
Fennel could be used instead of the celery. It has a delicious taste and goes well with salmon. Quarter and core a fennel bulb, saving the fronds to add to the garnish for the loaf. Chop the fennel finely and toss it with the lemon juice so that it doesn't discolour.

COOK'S TIP
Lining the base of the loaf tin (pan) with non-stick baking parchment will make it easier to unmould the loaf.

SALMON WITH ROASTED VEGETABLES

THIS COLOURFUL AND TASTY DISH IS PERFECT FOR A SUMMER MEAL, AND BECAUSE IT IS SO EASY TO COOK, YOU DON'T HAVE TO SPEND TIME IN THE KITCHEN WHEN YOU COULD BE SOAKING UP THE SUN.

SERVES 4

INGREDIENTS

175g/6oz green beans, trimmed
1 red (bell) pepper, seeded
   and sliced
1 yellow (bell) pepper, seeded
   and sliced
16 cherry tomatoes, halved
50g/2oz/½ cup pitted
   black olives
50g/2oz/½ cup pitted
   green olives
30ml/2 tbsp garlic-flavoured olive oil
4 salmon fillets, each about
   200g/7oz
juice of ½ lemon
30ml/2 tbsp olive oil
1 bunch fresh basil, leaves stripped
   from stems
salt and ground black pepper
walnut bread and olive oil, to serve

1 Preheat the oven to 220°C/425°F/ Gas 7. Bring a pan of lightly salted water to the boil. Add the trimmed green beans and cook them over a medium heat until they are just tender.

2 Drain the green beans very well, then put them into a large bowl. Add the red and yellow peppers, the tomatoes and the olives. Season well, drizzle the garlic oil over and stir to coat.

3 Place the salmon fillets in a single layer in a roasting pan. Pour over the lemon juice and olive oil. Turn the salmon fillets to coat them in the mixture. Season with salt and pepper.

4 Spoon the vegetable mixture into a separate roasting pan. Set aside eight basil leaves for the garnish, and tuck the rest among the vegetables.

5 Place both roasting pans in the oven, with the vegetables on a higher shelf than the fish. Bake for about 15 minutes or until the fish is opaque and the vegetables are just beginning to char at the edges.

6 To serve, arrange the vegetables on four serving plates. Top each portion with a salmon fillet and garnish with the reserved basil leaves. Serve with walnut bread and olive oil for dipping.

VARIATION
This dish works well with any thick fish fillets – try it with tuna or cod for a change.

BLUE TROUT

THE BLUE SHEEN OF BLAUE FORELLE IS A GERMAN SPECIALITY AND IS EASILY ACHIEVED BY FIRST SCALDING THE FISH AND THEN FANNING TO COOL IT. TRADITIONALLY, THE FISH WOULD BE LEFT TO COOL BY THE KITCHEN WINDOW IN A BREEZE OR DRAUGHT.

SERVES 4

INGREDIENTS

4 trout, about 175g/6oz each
5ml/1 tsp salt
600ml/1 pint/2½ cups white
   wine vinegar
1 onion, sliced
2 bay leaves
6 whole black peppercorns
bay leaves and lemon slices,
   to garnish
115g/4oz/½ cup melted butter,
   creamed horseradish sauce and
   green beans, to serve

1 Preheat the oven to 180°C/350°F/Gas 4. Rub both sides of the trout with salt and place in a non-aluminium roasting tin or fish kettle.

2 Bring the vinegar to the boil and slowly pour over the trout. Fan the fish as it cools or leave to stand in a draught for 5 minutes.

3 Bring the vinegar back to the boil, then add the sliced onion, bay leaves and peppercorns.

4 Cover the tin with foil and cook in the oven for 30 minutes, or until the fish is cooked through.

5 Transfer the fish to warmed serving dishes, garnish with bay leaves and lemon slices, and serve with melted butter, creamed horseradish sauce and green beans.

COOK'S TIPS
• This method of cooking is used for freshwater trout – as well as other types of freshwater fish, such as carp, trench or pike – that are either still alive or exceedingly fresh. If the fish is alive it should first be stunned by hitting the back of its head with a wooden mallet. It will then need to be cleaned through the gills and rinsed and dried before being rubbed with salt.
• Sprinkling boiling vinegar over the fish turns the slime on its skin a steely blue colour, hence the name "au bleu".
• The cooked fish can be served either hot or cold.
• If necessary, the fish should be scaled before being served. Using a fish scaler will make this task straightforward.

COMPRESSED SUSHI WITH SMOKED SALMON

THIS SIMPLE RECIPE OF VINEGARED RICE WITH SMOKED SALMON IS AN EXCELLENT INTRODUCTION TO THE ANCIENT ART OF SUSHI AND IS IDEAL FOR ANYONE NERVOUS ABOUT EATING RAW FISH.

MAKES ABOUT 12

INGREDIENTS

200g/7oz/1 cup Japanese short grain rice, soaked for 20 minutes in water to cover
250ml/8fl oz/1 cup water
40ml/8 tsp rice vinegar, plus extra for moulding
20ml/4 tsp caster (superfine) sugar
5ml/1 tsp salt
175g/6oz smoked salmon, thickly sliced
15ml/1 tbsp sake
15ml/1 tbsp water
30ml/2 tbsp shoyu (Japanese soy sauce)
1 lemon, thinly sliced into 6 x 3mm/⅛in rings

1 Drain the rice, then put it in a pan with the measured water. Bring to the boil, then reduce the heat, cover and simmer for 20 minutes, until all the water has been absorbed. Meanwhile, heat the vinegar, sugar and salt in a pan, stir well and cool. Fold into the hot rice, then remove from the heat, cover and leave to stand for 20 minutes.

2 Lay the smoked salmon on a chopping board and sprinkle with a mixture of the sake, water and shoyu. Leave to marinate for 1 hour, then wipe dry with kitchen paper.

3 Wet a wooden Japanese sushi mould or line a 25 x 7.5 x 5cm/10 x 3 x 2in plastic container with a large sheet of clear film (plastic wrap), allowing the edges to hang over.

4 Spread half the smoked salmon to evenly cover the bottom of the mould or container. Add one-quarter of the cooked rice and firmly press down with hands dampened with rice vinegar to make a layer 1cm/½in thick. Add the remainder of the salmon, and press the remaining rice on top.

5 Put the wet wooden lid on the mould, or cover the plastic container with the overhanging clear film. Place a weight, such as a heavy dinner plate, on top. Leave in a cool place overnight, or for at least 3 hours. If you use the refrigerator, place the mould in the least cool part, such as on the top shelf.

6 Remove the compressed sushi from the mould or container and unwrap. Cut into 2cm/¾in slices and serve on a Japanese lacquered tray or a large plate. Quarter the lemon rings. Garnish each piece of sushi with two pieces of lemon and serve.

SALMON AND VEGETABLES IN A PARCEL

FOR THIS DELIGHTFUL JAPANESE RECIPE, SALMON IS STEAMED WITH SAKE AND BEAUTIFULLY CARVED
VEGETABLES IN A FOIL PARCEL. WHEN THE PARCELS ARE OPENED, THE CONTENTS LOOK LOVELY.

SERVES 4

INGREDIENTS
500g/1¼lb salmon fillet, skinned
30ml/2 tbsp sake
15ml/1 tbsp shoyu (Japanese soy
  sauce), plus extra to serve (optional)
about 250g/9oz/3 cups fresh
  shimeji mushrooms
8 fresh shiitake mushrooms
2.5cm/1in piece of carrot
4 spring onions (scallions)
115g/4oz/1 cup mangetouts
  (snow peas)
salt

1 Preheat the oven to 190°C/375°F/Gas 5. Cut the salmon into bitesize pieces. Place in a shallow bowl and add the sake and shoyu. Marinate for about 15 minutes. Drain and reserve the marinade.

2 Clean the shimeji mushrooms and chop off the hard root from each. Remove and discard the stalks from the shiitake. Carve a shallow slit on the top of each shiitake with a sharp knife inserted at a slant. Repeat from the other side to cut out a notch about 4cm/1½in long. Rotate the shiitake 90° and carve another notch to make a small white cross in the brown top.

3 Slice the carrot very thinly, then use a Japanese vegetable cutter or sharp knife to cut out 8–12 maple-leaf or flower shapes. Carefully slice the spring onions in half lengthways with a sharp knife. Trim the mangetouts.

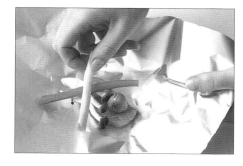

4 Cut four sheets of foil, each about 29 x 21cm/11½ x 8½in. With the long side of one sheet facing you, arrange the salmon and shimeji mushrooms in the centre, then place a spring onion diagonally across them. Put two shiitake on top, three or four mangetouts in a fan shape and then sprinkle with a few carrot shapes.

5 Sprinkle the marinade and a good pinch of salt over the top. Fold the two longer sides of the foil together, then fold the shorter sides to seal. Repeat to make four parcels.

6 Place the parcels on a baking sheet and bake for 15–20 minutes in the middle of the preheated oven. When the foil has expanded into a balloon, the dish is ready to serve. Take the parcels to the table unopened and offer a little extra shoyu, if required.

HAND-MOULDED SUSHI

IF YOU HAVE ACCESS TO QUALITY SEAFOOD AT THE PEAK OF FRESHNESS, THIS IS A WONDERFUL WAY OF APPRECIATING ITS SUPERB NATURAL FLAVOUR.

SERVES 4

INGREDIENTS
  400g/14oz/2 cups Japanese short
    grain rice, soaked for 20 minutes
    in water to cover
  500ml/18fl oz/2½ cups water
  55ml/3½ tbsp rice vinegar, plus
    extra for moulding
  30ml/2 tbsp caster (superfine) sugar
  10ml/2 tsp salt
  4 raw king prawns (jumbo shrimp),
    head and shell removed, tails intact
  4 scallops, white muscle only
  425g/15oz assorted very fresh fish,
    such as salmon, tuna, sea bass
    and mackerel, skinned, cleaned
    and filleted
  45ml/3 tbsp wasabi paste from
    a tube, or the same amount of
    wasabi powder mixed with 15ml/
    1 tbsp water
pickled ginger, to garnish
shoyu (Japanese soy sauce), to serve

COOK'S TIP
For moulding the vinegared rice, wet your fingers frequently, by dipping them in a bowl containing a mixture of 150ml/¼ pint/⅔ cup water and 15ml/1 tbsp rice vinegar.

1 Drain the rice, then put it in a pan with the measured water. Bring to the boil, then reduce the heat, cover and simmer for 20 minutes, until all the water has been absorbed. Meanwhile, heat the vinegar, sugar and salt in a pan, stir well and cool. Fold into the hot rice, then remove the pan from the heat, cover and leave to stand for 20 minutes.

2 Insert a bamboo skewer or cocktail stick (toothpick) into each prawn lengthways. This stops the prawns curling up when cooked. Boil them in lightly salted water for 2 minutes, or until they turn pink. Drain and cool, then pull out the skewers. Cut open from the belly side but do not slice in two. With the point of a sharp knife, remove the black vein running down the back. Open each prawn out flat and place on a tray.

3 Slice the scallops horizontally in half, but not quite through. Gently open each scallop at this "hinge" to make a butterfly shape. Place on the tray, cut side down. Use a sharp knife to cut all the fish fillets into 7.5 x 4cm/3 x 1½in pieces, 5mm/¼in thick. Place all the raw fish and shellfish on the tray, cover with clear film (plastic wrap), then chill in the refrigerator for at least 1 hour, or up to 4 hours.

4 Spoon the vinegared rice into a bowl. Have ready a small bowl filled with water acidulated with rice vinegar for moulding (see Cook's Tip). Take the tray of seafood from the refrigerator.

5 Wet your hand with the vinegared water and scoop about 25ml/1½ tbsp vinegared rice into your palm. Gently but firmly grip it to make a rectangular block. Do not squash the rice, but ensure that the grains stick together. The size of the blocks must be smaller than the toppings.

6 Put the rice block on a damp chopping board. Taking a piece of salmon topping in your palm, rub a little wasabi paste in the middle of it. Put the rice block on top of the salmon and gently press it. Form your palm into a cup and shape the topped rice to a smooth-surfaced mound. Place it on a serving tray. Work quickly, or the warmth of your hands may cause the salmon to lose its freshness.

7 Repeat this process until all of the rice and toppings are used. Serve immediately with a little shoyu dribbled on individual plates. To eat, pick up a hand-moulded sushi and dip the tip into the shoyu. Eat a little pickled ginger between tasting different sushi to refresh your mouth and prepare yourself for a new flavour sensation.

MOOLI LAYERED WITH SMOKED SALMON

THIS TRADITIONAL JAPANESE RECIPE ORIGINALLY CALLED FOR SALTED SLICED SALMON AND MOOLI TO BE PICKLED IN A WOODEN BARREL FOR A LONG TIME. THIS VERSION IS LESS SALTY AND FAR QUICKER.

1 Slice the mooli very thinly into rounds. Put in a shallow container, sprinkle with salt and vinegar, and add the chopped dashi-konbu. Mix and rub gently with your hands. Cover and leave in the refrigerator for 1 hour.

2 Drain in a sieve and squeeze out the excess liquid. If necessary, rinse with running water for 30 seconds, then drain and squeeze out again.

3 Cut the smoked salmon slices into 4cm/1½in squares. Take one slice of mooli, top with a salmon slice, then cover with another mooli slice. Repeat until all the salmon is used. Place in a shallow container, cover with clear film (plastic wrap), then leave to pickle at room temperature for up to 1 day.

4 Arrange the mooli rounds on a serving plate and put a pinch of poppy seeds in the centre.

SERVES 4

INGREDIENTS
  10cm/4in mooli (daikon), about
    6cm/2½in in diameter, peeled
  10ml/2 tsp salt
  5ml/1 tsp rice vinegar
  5cm/2in square dashi-konbu (dried
    kelp seaweed), chopped into
    1cm/½in strips
  50g/2oz smoked salmon, thinly sliced
  2.5ml/½ tsp white poppy seeds

COOK'S TIPS
• Use a good quality smoked salmon for this recipe as the flavour of cheaper varieties is often obscured, if not lost altogether, by the smoking process. The salmon must also be absolutely fresh.
• Nowadays mooli is available from most large supermarkets, but look in Japanese food stores and markets if you have difficulty finding it.
• You can use a mandoline, a food cutter or a vegetable slicer to make paper-thin slices of mooli.
• Taste the mooli after salting and squeezing to check whether it needs to be rinsed. The degree of saltiness will depend on its original water content.

SALMON TERIYAKI

SAKE TERIYAKI IS A WELL-KNOWN JAPANESE DISH, WHICH USES A SWEET AND SHINY SAUCE FOR MARINATING AS WELL AS FOR GLAZING THE INGREDIENTS.

SERVES 4

INGREDIENTS

4 small salmon fillets with skin on,
each weighing about 150g/5oz
50g/2oz/1 cup beansprouts, washed
50g/2oz mangetouts (snow peas)
20g/¾oz carrot, cut into thin strips
salt

For the teriyaki sauce
45ml/3 tbsp shoyu (Japanese soy sauce)
45ml/3 tbsp sake
45ml/3 tbsp mirin or sweet sherry
15ml/1 tbsp plus 10ml/2 tsp caster
(superfine) sugar

1 Make the teriyaki sauce. Mix the shoyu, sake, mirin and 15ml/1 tbsp caster sugar in a pan. Heat, stirring, to dissolve the sugar. Cool for 1 hour.

2 Place the salmon fillets, skin side down, in a shallow glass or china dish. Pour over the teriyaki sauce. Leave to marinate for 30 minutes.

3 Meanwhile, bring a pan of lightly salted water to the boil. Add the beansprouts, then after 1 minute, the mangetouts. Leave for 1 minute then add the thin carrot strips. Remove the pan from the heat after 1 minute, then drain the vegetables and keep warm.

4 Preheat the grill (broiler) to medium. Take the salmon fillet out of the sauce and pat dry with kitchen paper. Reserve the sauce. Lightly oil a grilling (broiling) tray. Grill (broil) the salmon for about 6 minutes, turning once, until golden.

5 Meanwhile, pour the remaining teriyaki sauce into a small pan, add the remaining sugar and heat until dissolved. Brush the salmon with the sauce.

6 Continue to grill the salmon until the surface of the fish bubbles. Turn over and repeat on the other side.

7 Heap the vegetables on to serving plates. Place the salmon on top and spoon over the rest of the sauce.

COOK'S TIP
To save time, you could use ready-made teriyaki sauce for the marinade. This useful ingredient comes in bottles and is handy for marinating chicken before cooking it on the barbecue. Add a splash of sake, if you have some.

ON THE GRILL

Anglers swear the best place to eat salmon or trout is in the open air, and if these superb recipes are anything to go by, they are probably right. All the recipes in this chapter are cooked either on the barbecue or under the grill, so that they can be enjoyed outdoors. As the sun goes down, tuck into Salmon and Scallop Brochettes or Hot and Fragrant Trout, or sit on the patio and sample Salmon with Spicy Pesto. Oily fish can be smoked in a kettle barbecue. If you have one of these, you've a treat in store when you tuck into Hot Smoked Salmon.

HOT AND FRAGRANT TROUT

THIS WICKEDLY HOT MARINADE COULD BE USED WITH ANY FIRM-FLESHED FISH OR MEAT. IT ALSO MAKES A WONDERFUL SPICY DIP FOR GRILLED OR BARBECUED MEAT.

SERVES 4

INGREDIENTS

2 large fresh green chillies, seeded and roughly chopped
5 shallots, peeled
5 garlic cloves, peeled
30ml/2 tbsp fresh lime juice
30ml/2 tbsp Thai fish sauce
15ml/1 tbsp palm sugar or light muscovado (molasses) sugar
4 kaffir lime leaves, rolled into cigarette shapes and finely sliced
2 trout, about 350g/12oz each, cleaned

VARIATION
Slightly sweet coconut rice is the perfect accompaniment to this spicy trout. To make it, simply substitute coconut milk for half of the water in your usual rice recipe. Ready-to-use coconut milk is available in cartons and cans but you can make your own using a block of creamed coconut. Dissolve one 200g/ 7oz block creamed coconut in 400ml/ 14fl oz/1⅔ cup hot water. Use this amount for coconut rice for four people. If you don't use the whole block of creamed coconut, store the remainder in the refrigerator.

1 Wrap the green chillies, shallots and garlic cloves in a foil package. Place under a hot grill (broiler) for 10 minutes, until the vegetables have softened.

2 As soon as the foil package is cool enough to handle, unwrap it and tip the contents into a mortar or food processor. Blend to a paste. Add the lime juice, fish sauce, sugar and lime leaves and mix well.

3 With a teaspoon, stuff this paste inside the fish. Smear a little on the skin too. Grill (broil) the fish for about 5 minutes on each side, until just cooked through. Carefully lift the fish on to a platter. Serve with rice.

COOK'S TIPS
• Thai fish sauce (*nam pla*) is made from anchovies, which are salted, then fermented in wooden barrels. The sauce, which is ubiquitous in Thai cooking, accentuates the flavour of food.
• Kaffir lime leaves release a distinctive lemony flavour when roughly chopped or torn. They are obtainable in Asian food stores. They will keep for several days, or can be frozen.

SALMON AND SCALLOP BROCHETTES

USING LEMON GRASS AS SKEWERS ISN'T A CULINARY GIMMICK. THE SUBTLE FLAVOUR GIVES THE INGREDIENTS — IN THIS CASE, SALMON AND SCALLOPS — A FRAGRANCE THAT SEEMS PERFECTLY IN KEEPING WITH THE DELICACY OF THIS SUPERB DINNER DISH.

SERVES 4

INGREDIENTS

8 lemon grass stalks
225g/8oz salmon fillet, skinned
8 queen scallops, with their corals
  if possible
8 baby onions, peeled and blanched
½ yellow (bell) pepper, cut into
  eight squares
100g/4oz/½ cup butter
juice of ½ lemon
30ml/2 tbsp dry vermouth
5ml/1 tsp chopped fresh tarragon
salt, ground white pepper
  and paprika

1 Preheat the grill (broiler) to medium-high. Cut off the top 7.5–10cm/3–4in of each lemon grass stalk. Reserve the bulb ends for another dish. Cut the salmon fillet into twelve 2cm/¾in cubes. Thread the salmon, scallops, corals if available, onions and pepper squares on to the lemon grass sticks and arrange the brochettes side by side in a grill (broiler) pan.

2 Melt half the butter in a small pan, add the lemon juice and a pinch of paprika and then brush all over the brochettes. Grill (broil) the skewers for about 2–3 minutes on each side, turning and basting the brochettes every minute, until the fish and scallops are just cooked, but are still very juicy. Transfer to a platter and keep hot while you make the tarragon butter sauce.

3 Pour the dry vermouth and all the leftover cooking juices from the brochettes into a small pan and boil quite fiercely to reduce by half. Add the remaining butter and melt, stirring all the time. Stir in the chopped fresh tarragon and add salt and ground white pepper to taste. Pour the tarragon butter sauce over the brochettes and serve immediately.

CHEESE-TOPPED TROUT

FOR THIS SIMPLE YET SOPHISTICATED SUPPER DISH, SUCCULENT STRIPS OF FILLETED TROUT ARE TOPPED WITH A MIXTURE OF PARMESAN CHEESE, PINE NUTS, HERBS AND BREADCRUMBS BEFORE BEING DRIZZLED WITH LEMON BUTTER AND GRILLED UNTIL TENDER.

SERVES 4

INGREDIENTS
 50g/2oz/1 cup fresh white
  breadcrumbs
 50g/2oz Parmesan cheese, finely
  grated
 25g/1oz/⅓ cup pine nuts, chopped
 15ml/1 tbsp chopped fresh parsley
 15ml/1 tbsp chopped fresh coriander
  (cilantro)
 30ml/2 tbsp olive oil
 4 thick trout fillets, each about
  225g/8oz
 40g/1½oz/3 tbsp butter
 juice of 1 lemon
 salt and ground black pepper
 lemon slices, to garnish
 steamed baby asparagus and carrots,
  to serve

1 In a mixing bowl, combine the breadcrumbs, Parmesan cheese, pine nuts, parsley and coriander. Add the oil.

2 Cut each trout fillet into two strips. Firmly press the breadcrumb mixture on to the top of each strip of trout.

3 Preheat the grill (broiler) to high. Grease the grill pan with 15g/½oz of the butter. Melt the remaining butter in a small pan and stir in the lemon juice.

4 Place the breadcrumb-topped fillets on the greased grill pan and pour the lemon butter over.

5 Grill (broil) the trout for 10 minutes or until the fillets are just cooked. Place two trout strips on each plate, garnish with lemon slices and serve with steamed asparagus and carrots.

VARIATIONS
• It isn't essential to use pine nuts in the stuffing. Almonds would work well, or you could try hazelnuts.
• If you don't have any fresh coriander (cilantro), increase the amount of fresh parsley.
• Dried peaches or apricots could be chopped finely and added to the stuffing, with perhaps a little finely grated lemon rind to enhance the fruity flavour.

TROUT <u>IN</u> WINE SAUCE <u>WITH</u> PLANTAIN

*IN THE WEST INDIES, WHERE THIS RECIPE ORIGINATED, THE FISH USED WOULD PROBABLY BE
DOLPHINFISH OR SNAPPER, BUT THIS IS ALSO A WONDERFUL TREATMENT FOR TROUT.*

SERVES 4

INGREDIENTS
  4 trout fillets
  15ml/1 tbsp crushed garlic
  7.5ml/1½ tsp coarse-grain black pepper
  7.5ml/1½ tsp paprika
  7.5ml/1½ tsp celery salt
  7.5ml/1½ tsp curry powder
  5ml/1 tsp caster (superfine) sugar
  25g/1oz/2 tbsp butter
  150ml/¼ pint/⅔ cup white wine
  150ml/¼ pint/⅔ cup fish stock
  10ml/2 tsp clear honey
  15–30ml/1–2 tbsp chopped fresh
    parsley
  1 yellow plantain
  oil, for frying

1 Put the trout fillets in a dish. Mix the garlic, pepper, paprika, celery salt, curry powder and sugar in a bowl. Sprinkle over the trout and marinate for 1 hour.

2 Melt the butter in a large frying pan and sauté the marinated trout fillets, in batches if necessary, for about 5 minutes or until cooked through, turning once. Transfer to a warm plate and keep hot.

3 Add the wine, fish stock and honey to the pan. Bring to the boil and simmer to reduce slightly. Return the fillets to the pan and spoon over the sauce. Sprinkle with parsley and simmer gently for a few minutes.

4 Peel the plantain and cut it into rounds. Heat a little oil in a frying pan and fry the plantain until soft and golden brown, turning once.

5 Transfer the fish to warmed serving plates, stir the sauce and pour it over. Garnish with the fried plantain.

COOK'S TIP
This recipe can also be prepared on a barbecue. Cook the fish and wine sauce in a frying pan but wrap the unpeeled plantain in foil and bake it on the barbecue for about 10 minutes, or until tender, before cutting it into rounds.

SALMON KEBABS WITH COCONUT

*INSPIRED BY FLAVOURS FROM THE WEST INDIES, THIS RECIPE
COMBINES COCONUT AND LIME TO PROVIDE A COUNTERPOINT
TO THE SUBTLE TASTE OF SALMON AND SCALLOPS.*

SERVES 6

INGREDIENTS

    450g/1lb salmon fillet, skinned
    1 small fresh coconut
    2 limes
    12 scallops
    45ml/3 tbsp freshly squeezed
      lime juice
    30ml/2 tbsp soy sauce
    30ml/2 tbsp clear honey
    15ml/1 tbsp soft light brown sugar
    ground black pepper

1 Using a sharp knife, cut the salmon into bitesize chunks and place these in a shallow bowl.

2 Halve the coconut and pour the liquor into a jug (pitcher). Using a small, sharp knife, remove the coconut flesh from the inside of the shell and cut it into chunks, making them about the same size as the salmon.

3 Cut each lime into six thick slices. Thread the coconut, salmon, scallops and pieces of lime alternately on to six skewers.

4 Add the lime juice, soy sauce, honey and sugar to the coconut liquor to make the marinade. Mix well and stir in some pepper. You will probably not need salt with the soy sauce.

5 Place the prepared kebabs in a single layer in a shallow non-metallic dish. Pour the marinade over. Cover and chill for at least 3 hours.

6 Preheat the grill (broiler) to high. Remove the kebabs from the marinade and place on the grill pan. Grill (broil) for 4 minutes on each side, turning once and basting occasionally with the marinade.

COOK'S TIP
The easiest way to open a coconut is to hold it in the palm of your left hand, with the "eyes" just above your thumb. The fault line lies between the eyes. Hold the coconut over a bowl to catch the liquid, then carefully hit the line with the blunt side of a cleaver or hammer. If you do this correctly, the coconut will split neatly into two halves.

SALMON WITH RED ONION MARMALADE

SALMON COOKS WELL ON THE BARBECUE BUT MAKE SURE IT IS AT LEAST 2.5CM/1IN THICK TO MAKE IT EASY TO TURN THE PIECES ON THE GRILL. THE RED ONION MARMALADE IS RICH AND DELICIOUS.

SERVES 4

INGREDIENTS
    30ml/2 tbsp olive oil
    4 salmon fillets, 2.5cm/1in thick
    salt and ground black pepper

For the red onion marmalade
    50g/2oz/¼ cup butter
    5 medium red onions, thinly sliced
      and separated into rings
    175ml/6fl oz/¾ cup red wine vinegar
    50ml/2fl oz/¼ cup crème de cassis
    50ml/2fl oz/¼ cup grenadine
    50ml/2fl oz/¼ cup red wine

1 Brush the olive oil over the salmon fillets, working it into the flesh. Grind sea salt over the fish then repeat the process using black pepper. Set the salmon fillets aside.

2 Make the red onion marmalade. Melt the butter in a large, heavy pan and add the onion rings. Stir to coat them in butter, then sauté for 5–10 minutes, until the onions have softened.

3 Stir in the vinegar, crème de cassis, grenadine and wine and continue to cook the onions over a medium heat until the liquid has reduced. It should take about 10 minutes for the liquid to evaporate, leaving the onions covered with a rich glaze. Season well.

4 Brush the fish with a little more oil. Cook on a hot ridged griddle pan or in a hinged grill on the barbecue for 4–6 minutes on each side, or until cooked through. Serve immediately.

SALMON <u>WITH</u> SPICY PESTO

THIS IS A GREAT WAY TO BONE SALMON STEAKS TO GIVE A SOLID PIECE OF FISH. THE PESTO USES SUNFLOWER KERNELS AND CHILLI AS ITS FLAVOURING RATHER THAN THE CLASSIC BASIL AND PINE NUTS.

SERVES 4

INGREDIENTS
4 salmon steaks, each about 225g/8oz
30ml/2 tbsp sunflower oil
finely grated rind and juice of 1 lime
salt and ground black pepper

For the pesto
6 fresh mild red chillies, seeded and
    roughly chopped
2 garlic cloves
30ml/2 tbsp pumpkin or
    sunflower seeds
finely grated rind and juice of 1 lime
75ml/5 tbsp olive oil

1 Place a salmon steak flat on a board. Insert a very sharp knife close to the top of the bone. Staying close to the bone all the time, cut to the end of the steak to release one side of the steak. Repeat with the other side.

2 Place one piece of salmon skin side down and hold it firmly with one hand. Insert a small sharp knife under the skin and, working away from you, cut the flesh off in a single piece. Repeat with the remaining salmon steaks.

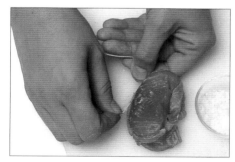

3 Wrap each piece of fish into a circle, with the thinner end wrapped around the fatter end. Tie with string (twine). Place in a shallow bowl.

4 Rub the oil into the boneless fish rounds. Add the lime juice and rind to the bowl. Cover and marinate in the refrigerator for 2 hours.

5 Make the pesto. Put the chillies, garlic, pumpkin or sunflower seeds, lime rind and juice and seasoning into a food processor. Process until well mixed. With the machine running, gradually add the olive oil through the feeder tube. The pesto will slowly thicken and emulsify. Scrape it into a bowl. Preheat the grill (broiler).

6 Drain the salmon and place the rounds in a grill pan. Grill (broil) for 5 minutes on each side or until opaque. Serve with the spicy pesto.

COOK'S TIP
If any small bones remain in the salmon steaks after preparation, remove them with fish tweezers or a pair of new eyebrow tweezers kept for the purpose.

MEXICAN BARBECUE SALMON

THESE SALMON FILLETS COOK QUICKLY ON THE BARBECUE, AND BECAUSE THEY'VE BEEN MARINATED IN THE TOMATO SAUCE, THEY REMAIN BEAUTIFULLY MOIST AND SUCCULENT.

SERVES 4

INGREDIENTS

25g/1oz/2 tbsp butter
1 small red onion, finely chopped
1 garlic clove, crushed
6 plum tomatoes, diced
45ml/3 tbsp tomato ketchup
30ml/2 tbsp Dijon mustard
30ml/2 tbsp soft dark brown sugar
15ml/1 tbsp clear honey
5ml/1 tsp ground cayenne pepper
15ml/1 tbsp ancho chilli powder
15ml/1 tbsp paprika
15ml/1 tbsp Worcestershire sauce
4 salmon fillets, each about 175g/6oz
fresh flat leaf parsley sprigs,
  to garnish

3 Add the tomato ketchup, Dijon mustard, brown sugar, honey, cayenne pepper, chilli powder, paprika and Worcestershire sauce. Stir well, then simmer for a further 20 minutes. Pour the mixture into a food processor and process until smooth. Leave to cool.

4 Put the salmon fillets in a shallow dish, brush generously with the sauce and chill for at least 2 hours. Cook the salmon fillets on an oiled barbecue grill over medium-hot coals for 2–3 minutes on each side, brushing frequently with the sauce. Garnish and serve.

1 Melt the butter in a large, heavy pan and cook the onion and garlic gently for about 5 minutes until softened and translucent. Do not let the onion brown.

2 Add the diced plum tomatoes. Bring to the boil, then reduce the heat and simmer for 15 minutes. Stir the tomatoes occasionally with a wooden spoon so that they do not catch on the base of the pan.

SALMON WITH TROPICAL FRUIT SALSA

FRESH SALMON, COOKED ON THE BARBECUE, IS GOOD ENOUGH TO SERVE ON ITS OWN, BUT TASTES EVEN BETTER WITH THIS COLOURFUL AND TASTY COMBINATION OF MANGO, PAPAYA AND CHILLI.

SERVES 4

INGREDIENTS

4 salmon steaks or fillets, each about
175g/6oz
finely grated rind and juice
of 1 lime
1 small, ripe mango
1 small, ripe papaya
1 fresh red chilli
45ml/3 tbsp chopped fresh
coriander (cilantro)
salt and ground black pepper

COOK'S TIP
If fresh red chillies are not available, use about 2.5ml/½ tsp of chilli paste from a jar, or add a dash of chilli sauce.

1 Lay the pieces of salmon side by side in a wide dish and sprinkle over half the lime rind and juice. Season well.

2 Take a thick slice off either side of the mango stone (pit), and then remove the stone. Finely chop the mango flesh and put it in a bowl. Halve the papaya, scoop out and discard the seeds and remove the skin. Chop the flesh finely and add it to the mango.

3 Cut the chilli in half lengthways. For a milder flavour, remove the seeds, or leave the seeds in to make the salsa hot and spicy. Finely chop the chilli and add to the chopped fruit. Add the chopped fresh coriander to the bowl and mix gently with a large spoon.

4 Stir in the remaining lime rind and juice. Season to taste.

5 Cook the salmon on an oiled barbecue grill over medium-hot coals for 5–8 minutes, turning once. Serve with the tropical fruit salsa.

THAI MARINATED SEA TROUT

SEA TROUT HAS A SUPERB TEXTURE AND A FLAVOUR LIKE THAT OF WILD SALMON. IT IS BEST SERVED WITH STRONG BUT COMPLEMENTARY FLAVOURS, SUCH AS CHILLIES AND LIME, THAT CUT THE RICHNESS OF ITS FLESH.

SERVES 6

INGREDIENTS

6 sea trout cutlets, each about
 115g/4oz, or wild or farmed salmon
2 garlic cloves, chopped
1 fresh long red chilli, seeded
 and chopped
45ml/3 tbsp chopped Thai basil
15ml/1 tbsp palm sugar or
 granulated sugar
3 limes
400ml/14fl oz/1⅔ cups
 coconut milk
15ml/1 tbsp Thai fish sauce

1 Place the sea trout cutlets side by side in a shallow dish. Using a pestle, pound the garlic and chilli in a large mortar to break both up roughly. Add 30ml/2 tbsp of the Thai basil with the sugar and continue to pound to a rough paste.

2 Grate the rind from 1 lime and squeeze it. Mix the rind and juice into the chilli paste, with the coconut milk. Pour the mixture over the cutlets. Cover and chill for about 1 hour. Cut the remaining limes into wedges.

3 Take the fish out of the refrigerator so that it can return to room temperature. Remove the cutlets from the marinade and place them in an oiled hinged wire fish basket or directly on the lightly oiled grill. Cook the fish for 4 minutes on each side, trying not to move them. They may stick to the grill rack if not seared first.

4 Strain the remaining marinade into a pan, reserving the contents of the sieve. Bring the marinade to the boil, then simmer gently for 5 minutes, stirring. Stir in the contents of the sieve and continue to simmer for 1 minute more. Add the Thai fish sauce and the remaining Thai basil.

5 Lift each fish cutlet on to a plate, pour over the sauce and serve with the lime wedges.

COOK'S TIP
Sea trout is best cooked when the barbecue is cool to medium hot, and the coals have a medium to thick coating of ash. Always remember to oil the barbecue rack or hinged grill lightly and take care when cooking any fish in a marinade, as the residue can cause flare-ups if it drips on to the coals.

BACON-WRAPPED TROUT WITH OATMEAL

THIS STUFFING IS BASED ON A SCOTTISH SPECIALITY, CALLED SKIRLIE, WHICH IS A MIXTURE OF OATMEAL AND ONION. COOK THIS TROUT ON A MEDIUM-HOT BARBECUE, IF YOU LIKE. BRUSH THE TROUT WITH OIL AND PUT IT IN A HINGED WIRE BARBECUE FISH BASKET TO MAKE IT EASIER TO TURN.

SERVES 4

INGREDIENTS

- 10 dry-cured streaky bacon rashers (fatty bacon slices)
- 40g/1½oz/3 tbsp butter or bacon fat
- 1 onion, finely chopped
- 115g/4oz/1 cup oatmeal
- 30ml/2 tbsp chopped fresh parsley
- 30ml/2 tbsp chopped fresh chives
- 4 trout, each about 350g/12oz, cleaned and boned
- juice of ½ lemon
- salt and ground black pepper
- watercress, cherry tomatoes and lemon wedges, to serve

For the herb mayonnaise
- 6 watercress sprigs
- 15ml/1 tbsp chopped fresh chives
- 30ml/2 tbsp roughly chopped fresh parsley
- 90ml/6 tbsp lemon mayonnaise
- 30ml/2 tbsp fromage frais, crème fraîche or sour cream
- 2.5–5ml/½–1 tsp tarragon mustard

1 Preheat the oven to 190°C/375°F/Gas 5. Chop two of the bacon rashers. Melt 25g/1oz/2 tbsp of the butter or bacon fat in a large frying pan and cook the chopped bacon briefly. Add the finely chopped onion and fry gently for 5–8 minutes, until softened.

2 Add the oatmeal and cook until the oatmeal darkens and absorbs the fat, but do not allow it to overbrown. Stir in the parsley and chives, with salt and pepper to taste. Cool.

3 Wash and dry the trout, then stuff with the oatmeal mixture. Wrap each fish in two bacon rashers and place in an ovenproof dish. Dot with the remaining butter and sprinkle with the lemon juice. Bake for 20–25 minutes, until the bacon browns and crisps a little.

4 Meanwhile, make the mayonnaise. Place the watercress, chives and parsley in a sieve and pour boiling water over them. Drain, rinse under cold water, and drain well on kitchen paper.

5 Purée the herbs in a mortar with a pestle. (This is easier than using a food processor for a quantity as small as this.) Stir the puréed herbs into the lemon mayonnaise with the fromage frais, crème fraîche or sour cream. Add tarragon mustard to taste and stir well.

6 When cooked, transfer the trout to warmed serving plates. Serve with watercress, cherry tomatoes and lemon wedges, accompanied by the herb mayonnaise.

HOT SMOKED SALMON

THIS IS A FANTASTIC WAY OF SMOKING SALMON ON A CHARCOAL BARBECUE, USING SOAKED HICKORY WOOD CHIPS. MOJO, A SPICY BUT NOT HOT SAUCE POPULAR IN CUBA, IS PERFECT TO CUT THE RICHNESS OF THE HOT SMOKED SALMON.

SERVES 6

INGREDIENTS
  6 salmon fillets, each about
    175g/6oz, with skin
  15ml/1 tbsp sunflower oil
  salt and ground black pepper
  2 handfuls hickory wood chips,
    soaked in cold water for at least
    30 minutes

For the mojo
  1 ripe mango, diced
  4 drained canned pineapple
    slices, diced
  1 small red onion, finely chopped
  1 fresh long mild red chilli, seeded
    and finely chopped
  15ml/1 tbsp good quality sweet
    chilli sauce
  grated rind and juice of 1 lime
  leaves from 1 small lemon basil plant
    or 45ml/3 tbsp fresh coriander
    (cilantro) leaves, chopped

1 Place the salmon fillets, skin side down, on a platter. Sprinkle the flesh lightly with salt. Cover and leave in a cool place for about 30 minutes.

2 Make the mojo by putting the mango, diced pineapple, chopped onion and seeded and chopped chilli in a bowl.

3 Add the chilli sauce, lime rind and juice, and the herb leaves. Stir to mix well. Cover tightly and leave in a cool place until needed.

COOK'S TIP
Although canned pineapple slices give a very satisfactory result, when sweet pineapples are in season, you may prefer to use fresh ones in the mojo. You will need about half a medium-sized pineapple. Slice off the skin, remove the core and cut into chunks.

4 Pat the salmon fillets with kitchen paper, then brush each one with a little oil. Place the salmon fillets skin side down on a lightly oiled grill rack over medium-hot coals. Cover the barbecue with a lid or tented heavy-duty foil and cook the fish for about 3 minutes.

5 Drain the hickory chips into a colander and sprinkle about a third of them as evenly as possible over the coals. Carefully drop them through the slats in the grill racks, taking care not to scatter the ash as you do so.

6 Replace the barbecue cover and continue cooking for a further 8 minutes, adding a small handful of hickory chips twice more during this time. Serve the salmon hot or cold, with the mojo.

TANGY GRILLED SALMON WITH PINEAPPLE

FRESH PINEAPPLE REALLY BRINGS OUT THE FLAVOUR OF SALMON. HERE, IT IS COMBINED WITH LIME JUICE TO MAKE A LIGHT AND REFRESHING DISH, WHICH TASTES GREAT WITH WILD RICE AND A SIMPLE GREEN SALAD TOSSED WITH A GRAPEFRUIT VINAIGRETTE DRESSING.

SERVES 4

INGREDIENTS
grated rind and juice of 2 limes
15ml/1 tbsp olive oil, plus extra
   for greasing
1cm/½in piece fresh root ginger,
   peeled and grated
1 garlic clove, crushed
30ml/2 tbsp clear honey
15ml/1 tbsp soy sauce
4 salmon fillets, each about
   200g/7oz
1 small pineapple
30ml/2 tbsp sesame seeds
ground black pepper
fresh chives, to garnish
wild rice and a green salad,
   to serve

COOK'S TIPS
• Watch the sesame seeds closely as they brown very quickly.
• To cook wild rice, put it in a pan of cold salted water. Bring to the boil, then simmer for 30–40 minutes, or as directed on the packet, until tender.
• Serve the grilled salmon with a mixed leaf salad. For the dressing, mix 45ml/3 tbsp grapefruit juice with 10ml/2 tsp balsamic vinegar and a pinch each of salt, ground black pepper and sugar, then whisk in 120ml/4fl oz/½ cup mild olive oil.

1 Make the marinade. Put the lime rind in a jug (pitcher) and stir in the lime juice, olive oil, ginger, garlic, honey and soy sauce. Taste and add a little ground black pepper. The inclusion of soy sauce in the marinade means that salt will probably not be needed.

2 Place the salmon fillets in a single layer in a shallow, non-metallic dish. Pour the marinade over the salmon. Cover and chill for at least 1 hour, turning the salmon halfway through.

3 Carefully cut the skin off the pineapple, removing as many of the small black "eyes" as possible. Cut the pineapple into four thick slices. Use an apple corer to remove the tough central core from each slice and cut away any remaining eyes with a small knife.

4 Preheat the grill (broiler) to high. Sprinkle the sesame seeds over a piece of foil and place under the grill for a minute or two until they turn golden brown. Set aside.

5 Grease the grill pan and cover with a layer of foil. Using a slotted spoon, remove the salmon fillets from the marinade and place them in a single layer on the foil. Add the pineapple rings, placing one on top of each piece of salmon.

6 Grill (broil) the fish and pineapple for 10 minutes, brushing occasionally with the marinade and turning everything over once, until the fish is cooked through and the pineapple rings are golden brown.

7 Transfer the fish to serving plates, placing each fillet on a bed of wild rice. Top with the pineapple slices. Sprinkle the sesame seeds over and garnish with the chives. Serve with a green salad.

SALMON IN A LEAF PARCEL

THIS IS AN INDIAN SPECIALITY FROM MUMBAI – OR, TO USE THE OLD NAME, BOMBAY. THERE IT WOULD BE MADE USING SILVER POMFRET, BUT SALMON, WITH ITS ROBUST FLAVOUR, ALSO WORKS WELL.

SERVES 6

INGREDIENTS

50g/2oz fresh coconut, skinned and finely grated, or 65g/2½oz/scant 1 cup desiccated (dry unsweetened shredded) coconut, soaked in 30ml/2 tbsp water

1 large lemon, skin, pith and seeds removed, roughly chopped

4 large garlic cloves, crushed

3 large fresh mild green chillies, seeded and chopped

50g/2oz/1 cup fresh coriander (cilantro), roughly chopped

25g/1oz/½ cup fresh mint leaves, roughly chopped

5ml/1 tsp ground cumin

5ml/1 tsp sugar

2.5ml/½ tsp fenugreek seeds, finely ground

5ml/1 tsp salt

2 large, whole banana leaves

6 salmon fillets, total weight about 1.2kg/2½lb, skinned

1 Place all the ingredients except the banana leaves and salmon in a food processor. Pulse to a fine paste. Scrape the mixture into a bowl, cover and chill for 30 minutes.

2 Make the parcels. Cut each banana leaf widthways into three and cut off the hard outside edge from each piece. Put the pieces of leaf and the edge strips in a bowl of hot water. Leave to soak for about 10 minutes.

3 Drain the leaf pieces and strips and gently wipe off any white residue. Rinse and pour over boiling water to soften. Drain again, then place the leaf pieces and strips, smooth side up, on a clean board to dry.

COOK'S TIP
Serve little rice parcels with the salmon. Fill six more banana leaf packages with cooked basmati rice, secure each one with a skewer and reheat on the grill.

4 Smear the top and bottom of each leaf with the coconut paste. Place one salmon fillet on each leaf. Bring the trimmed edge of the leaf over the salmon, then fold in the sides. Finally, bring up the remaining edge to cover the salmon and make a neat parcel. Tie each parcel securely with one of the soaked leaf strips.

5 Lay each parcel on a sheet of heavy-duty foil, bring up the edges and scrunch the tops together to seal. Position a lightly oiled grill rack over medium-hot coals to heat. Place the salmon parcels on the grill rack and cook for 10 minutes, turning over once.

6 Place the parcels on a board and leave to stand for 2–3 minutes – the salmon will continue to cook in the residual heat. Remove the foil, then transfer each banana leaf parcel to a plate, to be unwrapped at the table. Eat the fish straight out of the parcel.

TROUT <u>WITH</u> CURRIED ORANGE BUTTER

TROUT ARE PERFECT FOR MIDWEEK MEALS, ESPECIALLY SERVED WITH THIS DELICIOUS TANGY BUTTER. CHILDREN WILL LOVE THE BUTTERY CURRY FLAVOUR BUT IT WOULD BE AN IDEA TO FILLET THE COOKED TROUT TO REMOVE THE BONES BEFORE GIVING THIS TO YOUNG CHILDREN.

SERVES 4

INGREDIENTS

25g/1oz/2 tbsp butter, softened
5ml/1 tsp curry powder
5ml/1 tsp grated orange rind
4 small trout, gutted,
  heads removed
vegetable or sunflower oil,
  for brushing
salt and ground black pepper
orange wedges, to garnish
boiled new potatoes, to serve

1 Mix the softened butter, curry powder and orange rind together in a bowl with salt and plenty of ground black pepper. Wrap in foil and freeze for 10 minutes.

2 Brush the fish all over with oil and sprinkle well with seasoning. Make three diagonal slashes through the skin and flesh on each side of the fish.

3 Cut the flavoured butter into small pieces and carefully insert into the slashes made in the fish.

4 Place the fish on the grill (broiling) pan and cook under a preheated high grill (broiler) or hot barbecue for 3–4 minutes on each side, depending on the thickness of the fish. Garnish with wedges of orange before serving with boiled new potatoes.

COOK'S TIP
The curry powder for this recipe can be made at home from a blend of dry spices. The following mix could also be used as the basis for any curry dish. It is a fairly mild recipe but you could increase the quantity of dried chilli for a hotter taste.
  Place 50g/2oz/½ cup whole coriander seeds, 60ml/4 tbsp whole cumin seeds, 30ml/2 tbsp each of whole fennel seeds and fenugreek seeds, 4 dried red chillies and 5 curry leaves together in a large frying pan. Dry roast for 8–10 minutes, shaking the pan until the spices darken and release a rich aroma. Allow the roasted spices to cool, then grind to a fine powder in a spice mill. Place in a large glass bowl and add 15ml/1 tbsp chilli powder, 15ml/1 tbsp ground turmeric and 2.5ml/½ tsp salt and mix well. Store in an airtight container.

PARTY FOODS

Time to show off now, as you transform salmon and trout into impressive dinner party dishes. Elegant doesn't have to mean elaborate, though, and many of these recipes are easy to prepare, relying for their impact on the quality of the ingredients rather than complicated procedures. The chapter opens with a selection of simple but stunning canapés, and moves on to main attractions like Salmon Ceviche with Gin and Lime, and a Fish Terrine which will do wonders for your reputation as a fine cook. For the buffet table, choose Smoked Salmon and Herb Roulade or the stunning Trout Gougère.

SMOKED SALMON PARCELS

NOTHING COULD BE SIMPLER THAN THESE PRETTY SALMON ROLLS. THERE ARE TWO DIFFERENT FILLINGS BUT BOTH ARE SO GOOD THAT THEY'RE LIKELY TO DISAPPEAR AT THE SAME SPEED.

MAKES ABOUT 20

INGREDIENTS
    350g/12oz best quality
      smoked salmon
    2 lemons, cut in quarters and a
      bunch of fresh dill, to garnish

For the fish filling
    225g/8oz smoked mackerel
      fillet, skinned
    45ml/3 tbsp crème fraîche
    ground black pepper

For the cheese and herb filling
    bunch of fresh mixed herbs, such
      as chives, parsley and chervil
    225g/8oz/1 cup ricotta cheese
    salt and ground black pepper

1 For the fish filling, chop the mackerel roughly and place in a bowl. Mash with the crème fraîche. Season with pepper.

2 Make the cheese filling. Chop the herbs finely and stir them into the ricotta cheese in a bowl. Season with plenty of salt and pepper.

3 Cut the smoked salmon into strips, about 2.5 x 7.5cm/1 x 3in. Put a teaspoon of the fish filling at one end of a strip and roll up neatly. Continue until half the salmon has been used, then repeat the procedure with the cheese filling. Arrange the rolls on a platter and garnish with the lemon and dill.

SALMON TRIANGLES

THESE ELEGANT PARTY PIECES TAKE A LITTLE TIME TO MAKE, BUT THEY CAN BE PREPARED IN ADVANCE WITH THE FINAL TOUCHES ADDED JUST BEFORE YOUR GUESTS ARRIVE.

MAKES 12

INGREDIENTS
  2 eggs
  3–4 slices dark rye bread
  115g/4oz poached salmon
  coriander (cilantro) leaves, to garnish

For the lime and coriander mayonnaise
  45–60ml/3–4 tbsp mayonnaise
  5ml/1 tsp chopped fresh coriander
    (cilantro)
  5ml/1 tsp freshly squeezed
    lime juice
  salt and ground black pepper

1 Bring a pan of water to the boil. Reduce the heat, then add the eggs. Cook for 12 minutes, then plunge the eggs into cold water to arrest further cooking. When cold, shell the hard-boiled eggs and slice them.

2 Cut the rye bread into 12 triangular pieces, using a sharp knife.

3 Make the lime and coriander mayonnaise. Combine the mayonnaise, chopped coriander and lime juice, and season to taste.

4 Top each bread triangle with a slice of egg, a small portion of salmon and a teaspoon of mayonnaise. Garnish with a coriander leaf. Chill until ready to serve.

VARIATIONS
Using this recipe as a guide, many different canapés can be made. Try substituting cherry tomato slices for the egg and topping the salmon with a mixture of mayonnaise and red pesto, or use sliced cucumber and top the salmon with lemon-flavoured mayonnaise. For a luxury note, use a neutral mayonnaise and add a spoonful of caviar. The black roe looks very dramatic with the pale pink salmon.

SALMON AND TROUT CANAPÉS

THESE TINY LITTLE BITES ARE IDEAL FOR SERVING WITH A GLASS
OF CHILLED SPARKLING WINE OR AS PART OF A FINGER BUFFET.

MAKES 44

For the salmon and dill squares
   15ml/1 tbsp olive oil
   175g/6oz salmon fillet, skinned
   500g/1¼lb sliced pumpernickel
    bread
   mayonnaise, for spreading
   1 small cucumber, thinly sliced
   60ml/4 tbsp sour cream
   30ml/2 tbsp chopped fresh dill
   10ml/2 tsp lemon juice
   ½ red (bell) pepper, seeded and
    finely chopped
   salt and ground black pepper

For the smoked trout squares
   5 thin slices white bread, toasted
   75g/3oz/scant ½ cup cream cheese
    with garlic and herbs
   75g/3oz smoked trout, skinned
   finely grated rind of 2 lemons
   lemon wedges, to garnish

1 Heat the oil in a griddle pan. Season the salmon fillet well on both sides and fry for 5–8 minutes or until the flesh is opaque. Remove from the pan and leave to cool.

2 Using a fluted 5cm/2in cutter, cut out 24 squares from the sliced pumpernickel. Spread a little mayonnaise on each bread square and top with a cucumber slice.

3 Flake the salmon into bitesize pieces and remove any remaining bones. Put the fish in a bowl and mix with the sour cream, dill and lemon juice. Season with salt and pepper to taste.

4 Spread a little of the mixture on each pumpernickel square and top with pieces of red pepper.

5 Make the smoked trout squares. Trim the crusts from the toast and spread a fifth of the cheese on each slice. Cut each slice into four squares.

6 Cut the smoked trout into pieces and divide among the toast squares.

7 Sprinkle the lemon rind over the trout and season with plenty of black pepper.

8 Arrange the canapés on a large serving platter or separate plates and garnish with the lemon wedges. Chill until ready to serve.

SMOKED SALMON PANCAKES WITH PINE NUTS

THESE SIMPLE PANCAKES TAKE ONLY MINUTES TO PREPARE AND ARE PERFECT FOR A SPECIAL OCCASION. SMOKED SALMON IS DELICIOUS WITH FRESH BASIL AND COMBINES WELL WITH TOASTED PINE NUTS AND A SPOONFUL OF CRÈME FRAÎCHE OR SOUR CREAM.

MAKES 12–16

INGREDIENTS
  120ml/4fl oz/½ cup milk
  115g/4oz/1 cup self-raising
    (self-rising) flour
  1 egg
  30ml/2 tbsp pesto
  vegetable oil, for frying
  200ml/7fl oz/scant 1 cup crème
    fraîche or sour cream
  75g/3oz smoked salmon
  15ml/1 tbsp pine nuts, toasted
  salt and ground black pepper
  12–16 fresh basil sprigs, to garnish

1 Pour half the milk into a mixing bowl. Add the flour, egg and pesto and mix to a smooth batter.

2 Add the remainder of the milk and mix until evenly blended. Season the batter with salt and pepper.

3 Heat the vegetable oil in a large frying pan. Spoon the batter into the heated oil in small heaps. Allow about 30 seconds for the pancakes to cook, then turn and cook briefly on the other side. Continue cooking pancakes until all the batter has been used.

4 Arrange the pancakes on a serving plate and top each one with a spoonful of crème fraîche or sour cream.

5 Cut the salmon into pieces to fit the top of the pancakes and lightly place them on top of the cream.

6 Sprinkle each pancake with pine nuts and garnish with the fresh basil. Serve immediately.

COOK'S TIP
If not serving immediately, cover the pancakes with a dishtowel and keep warm in an oven preheated to 140°C/275°F/Gas 1.

SMOKED SALMON PIZZETTES

FOR A SOPHISTICATED MEAL, DISPENSE WITH THE APPETIZER AND SERVE THESE PIZZAS WITH PRE-MEAL DRINKS. BLACK LUMPFISH ROE MAKES A DRAMATIC CONTRAST TO THE COLOUR OF THE SALMON.

MAKES 10–12

INGREDIENTS
    15ml/1 tbsp olive oil
    75–115g/3–4oz smoked salmon,
      cut into strips
    60ml/4 tbsp crème fraîche or
      sour cream
    30ml/2 tbsp black lumpfish roe
    chives, to garnish

For the dough
    175g/6oz/1½ cups strong white
      (bread) flour
    1.5ml/¼ tsp salt
    5ml/1 tsp easy-blend (rapid-rise)
      dried yeast
    120–150ml/4–5fl oz/½–⅔ cup
      lukewarm water
    15ml/1 tbsp olive oil
    15ml/1 tbsp chopped fresh chives

1 Make the dough. Sift the flour and salt into a mixing bowl, stir in the yeast, then make a well in the centre and add the liquids. Mix with a spoon to a soft dough.

2 Knead the dough until smooth and elastic, then place in a bowl, cover with clear film (plastic wrap) and leave in a warm place for about 1 hour or until the dough has doubled in bulk.

3 Preheat the oven to 200°C/400°F/ Gas 6. Knock back (punch down) the dough and knead it gently, adding the chives until evenly mixed.

4 Roll out the dough on a lightly floured surface to about 3mm/⅛in thick. Using a 7.5cm/3in plain round cutter, stamp out 10–12 circles.

5 Place the bases well apart on two greased baking sheets, prick all over with a fork, then brush with the oil. Bake for 10–15 minutes until crisp.

6 Arrange the smoked salmon on top, then spoon on the crème fraîche or sour cream. Top with lumpfish roe and garnish with chives. Serve immediately.

POTATO BLINIS WITH SMOKED SALMON

THESE CRISP, LIGHT PANCAKES ORIGINATED IN RUSSIA, WHERE THEY ARE SERVED WITH THE FINEST CAVIAR, BUT THEY ARE ALSO GOOD WITH SALMON ROE.

SERVES 6 AS PART OF A BUFFET

INGREDIENTS

    1 potato, about 115g/4oz, boiled
      and mashed
    15ml/1 tbsp easy-blend (rapid-rise)
      dried yeast
    175g/6oz/1½ cups plain
      (all-purpose) flour
    300ml/½ pint/1¼ cups
      lukewarm water
    oil, for greasing
    90ml/6 tbsp sour cream
    6 slices smoked salmon
    salt and ground black pepper
    lemon slices, to garnish

1 Mix the potato, yeast, flour, salt and pepper with the water to make a smooth dough. Cover with clear film (plastic wrap) and leave to rise in a warm place for 30 minutes until doubled in bulk.

2 Heat a non-stick frying pan and add a little oil. Drop spoonfuls of the mixture on to the pan.

3 Cook the blinis for 2 minutes until lightly golden on the underside. Toss with a spatula and cook on the second side. Remove each batch as it cooks and keep warm.

4 To serve, top each blini with a little sour cream and a small folded slice of smoked salmon. Garnish with black pepper and a small slice of lemon.

VARIATION

For an alternative topping, mix 200g/7oz/ scant 1 cup cream cheese with 15ml/ 1 tbsp chopped parsley or dill. Spread on the blinis and top with the salmon. Add slivers of sweet pickled cherry chillies or a spoonful of salmon roe.

GRAVLAX

SERVES 12

INGREDIENTS
  1.2kg/2½lb salmon, cleaned and
    with head, tail and bones removed
  45ml/3 tbsp coarse sea salt
  30ml/2 tbsp caster (superfine)
    sugar
  12 black peppercorns, crushed
  large bunch of fresh dill, chopped

For the mustard sauce
  2 egg yolks
  30ml/2 tbsp white wine vinegar
  45ml/3 tbsp mild mustard
  50g/2oz soft light brown sugar
  300ml/½ pint/1¼ cups light olive oil
  30ml/2 tbsp chopped fresh dill
  salt and ground white pepper

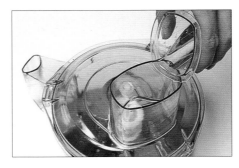

1 Place one fillet skin-side down in a non-metallic dish. Sprinkle over the salt, sugar and peppercorns. Cover with half the dill.

2 Lay the other fillet on top and cover with the remaining dill. Set a heavy weight on top of the fish. Cover and chill in the refrigerator for at least 72 hours, turning the salmon every 12 hours and basting it with the brine solution that collects in the dish.

3 Put the egg yolks and half the vinegar and mustard into a food processor. Add the brown sugar and a little salt and white pepper. Process until smooth.

4 With the motor running, gradually add the oil in a steady stream through the feeder tube, continuing to process the mixture until it thickens. Stir in the remaining vinegar and mustard with the dill, then scrape the sauce into a bowl and set it aside.

5 Drain the liquid from the salmon and scrape off any remaining salt. Pat the fish dry. Cut on the diagonal into thin slices and serve with the mustard sauce.

SALMON AND RICE TRIANGLES

IN JAPAN, WHERE THESE ORIGINATED, THEY ARE OFTEN USED FOR PACKED LUNCHES OR PICNICS, BUT WOULD ALSO MAKE ELEGANT PARTY PIECES. THEY ARE GREAT FUN TO MAKE AND LOOK MARVELLOUS.

SERVES 4 AS PART OF A BUFFET

INGREDIENTS
    1 salmon steak
    15ml/1 tbsp salt
    450g/1lb/4 cups freshly cooked
        Japanese short grain rice
    4 umeboshi (plum pickles)
    ½ sheet yaki-nori seaweed, cut into
        four equal strips
    white and black sesame seeds,
        for sprinkling

1 Grill (broil) the salmon steak for 4–5 minutes on each side, until the flesh flakes easily when it is tested with the tip of a sharp knife. Set aside to cool.

2 Put the salt in a bowl. Spoon a quarter of the warm cooked rice into a small rice bowl.

3 Make a hole in the middle of the rice and put in one umeboshi. Smooth the rice carefully over to cover it completely.

4 Wet the palms of both hands with cold water, then rub the salt evenly on to your palms.

5 Empty the rice and umeboshi from the bowl on to one hand. Use both hands to shape the rice into a triangular shape, using firm but not heavy pressure. Make three more rice triangles in the same way.

6 Flake the salmon, discarding any skin and any bones. Mix the flaked salmon into the remaining rice, then shape it into triangles as before.

7 Wrap a strip of yaki-nori around each of the umeboshi triangles. Sprinkle sesame seeds on the salmon triangles. Serve immediately or cool completely, then wrap each in foil or clear film (plastic wrap).

COOK'S TIP
Always use warm rice to make triangles as it is easier to mould.

SASHIMI MORIAWASE

THE ARRANGEMENT OF A DISH OF SASHIMI IS AS IMPORTANT AS THE FRESHNESS OF THE FISH. CHOOSE TWO TO FIVE KINDS OF FISH FROM EACH GROUP AND ONLY USE THE FRESHEST CATCH OF THE DAY.

SERVES 4

INGREDIENTS
500g/1¼lb total of fish from
the 4 groups

Group A
skinned fillets, cut lengthways
if possible
Maguro akami: lean tuna
Maguro toro: fatty tuna
Sake: salmon
Kajiki: swordfish
Tai: sea bream or red snapper
Suzuki: sea bass
Hamachi: yellowtail
Katsuo: skipjack tuna

Group B
skinned fillets
Hirame: flounder or sole
Karei: halibut or turbot

Group C
Ika: squid body, cleaned, boned
and skinned
Tako: cooked octopus tentacles
Hotate-gai: scallop, the coral, black
stomach and frill removed

Group D
Aka-ebi: sweet prawns (shrimp),
peeled, heads can be removed,
tails intact
Uni: sea urchin
Ikura: salted salmon roe

To serve
1 fresh mooli (daikon), peeled and
cut into 6cm/2½in lengths
1 Japanese or salad cucumber
4 shiso leaves
2 limes, halved (optional)
45ml/3 tbsp wasabi paste from
a tube, or the same amount of
wasabi powder mixed with 20ml/
4 tsp water
1 bottle tamari shoyu

1 Make the tsuma (the mooli strands). Slice the mooli pieces thinly lengthways, then cut the slices into very thin strips lengthways. Rinse under running water, drain and put in the refrigerator.

2 Prepare the cucumber. Trim and cut into 3cm/1¼in lengths, then cut each cucumber cylinder in half lengthways.

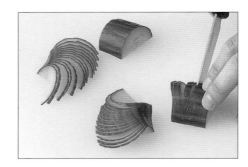

3 Place the cucumber on a chopping board, flat-side down. Make very fine cuts across each piece, leaving the slices joined together at one side. Then, gently squeeze the cucumber together between your fingers so that the slices fan out sideways. Set them aside and cover with clear film (plastic wrap).

4 Slice the fish. Group A needs hira giri, a thick cut. Trim the fillet into a long rectangular shape. With the fish skin side up, cut into 1cm/½in thick slices, cutting in the direction of the grain.

5 Group B needs usu zukuri, very thin slices. Place the fillet horizontally to you on its skinned side. Hold the knife almost horizontally to the fillet, shave it very thinly across the grain.

6 Group C fish each require different cutting styles. Slice the cooked octopus diagonally into 5mm/¼in thick ovals. Slice the scallops in half horizontally. If they are thicker than 4cm/1¼in, slice them into three.

7 Cut open the squid body and turn to lie on its skinned side, horizontally to you. Score lines 5mm/¼in apart over the surface, then cut into 5mm/¼in strips. Group D is all ready to arrange.

8 Arrange the sashimi creatively. First, take a handful of mooli and heap up on to the serving plate a large mound or several small mounds. Then, base your design on the following basic rules.
Group A and C: Put each slice of fish side by side like domino pieces. You can lay them on a shiso leaf.
Group B: Use the thin, soft slices to make a rose shape, or overlap the slices slightly, so that the texture of the plate can be seen through them.
Group D: Place the prawns by their tails, 2 or 3 at a time, in a bundle. If the sea urchins come tightly packed in a little box, try to get them out in one piece. The salmon roe can be heaped on thin cucumber slices or scooped into a lime case, made from a half lime, flesh removed. Fill the case with some mooli and place the roe on top.

9 Arrange the cucumber fans, heaped wasabi paste and shiso leaves to perfect your design. Serve immediately. Pour some shoyu into four dishes and mix in the wasabi. As the sauce is quite salty, only dip the edge of the sashimi into it.

RICE BALLS WITH FOUR FILLINGS

*ONIGIRI, THE JAPANESE NAME FOR THIS DISH, MEANS HAND-MOULDED RICE. JAPANESE RICE IS IDEAL
FOR MAKING RICE BALLS, WHICH ARE FILLED HERE WITH SALMON, MACKEREL, UMEBOSHI AND OLIVES.
THE NORI COATING MAKES THEM EASY TO PICK UP WITH YOUR FINGERS.*

SERVES 4

INGREDIENTS
    50g/2oz salmon fillet, skinned
    3 umeboshi, 50g/2oz in total weight
    45ml/3 tbsp sesame seeds
    2.5ml/½ tsp mirin
    50g/2oz smoked mackerel fillet
    2 nori sheets, each cut into 8 strips
    6 pitted black olives, wiped and
      finely chopped
    fine salt
    Japanese pickles, to serve

For the rice
    450g/1lb/2¼ cups Japanese
      short grain rice
    550ml/18fl oz/2½ cups water

1 To cook the rice, wash it thoroughly
with cold water. Drain and put into a
heavy pan. Pour in the water and leave
for 30 minutes. Put the lid on tightly
and bring the pan to the boil. Reduce
the heat and simmer for 12 minutes.
When you hear a crackling noise
remove from the heat and leave to
stand, covered, for about 15 minutes.

2 Stir carefully with a dampened rice
paddle or wooden spatula to aerate the
rice. Leave to cool for 30 minutes while
you prepare the fillings. Thoroughly salt
the salmon fillet and leave for at least
30 minutes.

3 Stone (pit) the umeboshi. With the
back of a fork, mash them slightly. Mix
with 15ml/1 tbsp of the sesame seeds
and the mirin to make a rough paste.

4 Wash the salt from the salmon.
Grill (broil) the salmon and smoked
mackerel under a high heat. Using a
fork, remove the skin and divide the
fish into loose, chunky flakes. Keep the
salmon and mackerel pieces separate.

5 Toast the remaining sesame seeds in
a dry frying pan over a low heat until
they start to pop.

6 Check the temperature of the rice.
It should be still quite warm but not hot.
To start moulding, you need a teacup
and a bowl of cold water to wet your
hands. Put the teacup and tablespoons
for measuring into the water. Put fine
salt into a small dish. Wipe a chopping
board with a very wet dishtowel. Wash
your hands thoroughly with unperfumed
soap and dry.

7 Remove the teacup from the bowl and
shake off excess water. Scoop about
30ml/2 tbsp rice into the teacup. With
your fingers, make a well in the centre
of the rice and put in a quarter of the
salmon flakes. Cover the salmon with
another 15ml/1 tbsp rice. Press well.

8 Wet your hands and sprinkle them
with a pinch of salt. Rub it all over your
palms. Turn the rice in the teacup out
into one hand and squeeze the rice
shape with both hands to make a
densely packed flat ball.

9 Wrap the rice ball with a nori strip.
Put on to the chopping board. Make
three more balls using the remaining
salmon, then make four balls using the
smoked mackerel and another four balls
using the umeboshi paste.

10 Scoop about 45ml/3 tbsp rice into
the teacup. Mix in a quarter of the
chopped olives. Press the rice with your
fingers. Wet your hands with water and
rub with a pinch of salt and a quarter
of the toasted sesame seeds. Hold the
teacup in one hand and shape the
rice mixture into a ball as above.
The sesame seeds should stick to the
rice. This time, do not wrap with nori.
Repeat, making three more balls.

11 Serve one of each kind of rice ball
on individual plates with a small helping
of Japanese pickles.

SALMON MARINATED <u>WITH</u> THAI SPICES

MARINATING THE FISH IN AN AROMATIC MIXTURE OF GINGER, LEMON GRASS, LIME LEAVES, CHILLIES AND SALT NOT ONLY CURES IT, BUT ALSO IMBUES THE SALMON WITH DELECTABLE FLAVOURS.

SERVES 4–6 AS PART OF A BUFFET

INGREDIENTS

tail piece of 1 salmon, about
    675g/1½lb, halved and boned
    to produce two fillets
20ml/4 tsp coarse sea salt
20ml/4 tsp sugar
2.5cm/1in piece fresh root
    ginger, grated
2 lemon grass stalks, coarse outer
    leaves removed, thinly sliced
4 kaffir lime leaves, finely chopped
    or shredded
grated rind of 1 lime
1 fresh red chilli, seeded and
    finely chopped
5ml/1 tsp black peppercorns,
    coarsely crushed
30ml/2 tbsp chopped fresh
    coriander (cilantro)
fresh coriander (cilantro) and kaffir
    limes, to garnish

For the dressing

150ml/¼ pint/⅔ cup mayonnaise
juice of ½ lime
10ml/2 tsp chopped fresh
    coriander (cilantro)

1 Remove any remaining bones from the salmon, using a pair of tweezers. In a bowl, mix together the salt, sugar, ginger, lemon grass, lime leaves, lime rind, chilli, peppercorns and chopped fresh coriander.

2 Place one-quarter of the spice mixture in a shallow non-metallic dish. Place one salmon fillet, skin side down, on top of the spices. Spread two-thirds of the remaining mixture over the flesh then place the remaining fillet on top, flesh side down. Sprinkle the rest of the spice mixture over the fish.

3 Cover the fish with foil, then place a board on top. Add some weights, such as clean cans of fruit. Chill for 4–5 days, turning the fish daily in the spicy brine that collects in the base of the dish.

4 Make the dressing by mixing the mayonnaise, lime juice and chopped coriander in a bowl.

5 Scrape the spices off the fish. Slice it as thinly as possible. Serve with the lime dressing, garnished with coriander and wedges of kaffir limes.

SALMON CEVICHE <u>WITH</u> GIN <u>AND</u> LIME

MARINATING RAW SALMON IN A MIXTURE OF GIN AND LIME JUICE CHANGES THE TEXTURE OF THE FISH, EFFECTIVELY "COOKING" IT. THE FLAVOUR IS SUPERB.

SERVES 4 AS PART OF A BUFFET

INGREDIENTS

675g/1½lb salmon fillet, skinned
1 small red onion, thinly sliced
6 chives
6 fennel sprigs
3 fresh parsley sprigs
2 limes
30ml/2 tbsp gin
45ml/3 tbsp olive oil
sea salt and ground black pepper
salad leaves, to serve

1 Cut the salmon fillet into thin slices, removing any remaining bones with tweezers. Lay the pieces in a wide, shallow non-metallic dish.

2 Sprinkle over the onion slices and strew with the chives, fennel and parsley sprigs. Using a canelle knife, remove a few fine strips of rind from the limes and reserve for the garnish. Cut off the remaining rind, avoiding the pith, and slice it roughly.

COOK'S TIP

• When preparing salmon in this way, it is vital to use very fresh fish from a reputable source. Tell the fishmonger you intend making ceviche, explaining that the fish will not be cooked in the conventional way, but that the texture will be altered by marinating it in lime juice, gin and olive oil.

• Serve the ceviche on the day you prepare it. It needs to be chilled for 4 hours, but do not leave it for much longer before serving.

3 Squeeze the lime juice into a jug (pitcher). Add the roughly sliced rind, with the gin and olive oil. Stir in sea salt and black pepper to taste. Pour the mixture over the fish and stir gently to coat each piece thoroughly.

4 Cover the dish and chill for 4 hours, stirring occasionally. To serve, arrange the slices of marinated fish on a platter, with the salad leaves. Sprinkle over the reserved strips of lime rind.

FISH TERRINE

THIS COLOURFUL LAYERED TERRINE MAKES A SPECTACULAR PRESENTATION FOR A SPECIAL OCCASION. IT IS PERFECT FOR ENTERTAINING SINCE IT IS BEST MADE THE DAY BEFORE AND CHILLED OVERNIGHT.

SERVES 6 AS PART OF A BUFFET

INGREDIENTS
    450g/1lb white fish fillets, skinned
    225–275g/8–10oz thinly sliced
      smoked salmon
    2 egg whites, chilled
    1.5ml/¼ tsp each salt and
      white pepper
    pinch of freshly grated nutmeg
    250ml/8fl oz/1 cup whipping cream
    60g/2oz baby spinach leaves
    lemon mayonnaise, to serve

1 Cut the white fish fillets into 2.5cm/1in pieces, removing any bones as you work. Spread out the fish pieces on a plate and cover with clear film (plastic wrap). Place in the freezer for about 15 minutes until very cold.

2 Lightly grease a 1.2 litre/2 pint/5 cup terrine or loaf pan. Line the base with baking parchment, then line the base and sides of the pan with smoked salmon slices, letting them hang over the edge. Preheat the oven to 180°C/350°F/Gas 4.

3 Put the pieces of chilled fish in a food processor and whizz to a very smooth purée, stopping the machine several times to scrape down the sides.

4 Add the egg whites, one at a time, then the salt, pepper and nutmeg. With the machine running, pour in the cream through the feeder tube. Stop as soon as it is blended. (If overprocessed, the cream will thicken too much.)

5 Transfer the fish mixture to a large glass bowl. Put the spinach leaves into the food processor and process to a purée. Add one-third of the fish mixture to the spinach and process until just combined, scraping down the sides once or twice.

6 Spread half the plain fish mixture in the base of the pan and smooth it level. Spoon the green fish mixture over the top and smooth the surface, then cover with the remaining plain mixture and smooth the top.

7 Fold the overhanging pieces of salmon over the top to enclose the fish mixture. Tap the pan to settle the mixture and remove any air pockets, then cover the terrine with a double layer of foil.

8 Put the terrine in a roasting pan and pour in enough boiling water to come halfway up the sides of the terrine. Bake for about 1 hour, until a skewer inserted in the centre comes out clean. Allow to cool, wrap well and chill for 3–4 hours or overnight, until firm.

9 To serve the terrine, invert on a board and slice. Arrange slices on individual plates and serve with lemon mayonnaise.

SMOKED SALMON AND HERB ROULADE

MAKE THE MOST OF A SMALL AMOUNT OF SMOKED SALMON BY USING IT IN THE FILLING FOR THIS DELICATELY FLAVOURED ROULADE. MAKE THE ROULADE IN ADVANCE TO GIVE IT TIME TO COOL, BUT DON'T PUT IT IN THE REFRIGERATOR OR IT WILL LOSE ITS LIGHT TEXTURE.

SERVES 6–8 AS PART OF A BUFFET

INGREDIENTS

25g/1oz/2 tbsp butter
25g/1oz/¼ cup plain
  (all-purpose) flour
175ml/6fl oz/¾ cup milk, warm
3 large eggs, separated
50g/2oz/⅔ cup freshly grated
  Parmesan cheese
60ml/4 tbsp chopped fresh dill
30ml/2 tbsp chopped fresh parsley
150ml/¼ pint/⅔ cup full fat crème
  fraîche or sour cream
115g/4oz smoked salmon
salt and ground black pepper
lamb's lettuce, to garnish

1 Melt the butter in a heavy pan, stir in the flour and cook over a low heat to a thick paste. Gradually add the milk, whisking constantly until the sauce boils and thickens, then cook for 1–2 minutes more. Stir in the egg yolks, two-thirds of the Parmesan cheese, the parsley and half the dill. Add salt and ground black pepper to taste.

2 Prepare a 33 x 28cm/13 x 11in Swiss roll tin (jelly roll pan) and preheat the oven to 180°C/350°F/Gas 4. Whisk the egg whites and fold into the yolk mixture, then pour into the tin or pan and bake for 12–15 minutes. Cover with baking parchment and set aside for 10–15 minutes, then tip out on to another sheet of parchment, this time sprinkled with a little Parmesan. Leave to cool.

3 Coarsely chop the smoked salmon, then mix it in a bowl with the crème fraîche or sour cream and remaining chopped dill. Stir gently but thoroughly, then taste and add salt and pepper as needed.

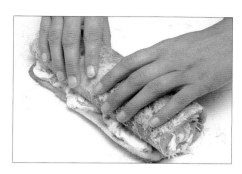

4 Peel off the lining paper from the roulade, spread the filling evenly over the surface and roll up, then leave to firm up in a cold place. Sprinkle with the rest of the Parmesan and garnish with the lamb's lettuce.

SALMON PASTRY WITH CHANTERELLE CREAM

SPECTACULAR IS AN APT ADJECTIVE TO DESCRIBE THIS DISH, WHICH NOT ONLY LOOKS MAGNIFICENT BUT ALSO TASTES SUPERB, WITH THE CRISP PUFF PASTRY PROVIDING A CONTRAST TO THE CREAMY MUSHROOM FILLING AND FLAVOURSOME FISH.

SERVES 6

INGREDIENTS

  2 packets puff pastry, each
    350g/12oz, thawed if frozen
  1 egg, beaten, to glaze
  2 large salmon fillets, total weight
    about 900g/2lb, skinned
  375ml/13fl oz/generous 1½ cups dry
    white wine
  1 small carrot
  1 small onion, halved
  ½ celery stick, chopped
  1 fresh thyme sprig

For the chanterelle cream

  25g/1oz/2 tbsp unsalted
    (sweet) butter
  2 shallots, chopped
  225g/8oz/3 cups chanterelles or
    mixed wild mushrooms, trimmed
    and sliced
  75ml/5 tbsp white wine
  150ml/¼ pint/⅔ cup double
    (heavy) cream
  45ml/3 tbsp chopped fresh chervil
  30ml/2 tbsp chopped fresh chives

For the hollandaise sauce

  2 egg yolks
  10ml/2 tsp lemon juice, plus more
    to taste, if needed
  115g/4oz/½ cup unsalted (sweet)
    butter, melted
  salt and ground black pepper

COOK'S TIP

If the salmon fillet breaks in half as you lift it out of the roasting pan, don't worry. Just reassemble the fish on the pastry. The mushroom cream will mask any obvious joins.

VARIATION

Instead of adding the butter to the egg mixture in the bowl, you could put the mixture in a food processor and add the butter through the feeder tube with the motor running.

1 Roll out the pastry on a floured surface to a rectangle 10cm/4in longer and 5cm/2in wider than the salmon fillets. Trim into a fish shape, support on a large baking sheet, decorate with a pastry cutter and glaze with beaten egg. Chill for 1 hour.

2 Preheat the oven to 200°C/400°F/ Gas 6. Bake the pastry for 30–35 minutes until well risen and golden. Remove from the oven and carefully split in half horizontally to provide two matching fish shapes. Reduce the oven temperature to 160°C/325°F/Gas 3.

3 Make the chanterelle cream. Melt the butter in a heavy pan and fry the shallots gently until soft but not coloured. Add the mushrooms and cook until their juices begin to run.

4 Pour in the wine, increase the heat and cook until the juices have evaporated. When the mushroom mixture is quite dry, stir in the cream and herbs and bring to a simmer. Season well, transfer to a bowl, cover and keep warm.

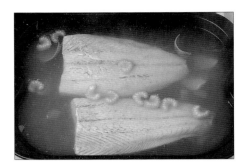

5 To poach the salmon fillets, place them in a roasting pan. Add the wine, carrot, onion, celery, thyme and enough water to cover the fish completely.

6 Bring to the boil slowly. As soon as the water begins to tremble, remove from the heat, cover with a tight-fitting lid or foil and set the pan aside for 30 minutes. The fish will continue to cook in the residual heat.

7 Carefully lift out the salmon fillets, draining them well. Put the base of the pastry on a baking sheet and lay a salmon fillet on top. Spread with the chanterelle cream and cover with a second salmon fillet. Cover with the top of the pastry "fish" and warm through in the oven for 10–15 minutes.

8 For the hollandaise sauce, pour the melted butter in a steady stream on to the egg yolk mixture in a heatproof bowl set over a pan of boiling water. Beat vigorously with a whisk to make a smooth, creamy sauce. Taste the sauce and add salt, pepper and more lemon juice if needed. Serve with the pastry.

SALMON WITH RICE IN PUFF PASTRY

THIS VARIATION ON THE FAMOUS KOULIBIAK MAKES A DRAMATIC PARTY DISH. LIKE THE ORIGINAL, IT ENCASES SALMON, RICE AND HARD-BOILED EGGS IN PASTRY.

SERVES 6 AS PART OF A BUFFET

INGREDIENTS
    450g/1lb puff pastry, thawed
      if frozen
    1 egg, beaten
    3 hard-boiled eggs
    90ml/6 tbsp single (light) cream
    200g/7oz/1¾ cups cooked long
      grain rice
    30ml/2 tbsp finely chopped fresh
      parsley
    10ml/2 tsp chopped fresh tarragon
    675g/1½lb fresh salmon fillets
    40g/1½oz/3 tbsp butter
    juice of ½ lemon
    salt and ground black pepper

1 Preheat the oven to 190°C/375°F/ Gas 5. Roll out two-thirds of the pastry into a large oval, measuring about 35cm/14in in length. Cut into a curved fish shape and place on a baking sheet. Cut narrow strips from the trimmings.

2 Brush one side of each strip with a little of the beaten egg and secure in place around the rim of the pastry to make a raised edge. Prick the base all over with a fork, then bake for 8–10 minutes until the sides have risen well and the pastry is lightly golden. Leave to cool.

COOK'S TIP
If the pastry seems to be browning too quickly, cover it with foil during cooking and remove from the oven for the last 5 minutes. It is important that the "fish" cooks for the recommended time, so that the salmon is cooked through.

3 In a bowl, mash the hard-boiled eggs with the cream, then stir in the cooked rice. Add the parsley and tarragon and season well. Spoon this mixture on to the prepared pastry.

4 Cut the salmon into 2cm/¾in chunks. Melt the butter until it starts to sizzle, then add the salmon. Turn the pieces over in the butter so that they begin to colour but do not cook through.

5 Remove from the heat and arrange the salmon pieces on top of the rice, piled in the centre. Stir the lemon juice into the butter in the pan, then spoon the mixture over the salmon pieces.

6 Roll out the remaining pastry and cut out a semi-circular piece to cover the head portion and a tail shape to cover the tail. Brush both pieces of pastry with a little beaten egg and place on top of the fish, pressing down firmly to secure. Score a criss-cross pattern on the tail.

7 Cut the remaining pastry into small circles and, starting from the tail end, arrange the circles in overlapping lines to represent scales. Add an extra one for an eye. Brush the whole fish shape with the remaining beaten egg.

8 Bake for 10 minutes, then reduce the temperature to 160°C/325°F/Gas 3 and cook for a further 15–20 minutes until the pastry is evenly golden. Slide the fish on to a serving plate and serve.

VARIATION
If time is short you may prefer to use this simplified version of the recipe. Roll two-thirds of the pastry into a rectangle, then make pastry edges to contain the filling. Part bake the pastry shape, then add the filling. Top with plain, rolled out pastry and bake as above.

TROUT GOUGÈRE

A GOUGÈRE IS A CHOUX PASTRY RING FLAVOURED WITH CHEESE. THIS ONE IS SERVED HOT, WITH A RICH, CREAMY TROUT AND WATERCRESS FILLING. ALTHOUGH IT IS EASY TO PREPARE, THIS MAKES AN IMPRESSIVE LUNCH OR SUPPER DISH.

SERVES 4

INGREDIENTS
For the gougère
    50g/2oz/¼ cup butter
    150ml/¼ pint/⅔ cup water
    65g/2½oz/generous ½ cup plain
      (all-purpose) flour
    2 eggs, beaten
    75g/3oz Gruyère cheese, grated
    butter, for greasing

For the filling
    350g/12oz trout fillet
    150ml/¼ pint/⅔ cup dry white wine
    4 fresh parsley sprigs
    ½ lemon, sliced
    1 bay leaf
    25g/1oz/2 tbsp butter
    1 small onion, chopped
    25g/1oz/¼ cup plain
      (all-purpose) flour
    150ml/¼ pint/⅔ cup milk
    60ml/4 tbsp double (heavy) cream
    50g/2oz Gruyère cheese, grated
    50g/2oz watercress, finely chopped
    salt and ground black pepper

1 Preheat the oven to 200°C/400°F/ Gas 6. Sift the flour on to a sheet of non-stick baking parchment. Draw a 20cm/8in circle on a separate sheet of baking parchment. Grease a baking sheet and place the parchment on it.

2 Make the choux paste for the ring. Put the butter and water in a medium pan and heat gently until the butter melts. Bring to the boil then remove the pan from the heat.

3 Quickly tip in all the sifted flour and beat the mixture with a wooden spoon until a smooth, glossy paste forms. Leave to cool for 5 minutes.

4 Add the beaten egg to the cooled paste gradually, stirring all the time to prevent the mixture from curdling. Stir in three-quarters of the grated Gruyère cheese.

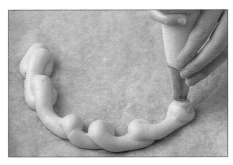

5 Carefully spoon the choux paste into a piping (pastry) bag fitted with a 1cm/½in plain round nozzle and pipe just inside the circle to form a ring. Sprinkle with the remaining cheese. Bake in the oven for 20–25 minutes or until golden brown and crisp.

6 Meanwhile, make the filling. Place the trout fillet, wine, parsley, lemon slices and bay leaf in a large frying pan. Gently poach the fish for 4–6 minutes, until it is cooked. Remove the fish from the pan. Strain the cooking liquid and reserve. Skin the fish, remove any bones and flake it into bitesize pieces.

7 Heat the butter in a pan, add the onion and fry gently for about 5 minutes until softened.

8 Stir the flour into the pan and cook for 1 minute, stirring. Gradually add the reserved cooking liquid and the milk, stirring constantly to form a thick sauce. Add the flaked trout, cream, cheese and watercress to the sauce and season well. Heat gently until piping hot.

9 When the choux ring is cooked, remove it from the oven and place on a warmed serving plate. Slice the gougère in half horizontally and spoon in the hot trout and watercress filling. Replace the pastry lid on the ring and serve immediately.

COOK'S TIP
Instead of using a piping bag, you can place large spoonfuls of choux pastry in a circle on the baking parchment. Position them close together so that they will join into a ring as they cook.

TROUT AND ASPARAGUS PIE

CRISP FILO PASTRY FILLED WITH LAYERS OF TROUT, RICOTTA CHEESE, ASPARAGUS AND MUSHROOMS MAKES A DRAMATIC-LOOKING DISH THAT IS ABSURDLY EASY TO MAKE.

SERVES 6–8

INGREDIENTS

115g/4oz asparagus
75g/3oz/6 tbsp butter
1 small onion, chopped
115g/4oz/1½ cups button (white)
  mushrooms, sliced
30ml/2 tbsp chopped fresh flat
  leaf parsley
250g/9oz/generous 1 cup ricotta
  cheese
115g/4oz/½ cup mascarpone
  cheese
450g/1lb trout fillet, skinned
8 filo pastry sheets, each measuring
  45 x 25cm/18 x 10in
salt and ground black pepper
butter, for greasing
flat leaf parsley, to garnish

1 Preheat the oven to 200°C/400°F/ Gas 6. Grease a 23cm/9in springform cake tin (pan). Bring a pan of water to the boil, add the asparagus and blanch for 3 minutes. Drain, refresh under cold water and drain again.

2 Heat 25g/1oz/2 tbsp of the butter in a frying pan and add the onion. Cook for 3–5 minutes or until softened. Add the mushrooms and cook for 2 minutes more. Stir in the parsley and season well with salt and black pepper.

3 In a mixing bowl combine the ricotta and mascarpone cheeses. Stir in the onion mixture. Melt the remaining butter in a small pan.

4 Line the cake tin with the filo pastry sheets, brushing each layer with melted butter and leaving the edges hanging over the sides of the tin. While you are working with one filo pastry sheet, keep the rest covered with a damp, clean dishtowel so that they do not dry out.

5 Place half the ricotta mixture in the base of the filo-lined tin. Remove any remaining pin bones from the trout fillets, then arrange them in a single layer over the ricotta. Season well.

6 Top with the asparagus and the remaining ricotta mixture. Bring the overhanging edges of the pastry over the top, and brush the layers with the remaining butter.

7 Bake the pie for 25 minutes or until golden brown. Cover loosely with foil and cook for a further 15 minutes.

8 To serve, remove the pie from the tin and place it on a warmed serving plate. Serve in slices, garnished with flat leaf parsley.

MONGOLIAN FIREPOT

A FIREPOT PROVIDES A WONDERFUL WAY TO ENTERTAIN. AS WITH FONDUE RECIPES, THE FOOD IS COOKED AT THE TABLE, BUT IN THE HEALTHIER MEDIUM OF STOCK RATHER THAN OIL. AS A BONUS, THIS BECOMES A FLAVOURSOME BROTH WHICH IS DRUNK AT THE CONCLUSION OF THE MEAL.

SERVES 4–6

INGREDIENTS
    2 salmon or tuna fillets, each about
        150g/5oz, skinned
    8–12 whole raw tiger or king prawns
        (jumbo shrimp), peeled and
        deveined, with tails on
    6 sachets instant miso soup mixed
        with 1.75 litres/3 pints/7½ cups
        water or the same quantity of fish,
        chicken or vegetable stock
    handful of coriander (cilantro) leaves
    2–3 spring onions (scallions), sliced
    small bunch watercress, rocket
        (arugula) or young mizuna greens
    50g/2oz/¾ cup enoki mushrooms
    200g/7oz fine egg noodles
    8–12 lemon grass stalks or
        wooden skewers
    soy sauce and wasabi paste or
        horseradish sauce, to serve

For the marinade
    grated rind and juice of 2 limes
    30ml/2 tbsp soy sauce
    2.5cm/1in piece fresh root ginger,
        peeled and finely chopped
    2 garlic cloves, finely chopped
    15ml/1 tbsp clear honey
    1 fresh red chilli, seeded
        and chopped

1 Cut the salmon or tuna fillets into 2.5cm/1in cubes and place in a deep serving bowl. Wash the prawns, pat them dry using kitchen paper, then add them to the fish cubes.

2 Mix all the marinade ingredients together and add to the bowl of seafood. Toss gently to coat, then cover and leave the seafood to marinate in the refrigerator for a minimum of 10 minutes, or 2 hours if possible.

3 Pour the stock into a pan, add the coriander and spring onions and bring to the boil. Transfer to a fondue pot and place on a burner at the table or pour the stock into a firepot at the table and keep hot.

4 Arrange the salad leaves and mushrooms on serving plates, and put the soy sauce and wasabi or horseradish into small bowls. Add the noodles to the stock at the table and leave to cook.

5 Invite each diner to spear a cube of fish or a prawn on a lemon grass stalk or skewer with a salad leaf and a mushroom. This is then submerged in the stock for 1 minute, or until the fish or prawn is cooked, then dipped into the soy sauce and wasabi or horseradish.

6 When the fish and vegetables have all been eaten, serve the remaining stock and noodles in soup bowls.

COOK'S TIP
To make them easier to eat, snip the noodles into short lengths using a pair of scissors.

SAUCES

The perfect sauce neither makes nor mars a dish but simply supports the main ingredients in such a way that it would be inconceivable to serve one without the other. Sorrel Sauce is a good example of this. Its tangy flavour and creamy consistency make it the perfect companion for grilled or fried salmon steaks, while Watercress Cream is a winner with either salmon or trout.

YOGURT AND MINT SAUCE

THIS LIGHT AND DELICATE SAUCE IS A PERFECT BALANCE FOR THE RICHNESS OF SALMON. IT WOULD ALSO BE VERY GOOD WITH EITHER FRESH OR SMOKED TROUT. A MIXED GREEN LEAF AND HERB SALAD MAKES A PERFECT ACCOMPANIMENT.

MAKES ABOUT 150ML/¼ PINT/⅔ CUP

INGREDIENTS
  ½ large cucumber
  6 fresh mint leaves
  150ml/¼ pint/⅔ cup natural Greek
    (US strained plain) yogurt
  salt and ground black pepper

COOK'S TIP
This sauce is delicious with smoked salmon or griddled fresh salmon in a pitta pocket. Toast pitta breads briefly, split in half widthways, then open out each pocket and fill with salmon, salad leaves and the yogurt and mint sauce.

1 Peel the cucumber, slice it in half lengthways and scoop out the seeds with a teaspoon.

2 Chop the mint leaves and put them in a bowl. Grate the cucumber into a sieve, salt lightly and drain for about 30 minutes.

3 Add the yogurt to the chopped mint leaves and mix well. Squeeze out any excess juice from the cucumber, then stir it into the bowl with the yogurt and mint. Season with black pepper to taste. Cover and chill until ready to serve.

SORREL SAUCE

THE SHARP, ALMOST LEMONY FLAVOUR OF THE SORREL SAUCE MAKES IT IDEAL FOR SERVING WITH SALMON OR TROUT. YOUNG SORREL LEAVES HAVE THE BEST FLAVOUR, BUT CAN BE DIFFICULT TO OBTAIN, SO IT IS WORTH GROWING THE HERB IN A POT OR KITCHEN GARDEN.

MAKES ABOUT 120ML/4FL OZ/½ CUP

INGREDIENTS
   25g/1oz/2 tbsp butter
   4 shallots, finely chopped
   90ml/6 tbsp crème fraîche or double
      (heavy) cream
   100g/3½oz fresh sorrel leaves,
      washed and patted dry
   salt and ground black pepper

1 Melt the butter in a heavy pan over a medium heat.

2 Add the shallots and fry for 2–3 minutes, stirring frequently, until just softened.

3 Stir in the crème fraîche or double (heavy) cream. Add the sorrel leaves to the shallots and cook until the sorrel is completely wilted, stirring constantly.

4 Spoon the cream and sorrel mixture into a food processor and process for just long enough to chop the sorrel and distribute the pieces evenly throughout the sauce.

5 Return the sauce to the clean pan, season with salt and pepper and heat gently. Serve hot.

VARIATION
If sorrel is not available, use finely chopped watercress instead.

BUTTER SAUCE

THE LEMONY BUTTER SAUCE IS A QUICK AND EASY ACCOMPANIMENT TO VIRTUALLY ANY FISH BUT IS ESPECIALLY GOOD WITH SALMON OR FILLETS OF TROUT.

MAKES ABOUT 120ML/4FL OZ/½ CUP

INGREDIENTS
  75g/3oz/6 tbsp butter
  grated rind and juice of ½ lemon
  15–30ml/1–2 tbsp cold water

VARIATION

If you like, use a lime instead of the half lemon for a change of flavour.

1 Melt the butter, then whisk in the lemon rind, lemon juice and cold water.

2 Season the sauce with salt and ground black pepper to taste. Simmer for 2–3 minutes and serve.

COOK'S TIP

It is important not to let the butter get too hot when making the sauce. If it darkens, it will not only spoil the appearance of the sauce, but will also ruin the delicate flavour.

SUMMER HERB MARINADE

RAID THE HERB GARDEN AND MAKE THIS FRESH-TASTING MARINADE. IT IS GREAT FOR SALMON OR TROUT, BUT ALSO WORKS WELL WITH CHICKEN, PORK OR LAMB.

MAKES ABOUT 150ML/¼ PINT/⅔ CUP

INGREDIENTS
  large handful of fresh herb sprigs,
    such as chervil, thyme, parsley,
    sage, chives, rosemary or oregano
  45ml/3 tbsp tarragon vinegar
  1 garlic clove, crushed
  2 spring onions (scallions), chopped
  90ml/6 tbsp olive oil
  salt and ground black pepper

COOK'S TIP

Use a sharp cook's knife or a mezzaluna to chop the herbs. It is best to avoid using a food processor. Unless you are very careful, the blade of a food processor will rapidly reduce the herbs to a soggy mess by releasing their natural moisture. This not only looks unattractive, but also muddies the flavour of the marinade.

1 Remove and discard any coarse stalks or damaged leaves from the herbs, then chop them very finely.

2 Mix the vinegar, garlic and spring onions in a bowl. Whisk in the olive oil, then add the chopped herbs and mix well. Season with salt and pepper.

3 Use as a marinade for salmon, pork, chicken, or lamb. Spread the fish or meat in a single layer in a dish. Pour over the marinade and mix. Marinate fish for 2–3 hours; meat for 4–6 hours.

4 Use the marinade to baste the fish or meat occasionally during cooking.

WATERCRESS CREAM

THE DELICATE GREEN COLOUR OF THIS CREAM SAUCE LOOKS WONDERFUL AGAINST PINK-FLESHED FISH SUCH AS SALMON OR SEA TROUT. THE FLAVOUR IS COMPLEMENTARY, TOO.

MAKES ABOUT 250ML/8FL OZ/1 CUP

INGREDIENTS
    2 bunches watercress or
    rocket (arugula)
    25g/1oz/2 tbsp butter
    2 shallots, chopped
    25g/1oz/¼ cup plain
    (all-purpose) flour
    150ml/¼ pint/⅔ cup hot
    fish stock
    150ml/¼ pint/⅔ cup dry
    white wine
    5ml/1 tsp anchovy essence
    (extract)
    150ml/¼ pint/⅔ cup single
    (light) cream
    lemon juice
    salt and cayenne pepper

3 Remove the pan from the heat and gradually stir in the fish stock and wine. Return the pan to the heat and bring the sauce to the boil, stirring constantly. Reduce the heat and simmer gently for 2–3 minutes, stirring occasionally.

4 Strain the sauce into a clean pan, then stir in the watercress or rocket, with the anchovy essence and cream. Warm over a low heat. Season with salt and cayenne pepper and sharpen with lemon juice to taste. Serve immediately.

1 Trim the watercress or rocket of any bruised leaves and coarse stalks. Blanch in boiling water for 5 minutes. Drain, refresh under cold running water, and drain again in a sieve or colander. Press the watercress or rocket against the sides of the sieve or colander with a spoon to remove excess moisture. Chop finely and set aside.

2 Melt the butter in a pan and fry the shallots over a medium heat for 3–4 minutes, until soft. Stir in the flour and cook for 1–2 minutes.

NEVER-FAIL MAYONNAISE

SOME PEOPLE FIND CLASSIC MAYONNAISE DIFFICULT TO MAKE, BUT THIS VERSION COULDN'T BE EASIER. THE ESSENTIAL THING IS TO HAVE ALL THE INGREDIENTS AT ROOM TEMPERATURE.

MAKES ABOUT 350ML/12FL OZ/1½ CUPS

INGREDIENTS
    1 egg, plus 1 egg yolk
    5ml/1 tsp Dijon mustard
    juice of 1 large lemon
    175ml/6fl oz/¾ cup olive oil
    175ml/6fl oz/¾ cup grapeseed,
      sunflower or corn oil
    salt and ground white pepper

COOK'S TIPS
• Be aware that this recipe contains raw eggs. If this is a concern, use bought mayonnaise instead.
• To make the mayonnaise even more glossy, beat in about 15ml/1 tbsp boiling water at the end, if you like.

1 Put the whole egg and yolk in a food processor and process for 20 seconds. Add the mustard, half the lemon juice and a generous pinch of salt and pepper. Put on the lid, then process the mixture for about 30 seconds more, until thoroughly mixed.

2 With the motor running, pour in the oils through the feeder tube in a thin, steady stream. When both oils have been incorporated and the mayonnaise is pale and thick, taste and add more lemon juice and seasoning if necessary. Scrape the mayonnaise into a bowl.

BEURRE BLANC

LEGEND HAS IT THAT THIS EXQUISITE SAUCE WAS INVENTED BY A COOK WHO FORGOT TO PUT EGG YOLKS INTO A BÉARNAISE SAUCE. WHETHER OR NOT THIS IS TRUE DOESN'T MATTER: THIS LIGHT SAUCE GOES PERFECTLY WITH POACHED OR GRILLED SALMON OR TROUT.

MAKES ABOUT 150ML/¼ PINT/⅔ CUP

INGREDIENTS
    3 shallots, very finely chopped
    45ml/3 tbsp dry white wine or
      court-bouillon
    45ml/3 tbsp white wine vinegar or
      tarragon vinegar
    115g/4oz/½ cup chilled unsalted
      (sweet) butter, diced
    lemon juice (optional)
    salt and ground white pepper

1 Put the shallots in a small pan with the wine or court-bouillon and vinegar. Bring to the boil and cook over a high heat until only about 30ml/2 tbsp liquid remains in the pan.

2 Remove the pan from the heat and leave to cool until the reduced liquid is just lukewarm.

3 Whisk in the chilled butter, one piece at a time, to make a pale, creamy sauce. Taste the sauce, then season with salt and pepper and add a little lemon juice to taste if you like.

4 If you are not serving the sauce immediately, keep it warm in the top of a double boiler set over barely simmering water.

HOLLANDAISE SAUCE

THIS RICH SAUCE GOES WELL WITH ANY POACHED FISH. SERVE IT WARM. AS THE EGG YOLKS ARE BARELY COOKED, IT IS NOT A GOOD IDEA TO SERVE THIS SAUCE TO CHILDREN, PREGNANT WOMEN, THE ELDERLY OR ANYONE WITH A WEAKENED IMMUNE SYSTEM.

MAKES ABOUT 135ML/4FL OZ/½ CUP

INGREDIENTS
    115g/4oz/½ cup unsalted
      (sweet) butter
    2 egg yolks
    15–30ml/1–2 tbsp lemon juice,
      white wine vinegar or tarragon
      vinegar
    salt and ground white pepper

COOK'S TIP
Instead of adding the butter to the egg mixture in the bowl, you could put the mixture in a food processor and add the butter through the feeder tube, with the motor running.

1 Melt the butter in a small pan. Put the egg yolks and lemon juice or vinegar in a bowl. Add salt and pepper and whisk until completely smooth.

2 Pour the melted butter in a steady stream on to the egg yolk mixture, beating vigorously with a wooden spoon to make a smooth, creamy sauce. Taste the sauce and add more lemon juice or vinegar if necessary.

MUSTARD AND DILL SAUCE

SERVE THIS FRESH-TASTING SAUCE WITH ANY COLD, SMOKED OR RAW MARINATED SALMON. NOTE THAT IT CONTAINS RAW EGG YOLK, SO, AS WITH HOLLANDAISE SAUCE, IT IS BEST TO AVOID SERVING IT TO CHILDREN, PREGNANT WOMEN, THE ELDERLY OR ANYONE WITH A WEAKENED IMMUNE SYSTEM.

MAKES ABOUT 120ML/4FL OZ/½ CUP

INGREDIENTS
  1 egg yolk
  30ml/2 tbsp brown French mustard
  2.5–5ml/½–1 tsp soft dark brown
    sugar
  15ml/1 tbsp white wine vinegar
  90ml/6 tbsp sunflower or vegetable oil
  30ml/2 tbsp finely chopped fresh dill
  salt and ground black pepper

1 Put the egg yolk in a small bowl and add the mustard with a little soft brown sugar to taste. Beat with a wooden spoon until smooth.

2 Stir in the white wine vinegar, then whisk in the oil, drop by drop at the start, then in a steady stream. As the oil is added, the dressing will start to thicken and emulsify.

3 When the oil has been completely amalgamated, season the sauce with salt and pepper, then stir in the finely chopped dill. Cover and chill for 1–2 hours before serving.

OLIVE OIL, TOMATO AND HERB SAUCE

THIS AROMATIC SAUCE IS SERVED WARM, RATHER THAN HOT, WITH GRILLED OR POACHED SALMON OR TROUT. IT TASTES SO GREAT YOU'LL WANT TO PROVIDE PLENTY OF GOOD BREAD OR BOILED NEW POTATOES TO MOP UP ANY SAUCE REMAINING ON THE PLATE.

MAKES ABOUT 350ML/12FL OZ/1½ CUPS

INGREDIENTS
    225g/8oz tomatoes
    15ml/1 tbsp finely chopped shallot
    2 garlic cloves, finely sliced
    120ml/4fl oz/½ cup extra virgin
       olive oil
    30ml/2 tbsp cold water
    15ml/1 tbsp lemon juice
    caster (superfine) sugar
    15ml/1 tbsp chopped fresh chervil
    15ml/1 tbsp chopped fresh chives
    30ml/2 tbsp torn fresh basil leaves
    salt and ground black pepper

COOK'S TIP
It is essential to the flavour of this sauce that you use the best quality olive oil.

1 Peel and seed the tomatoes, then cut them into fine dice.

2 Place the shallot, garlic and oil in a small pan over a very gentle heat and allow to infuse for a few minutes. The ingredients should warm through, but definitely not fry or cook.

3 Whisk in the cold water and lemon juice. Remove from the heat and stir in the tomatoes. Add a pinch of salt, pepper and caster sugar, then whisk in the chervil and chives. Leave the sauce to stand for about 10–15 minutes. Reheat gently until just warm, then stir in the basil just before serving.

USEFUL INFORMATION

INFORMATION SERVICES

For more information about salmon and trout, including conservation, the following organizations may be helpful:

United Kingdom
British Trout Association
8–9 Lambton Place
London W11 2SH
Tel: 020 7221 6065
www.britishtrout.co.uk

Environment Agency
www.environment-agency.org.uk

Fleetwood Fish Merchants
    Association Limited
6 Station Road
Fleetwood
Lancs FY7 6NW
Tel: 01253 873358

Marine Conservation Society
9 Gloucester Road
Ross-on-Wye
Herefordshire HR9 5BU
Tel: 01989 566017
www.mcsuk.org
(If you are concerned about choosing eco-friendly fish when shopping or eating out, the Marine Conservation Society publishes a Good Fish Guide)

North Atlantic Salmon Conservation
    Organization
1 Rutland Square

Edinburgh EH1 2AS
Tel: 0131 228 2551
www.nasco.org.uk

Sea Trout Conservation
www.seatrout.org

The Salmon & Trout Association
Fishmongers' Hall
London Bridge
London EC4R 9EL
Tel: 020 7283 5838

Wild Trout Trust
www.wildtrout.org

New Zealand Trade
    Development Board
New Zealand House
80 Haymarket
London SW1Y 4TE
Tel: 020 7973 0380
Fax: 020 7973 0104

United States and Canada
Bureau of Seafood & Aquaculture
    Marketing
2061 East Dirac Drive
Tallahassee
Florida 32310
Tel: (850) 488-0163
www.fl-seafood.com

Norwegian Seafood Export
    Council
Flagship Wharf, Suite 600
197 Eighth Street
Charlestown
MA 02129
Tel: 1-888-NORSKFISH
www.seafoodfromnorway.com/usa

Pacific Salmon Commission
600-1155 Robson Street
Vancouver
Canada V6E 1B5
Tel: (604) 684-8081
www.psc.org

The Wild Salmon Center
www.wildsalmoncenter.org

The Atlantic Salmon Federation
asf@nbnet.nb.ca

Trout Unlimited
1500 Wilson Boulevard 310
Arlington
WA 22209-2404
Tel: (800) 834-2419
trout@tu.org

Washington Trout
15629 Main Street NE
PO Box 402
Duvall
WA 98019
Tel: (425) 788-1167
wildfish@washingtontrout.org

Australia
Australia Fishing
www.ausfish.com.au
(Australian and New Zealand fishing related sites)

Sydney Fish Markets
Gipps Street
Pyrmont NSW 2009
Tel: (02) 9660 3652

New Zealand
New Zealand Fishing
    Industry Board
Private Bag 24091
Manners Street Post Office
Wellington
Tel: (04) 385 4005/8115
www.seafood.co.nz

MAIL ORDER COMPANIES

United Kingdom

Atlantic Harvest Limited
Pennyburn Industrial Estate
Buncrana Road
Londonderry
Co Londonderry
BT48 0LU
Tel: 028 7126 4275

Atlantis Smoked Fish
Fore Street
Grampound
Truro
Cornwall TR2 4SB
Tel: 01726 883201

Bridfish
Unit 1
The Old Laundry Industrial Estate
Sea Road North
Bridport
Dorset DT6 3BD
Tel: 01308 456306
(Smoked trout)

Cornish Smoked Fish
   Company Limited
Charlestown
St Austell
Cornwall PL25 3NY
Tel: 01726 72356
Fax: 01726 72360

Graig Farm Organics
Tel: 01597 851655
www.graigfarm.co.uk

Rhydlewis Fishery
Rhydlewis
Llandysul
Ceredigion SA44 5QS
Tel/Fax: 01239 851224

The Taste of Moray
www.scottishgourmetfood.co.uk

Ugie Salmon Fishings
Golf Road
Peterhead
Scotland AB42 6NF
Tel: (01779) 476 209
Fax: (01779) 471 475
sales@ugie-salmon.co.uk

United States

Always Fresh Fish
1889 Hwy 9, Unit 41
Toms River
NJ 08755
Tel: 732 349-0518
www.alwaysfreshfish.com

Great Alaska Seafood
Tel: (866) 262 8846
www.great-alaska-seafood.com

Smoked Salmon Company
19112 Bloomfield Road
Olney
MD 20832
Tel: 1-800-278-4050
Fax: (301) 924-2085
www.salmonlady.com

Australia

Aquatas Pty Limited
Marina Drive
Margate
Tasmania 7054
Tel: (03) 6267 6767
Fax: (03) 6267 9408
www.aquatas.com

Cairns Fish Marketing Agency
PO Box 201B
Bungalow
Cairns
Queensland 4870
Tel: (61) 7 40318455
Fax: (61) 7 40318355
www.cfma.com.au

Sydney Fish Market Pty Ltd
Locked Bag 247
Bank Street
Pyrmont
NSW 2009
Tel: (61) 2 9004 1100
Fax: (61) 2 9004 1177
www.sydneyfishmarket.com.au

New Zealand

New Zealand Fishing
   Industry Board
Private Bag 24091
Manners Street Post Office
Wellington
Tel: (04) 385 4005/8115
www.seafood.co.nz

GLOSSARY

Adipose fin The small fin between the dorsal fin and the tail fin on the back of a salmon or trout.

Alevin A newly hatched salmon, which is nourished by its yolk sac until it has developed and can feed naturally.

Anadromous Describes fish that migrate from the sea to fresh water to spawn. This contrasts with catadromous, which refers to fish like eels, which leave their fresh water habitat to spawn in the sea.

Anal fin A fairly large single fin close to the tail on the underbelly of a salmon or trout.

Cock salmon Adult male. The term is also used for trout.

Dapping A technique used in fly fishing, this involves suspending an imitation fly from a long rod so that it blows in the breeze before being delicately dropped or dappled on to the

water, imitating nature so expertly that the fish is fooled into thinking it is a real insect.

Dorsal fin Single large fin on the back of a salmon or trout.

Fry A very young salmon or trout, whose digestive tract has matured sufficiently to allow it to feed naturally.

Grilse A salmon that has spent one winter at sea and is returning to its native river.

Hen salmon Adult female. Adult female trout are also called hens.

Kelt Most adult salmon die after spawning. Those who survive to return to the marine feeding grounds are known as kelts.

Kype Hook-like protrusion on the lower jaw of a mature male salmon.

Parr When they are several months old, young salmon become known as parr. The name refers to the finger-like markings they acquire on their flanks at this time – parr being an old English word for finger. Immature trout are also called parr.

Pectoral fin One of a pair of fins on the underbelly of the fish, near the head.

Pelvic fin One of a pair of fins on the underbelly of the fish, more or less immediately below the dorsal fin.

Redds Gravel pits on the river bed where salmon and trout are spawned.

Smolt Salmon parr under a process called smotification, turning silver and losing their distinctive markings, when they are mature enough to migrate to sea in the spring. The term is also used for anadromous trout.

INDEX

Simple Rolled Sushi 49